This book contain
It also contains conten
sensitive readers. Reader discretion is advised. ...
words used here are **NOT** misspelled. They are written
as they were spoken and were used in the true
definition of Ebonics. This was my life. The names
have been changed to protect the identities of the
deceased and the privacy of those mentioned in my
story.

In believing we'll survive, makes us survive.
We take our miracles where we find them. Just as the
two worlds collide, theirs of discrimination, ours of
determination, we reach out. Against all odds and
against all logic we reach across the gap..... and
touch.

Brenda Costanzo

Dedications

To you, Doctor Albert Keating, who gave me what I could not provide for myself; Faith and support for this book by saying over and over, "You have a story to tell, one that others need to hear," for being there for my encouragement and last for helping me to deliver my story into the light.

Acknowledgements

I am deeply grateful to my own writing mentor and editor, Lucy Nagy, who offered me understanding, love and at times a shoulder to cry on when I became overwhelmed or discouraged and has continued to be a big part of my life.

I am most indebted to my beloved daughter Hali, for the time I took away from her and never complained. For showing me in her young years something I knew but thought that she was too young to understand. That that missed time I could never return. And even now as she has matured she continues to be my cheerleader in the stand.

To my friend, Courtney L. Sherrod, whose technical knowledge is uncanny and tediously transcribed endless hours to make this possible. His patience, understanding and nimble fingers kept me from losing my computer illiterate mind.

To my Fiancé' Richard, my rock, my friend, the person whose love for me goes far beyond that which any words could every say and has been by my side every step of the way.

I wish to give thanks to Dr. Balin Durr, Mr. Drabic and their staff. For keeping me sane when I had to recall events that happened to me during periods of my life that were very painful to recall. Trauma has a tendency to chase you and torment you. They helped me to embrace the past, to stop running and to let it go.

To my loving sister Felicia whose mind is liken to that of a calendar, which assisted me in the finer details that I had lost.

To everyone in Robert Taylor that I knew who lived and died but will never be forgotten.

My thanks to Mr. Jack Bridges, for allowing me to use his copyrighted pictures for my book. His photos gives a true and close up look in the faces of the people and the accounts of our lives that show what we endured. They say a picture is worth a thousand words, may these pictures be burned in our hearts and minds forever. I Thank you Mr. Bridges, for giving us all back a part of that history.

In memory of my Step-dad James, who was the father that I never had. He gave me the strength and courage to do the things that I didn't think that I could do. For everything that he did for me up until his passing. He will always be in my heart forever.

Most of all I wish to acknowledge my mother, Dora who gave me life, my name, and did all that she could for us. Because of her I was able to write this story, one that only I could tell.

Table of Contents

Chapter One: The Robert Taylor Homes

POW! POW! POW! The bullets from the guns made a deafening identifiable, but familiar sound. Sometimes the sounds from the guns went on from dusk till dawn. If you were down stairs in the playground, on your own porch, anywhere near or around the building, you would stop, drop to the ground, cover your head, and hope for the best until the sounds stopped. Usually, during the early part of the day or afternoon, the gun fire never went on for long. There were usually too many women with their children outside; when it stopped, everyone returned to their own mundane way of life.

Chapter Two: Robert Taylor Homes

The Robert Taylor Homes were known as the most infamous buildings in the City of Chicago followed by The Cabrini Green Housing Projects. The Robert Taylor Homes Projects sat on a narrow, 24 drab by 16 story slab. The buildings sat on a two-block by two-mile radius. All of the buildings were painted either red or white and all had sixteen floors, each floor had ten apartments per floor, a stairwell on each side with two elevators that never worked.

An incinerator, which I called, "The Dragon." On the left side of every wall was an incinerator and beyond that was a laundry room. It had two concrete tubs and a cage that was always kept locked so no one ever used it.

It was said that at one time there were twenty seven thousand residents; twenty thousand were to be children and babies. That came to roughly 5.8 people per unit. More than half were on public aid and everyone lived there knew that more than half were on public aid. Everyone that lived there knew that there was only one landlord which was The Chicago Housing Authority. They were the landlords over our city within a city. It had been stated by a journalist from the Sun Times and I quote," There has emerged from the south and west side a culture of complacency which was marked by a sad acceptance that crime and the shootings were as much of life as the sun rising in the east and setting in the west."

It was that type of culture that should have made cries for their outrage. Instead those cries muted to tolerance and resignation. So pitiful, so sad, but yet so true. The residences for the most part became tolerant of the gangs and blissful to their ignorance to the plight.

Chapter Three:
The Walls Came Tumbling Down

As I stood across the street I watched the wrecking ball as it slammed against the bricks the building that once-so long ago had been the place that I had called "home." With every hit I seemed to feel a kick to my stomach adding to the lump that had started to form in my throat making it harder and harder to swallow. As the trucks hauled away countless stacks of bricks and debris, the drivers had no way of knowing that they, in part, were severing the ties that bound a piece of history-- mine, and that once that last brick had been hauled away, my connection with the past would be lost--forever. As I continued to watch, they were already three fourths of the way from removing any evidence of the building having existed-- at all.

That Building had held for me many memories, some were good, the others had been bad. It was not so much the emphasis that was placed on its historical influence but for the personal impact that it had on me, I knew that I would always remember. Never in a million years would I nor anyone else who had lived there ever believed that after all of the years of the Chicago Housing Authority threatening to have it torn down, they finally did it. It was finally coming to pass. Everyone got the reality check of our lives! As my building was being torn down I felt at that point, what affluent people had been saying and quoting about the projects all along. The people in the media were always giving their opinions about how poor people's lives should have been run.

They could say it, because they didn't have to live it. But even with the statistics and books that had been written so very long ago, the pen then, as it is now, is mightier than the sword. And their words cut like a knife. No one knew how to write a proper letter to let the media know what was going on, let alone, who to send it to. And if they did, what would be the retribution for them or their families? The Chicago Housing Authority was too powerful, they had clout, and they made the rules. In all reality -- they ran The Robert Taylor Homes.

Chapter Four: Memories

But even through the deafening sound of the trucks coming and going, hauling and tearing through my mind's eye, I could envision the building as if it was still there. I thought of things that were long gone and thought to have been forgotten. Faces, and events and that would be frozen in time, the lives which had been lost to violence. Most, whose lives came from generation upon generation which occurred mainly due to ignorance. From floor to floor starting from the 16th floor, and the many people that I had had contact with. Not to mention the people that I have known of from the other buildings that surrounded mine.

The ghostly faces of people that I had known passed by my face and were exactly as I had remembered them quickly faded. Some brought memories of laughter, others reflected tears and sorrow.

It was supposed to be my last time returning but I knew that I would return again at a later time to see how the area had changed and what the changes had brought with it. The backhoes and wrecking balls continued doing their job. So I blanked out all of their sounds to help me ignore the fact that they were really there. I looked up, imagining that I was looking at a side view of my building. I could almost hear the music through the open windows. I could hear the music of Al Green, The Ohio Players, The Temptations and other musical groups with songs that had a funky beat.

Those were the days of vinyl LPS, and 45speed records. Not much late the Boom Boxes came along. They were basically large versions of radios that you carried on your shoulder. The speakers allowed the music to play so loud that you could feel the beat from the song from its rhythm through your heart. The sound was so loud that standing next to it long enough would make your ears ring.

And for a while we wouldn't be able to hear anything but we loved it. Now it was all gone. After all of those years I never would've believed that one day it would all be gone. That thought repeated itself like a loop that refused to stop playing in my mind.

After moving away, I still ran into people who had lived in the buildings. We would laugh as we hugged each other saying, "I remember you, you used to live in The Robert Taylor Homes!" When I lived there no one would use the complete name unless they were distinguishing them from other C.H.A properties, like The Cabrini-Green, Or the Ida B. Wells.

We always referred to them as the projects or the jets. We would laugh and talk awhile about how things had changed in our lives, if we had families of our own, and if we had seen or had spoken to anyone else from any of the buildings.

We would try to remember songs that were popular, and who we were dating when a particular song came out. We even tried, and sometimes did, remember the dances that we had done with each song.

It seemed so funny to us now. Giggling like school girls as we sang a song, like the funky chicken. We tucked our fist into our arm pits while flapping them like wings to do the dance. It made us laugh until we ended up wiping the tears from our eyes. We would end up saying the same thing that we had all heard at one time or another from our grand-mothers or other older women when they would talk about how it used to be when they were girls. They would sigh and say, "Yes LORD, those were the days." We referred to something that was either good or bad "as back in the day."

We had moved from the jets and remembered different things from long ago slowly other memories started to come back to our minds as well, the smiles slowly went away and the looks in our faces became sad. I said, "It was good for a while wasn't it?" But then we were all quiet for a second as we all remembered that it had been good in the beginning, but for most in the end it had been bad. It had been very bad. We laughed and talked about growing older, how we should have listen to our mothers when they told us things and how we didn't listen because those that had kids were trying to get their own kids to listen, getting the same response that they had given to their mothers. We talked about people we had run into and how they looked, better or worse as time had gone by.

When I lived there I could remember seeing generations that had lived right in the building with me. Usually, the Grandmothers took care of the kids of her daughter, sometimes she and her daughter would help to raise the daughter's kids. And when the young ones got pregnant after she had her baby, everyone would help her to raise it because she was still one herself.

It wasn't the trucks that snapped me back, away from where I had been. It was the pain in my feet, which told me that although they didn't mind my reminiscing, I would have to do it another way, like by finding a place sit down. I had been standing in front of my old high school, "Jean Baptist Point DuSable." So I walked the few steps over to the flat part of the stone that we used to sit on. It was an extension of the school that sat a few inches away from the door. I smiled and signed "as I thought to myself that I should have done so a long time ago". It had the same stairs and a medium stoop. It was weatherworn, and had even more noticeable cracks in the concrete then when we sat there in my high school years.

After rubbing my feet for a minute I continued to pick up where I left off, but now, I knew why it was different. When you are young you don't think of families as generations. You said so-in so had a baby, now her sister, so-in so is gonna have a baby. I hung my head down and shook my head as a sad smile came across my face. Actually it was a pathetic one, the look that you give to someone when you have said I told you so. It was getting clearer and clearer. As an adult, the how's and why's had always been clear.

Back then the adults didn't see the writing on the wall. It had been easy to hit the stop button in my mind for a minute and walk over to the stoop to take off my shoes to stop the pain in my feet. But to see my home being demolished, just to see it happening made me cry. So I left the reality of looking at what was taking place. I left that place; in my mind I hit the rewind button and returned to the place where everything was the way it used to be. It was impossible to see through an adult's eyes of how it had been as a child. Even then it wasn't a question; the only eyes you looked through were your own. Trying to grow up and not die in the processes even up to the very day that my family moved out. So I hit the continue button and returned to the place where I left off.

Chapter Five: How it Began

As my movie began to play through in my mind it showed how it looked in the beginning, when my family first moved there. There were trees neatly spaced behind every building from 51st street all the way down to 47th street. I remembered how beautiful everything looked. On the limbs of the trees were small white buds that blossomed into even more beautiful flowers. The lawns were all manicured; the maintenance men rode lawn mowers to cut all of the grass in the front and backs of the buildings. They had placed small white post with connecting chain to protect the trees. That was also done for every building I lived on the tenth floor and when looking out of my back window I could see into the parking lot as people stood and talked and as others came and went.

What I did notice was that I never saw any animals. No stray dogs, cats, or even squirrels. The one and only birds that were always around were pigeons. Pigeons and more pigeons they were always everywhere. Behind the building, a brand new paved black top area was put down. There, a large grocery store was built there. Its name was in large letters it was called, Nationals. Basically it became a strip-mall. At that time there was no name for it and the lines of other stores that were connected to it. We would just say the name of the place that we were going to that was where all of the other stores were. There was a laundry mat, and next to it was a small lounge where the older crowd would go at night. It was always dimly lit and the music that came from it was loud and the records always talked about someone leaving someone for one reason or another.

After a year or so, on the very opposite end of the food store they opened up a Walgreen's. Connected to the end wall of its store they added room enough for a medical and dental center. In the very middle of the two were a fast food takeout restaurant and the liquor store. At the adjacent corner from Walgreens construction workers built a hotdog stand shaped like a metal hotdog. I had cousins who lived a building away from mine but our family didn't visit their building much.

Everyone had been saying that on that weekend, MUHAMMAD ALI, the famous boxing champion was coming to sign autographs there. The hot dog stand had been named and dedicated to him. I came but he didn't show so after a while I just left. Years later as my sister and I spoke about it she said that he did show up in a limo. He had bodyguards all around him as he signed three or four autographs then was quickly whisked away. It must have been for publicity. Some said he didn't seem to really want to be around the crowds of poor
people and having his picture taken but did so, so he could be seen on all of the magazines. The next day the hotdog stand with his name on it was gone.

Chapter Six: What It Became

Eventually the maintenance men quickly removed all that was left of the trees that had been planted behind every building along with what was left of the posts which had been stolen a long time ago. Afterwards the landscapers stopped manicuring the lawn and sweeping along the sides of the curbs.

Without having anyone to water, fertilize or continue with the maintenance of the lawns the grass became strangled by the weeds. Even they, weren't hardy enough to withstand the continuous traffic by people who had started using the grass as a path to make a shortcut to get from one place to another.

In the end there were only sparse patches of weeds left around all of the buildings. Eventually, everything just went to the way side and in the end after the grass was gone, all that was left from the beautiful landscaping became desolation. It seemed to have happened so quickly when everything started to change. Kids started hanging, climbing, and even swinging from the branches. The trees eventually died from the constant climbing stripped away the bark. The parking lot behind all of the buildings became strewn with glass from broken bottles of wine, beer, and whiskey. Along with the broken bottles came the candy wrappers, potato chip bags, and bags for discarded food. Everything blew all around the parking lot as a whirling circle. That made it look like the formation that started to look like a small tornado.

The playground became just a place to chase your friends and play. I could almost see the children playing. If someone that didn't live in the projects had seen it they would never have referred to it as a playground because it really wasn't anymore. Without any swings or seats that were no longer attached, in the blink of an eye so were the chains that had originally held the seats were stolen. All that was left was an old rusty sliding board which swayed slightly as we climbed its stairs because the screws that held it tightly to the ground had started to loosen, due to the wear and tear from so many kids playing on it. There were the two monkey bars, each one sat at opposite ends of the playground.

On the monkey bars we played a game called King of The Hill you could climb to the top of it without

15

falling off. Whoever did it first would be called the king. We didn't think of the consequences of falling we didn't even know what the word consequences meant, because we had never even heard of that word being used. We did know there was nothing to break your fall. It was only the ground and you. We never thought of getting our skulls cracked open even though there was not sand, wood chips or dirt to break our fall just the concrete. Since we were kids when we hung upside down from the monkey bars the word (paralyzed) was another word we didn't know, understood or care what that word meant either. But we sure knew about broken arms and legs, skinned shins, sprained ankles and a lot about band aids it was what we as kids would do.

Sometimes you would see kids' with bikes, but not very many. Some had skates, basketballs, bats and softballs. Not many kids had the red wagons to pull their brothers and sisters in. The only thing most of us got lucky with was when someone's mother went and bought a clothes line. That's when the real fun started because we would go downstairs and play double-dutch. Some of the girls were really good. There would be two girls jumping at the same time. While jumping rope one would do a flip without missing a beat. They did great things in double-dutch which caught on so well that people started to have tournaments giving out trophies to the best ones. Sometimes we'd get lucky when someone got a softball for their birthday and someone else got a bat we would then play softball in the playground. But as we got older we started playing softball outside of the playground towards the street. When the boys rough housed, it became popular if they had to have a doctor apply a cast to a fractured part of their body. It became sort of a merit badge. Before you got to the doctor to get your injury fixed, you had to go to your mother first who would get really pissed off because you had hurt yourself, doing something stupid.

The first thing to worry about after she finished with you was if you were going to be alive to get a chance to get your cast put on. At that time a whipping wasn't called "corporal punishment." It was just called, "Getting your ass whipped" and that didn't happen just in the projects it was pretty much the norm inside of the projects as well as anywhere else. Sometimes when we were in the playground

16

playing, we would dance to the sounds of James Brown, and the boys were trying to imitate him, and the girls tried to imitate Dianna Ross and the Supremes, or Aretha Franklin.

We did all of those things in the playground. We made up our own games, we were kids in the projects and at our ages we were naive. We didn't call what the adults called playing dangerous with nothing else to play with-there was nothing else to do. Playing dangerously was the only thing to do. What we had to play with was no good and it wasn't safe it was just as dangerous and we played on it. We made do a lot with what we had. Our imaginations and the ragged things in the playground were all that we did have.

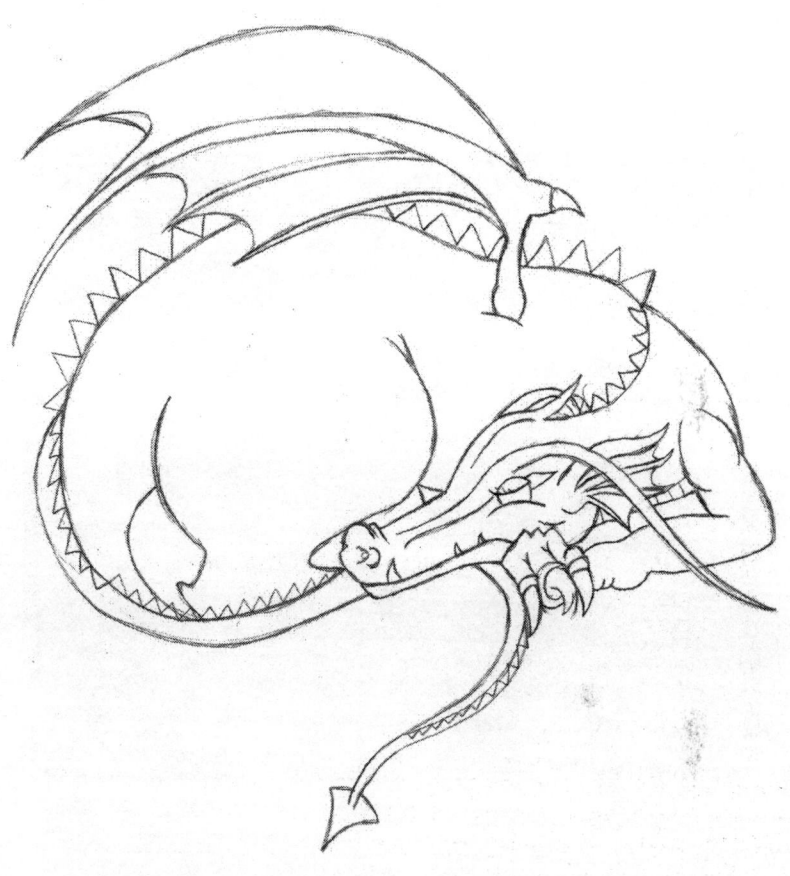

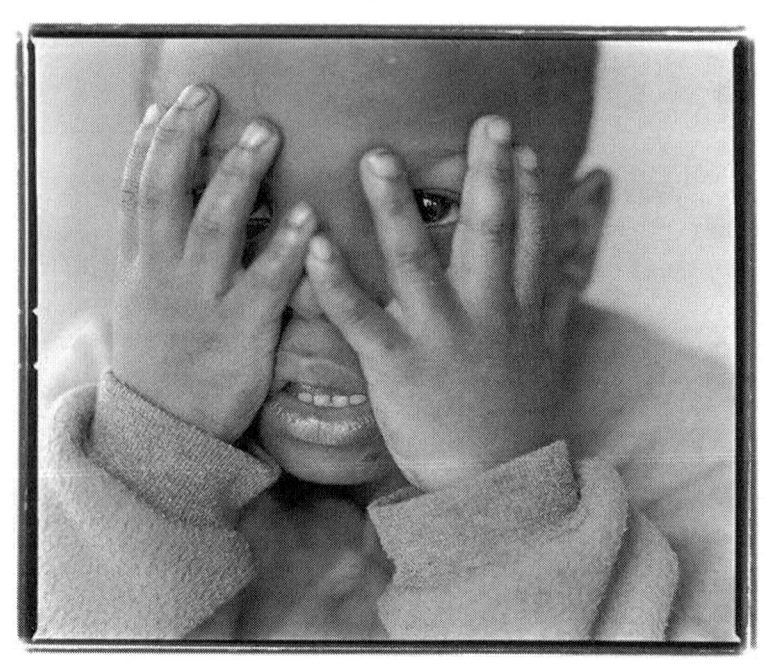

Chapter Seven: Death

As kids we didn't know what being superstitious was-only the little bits and pieces of things that were not talked about in detail when we were around. Some women would call them wives tales; others called it being superstitious when they sat in chairs on the porches. They talked about all sorts of things as they fanned themselves with whatever they had around, usually a dustpan. The windows in the apartments were kept open but only blew in hot air and so did the box fans. When it was too hot to play out in the sun we played paddle ball and jacks or hopscotch on the porch. When we played jacks there were so many waiting to play that we had to take Once when I was outside waiting for my turn to play the women got so involved in their conversation that they weren't paying attention to us, I was sitting next to them and had started to listen to them talk.

I pretended to be looking at people that were in the playground through holes in the fence. That was the first time I heard the name that the adults referred to as Death. But that day I learned that there was a reason that kids shouldn't listen when told not to. I overheard one woman say to the other "girl you know damn well he's the reaper girl, Death." They described him; each telling the other what they had heard when they were growing up. One said, "He wore a black robe with a black hood."

He had no face and carried a long knife attached to long stick. And once he decided to come for you, he didn't change; it didn't matter if you were a man, a woman, or a kid. And when he found not even God could save you. I had been sitting Indian-style and had completely forgotten that I was supposed to be looking through the holes in the porch.

But I was no longer looking out of the fence I was looking straight at them and had become so scared at what they were saying that I had started to tremble. The only reason that they caught me ease dropping was because one of the girls had been calling me for a while because it had been my turn to play. I hadn't moved! I couldn't one of the women laughed as I half crawled and half scooted away. She continued to laugh as she said "He only came for the bad kids."

They knew that I had been listening all of the

time! The word Death or the grim reaper, which ever name you gave him had been handed down and continued from one generation to another. But he was not known just to the black people in the projects. Later, after I had grown up I found out that a lot of different cultures believed in death also. He just had a different name.

The next day at school, I made myself fiddle around with my book till everyone left the classroom. I asked my teacher who the grim reaper was and what he had looked like. She took my chin in her hand and asked me where I had heard about him. And then she shook her head and said, "never mind, I'll bring a picture of him to you if you give me a few days." I counted the days for her to bring the picture of what it was that made me scared to walk or even sleep by myself after hearing about him. It seemed to take forever.

At one point I thought that maybe she had forgotten.

Finally that day came; she waited for the class to clear out and asked me to bring my chair next to hers. Slowly she placed the picture of what the grim reaper looked like in my hands. Just to look at the picture made the hairs on my neck stand out and I felt little goose pimples on my arms. She patted my shoulder as she told me that it was made from someone's imagination.

She put her arms around me to try and comfort me; it didn't. Looking at the picture was exactly as the woman on the porch described him. The figure in that picture was nothing like any of the scary movies that I had ever seen I asked my teacher "what is the stick that it was holding?" She called it "a scythe." Then she told me what it was really made for. Part of the myth was that only the person dying could see him.

I had not seen him but the description of his work was well known, throughout the entire projects. Death showed clarity and with it came the ability and the realization that he was real and had lurked in the darkness. He was in the elevator shaft, the hallways, the unused laundry roams and few vacant apartments that were usually on the 15th and 16th floors. Death was the candy man who was responsible for the small children who fell to their deaths chasing a dime that he had rolled out from nowhere, just out of their reach into so the elevator shaft. Some of the older boys who wanted to be like Bruce Lee and felt they could emulate his death-defying leaps and quick moves that Bruce Lee did with his hands while doing a judo chop.

Sometimes they took it too far and weren't able to pull their hand out of the elevator doors before it closed. It was probably unimaginable to stand and see their hand caught and then detach as the elevator continued to descend and the scream as they held what was left of their arm as they either fainted or had tried to make it to their house with one of their friends helping him to walk. I thank GOD that I was never there to see it when that happened. There were those who attempted to catch and climb the chains underneath the elevator to impress the other people who watched only to realize at the very last minute of their young lives that due to their poor timing a piece of their clothing had gotten caught and had prevented them from rolling free as planned.

While still holding on to the chains. Everyone watching knew that if they missed that moment that was it. It wouldn't have mattered whether one of the more experienced boys was there or not. The only thing that you could do was cover your mouth as you had when the other boy had lost his hand as they also held on for their life. You could hear their screams for help. They were very loud at the beginning but those friends knew that they could do nothing for their friend. The only thing they could do was to watch the bottom of the elevator descend as the screams for help became fainter and fainter as the bottom of the elevator come down. Crushing him as it made its final stop at the bottom of the shaft.

I'm sure death had known exactly when to reach out his hand and for the trapped one to feel that in being able to grab hold of the outstretched hand there may have been a glimmer of hope.

Maybe, in wanting to live so badly, they were willing to reach for something that was not able to be seen by the living. Those who tried to hold on to the out stretched hand that really wasn't there that they realized that there would be no chance to make it out, that their friends were not going to be able to help them and that they were really going to die. For the small ones, death released them quickly to perhaps end their suffering. By not letting them hold on to the chain they would not feel the sensation of being crushed as they fell down the empty elevator shaft.

In the meantime, Death was who he was, and no matter when he did it, he still did his job, and he did it very well. Maybe that's why he had had it since the beginning of time as the two women on the porch had said. Nope, no one that he was after never got another chance. Sometimes Death was cruel. He allowed them to look at him because for them, there was no going back, no one to tell how he really looked. His would be the last face that they would see.

Death was always busy. He had many buildings and floors to attend to so he could afford to take his time. After all, -- that's all he had. He had patience and as much time as he needed to get his job done.

Chapter Eight: Death's Pet—the Dragon

There was another type of evil of sorts. Although Death moved through the projects alone, it had a pet and his pet lived out in the open. No one was afraid of it. Most people called it "The Incinerator," It could be accessed from every floor - It lived on every floor. Death did not want to miss a thing. I called it "The Dragon." The Dragon had a dual purpose; it burned and ate the garbage but also served as a crematory for the unwanted babies and the occasional unfortunate soul that had been killed and then dropped down the chute it also helped to erase the fact that any person, or what was left of them had ever existed at all. It usually worked.

Its mouth opened by way of a single handle. Once the handle was opened it spewed clouds of smoke and flames from the garbage and anything else were thrown into it. The dragon didn't discriminate, nor was it particular. It would eat anything unusable or unwanted. Anything at all could be put into its greedy, toothless mouth. All of the garbage would be its meal. The ashes were the remnants of what it had eaten, and it would eat anything that it was given. It spewed smoke and flames six   days a week, eight hours a day every day. The garbage came from every tenant in every apartment on every floor from the first to the 16th.

Although it was always fed, it seemed to stay hungry. It wasn't an active predator; in fact, it was very sedate, almost like a giant pet. It only ate what it was fed, and--it was always well fed. On Monday mornings the janitor would come in to the boiler room and room and he would flip the make the dragon sleep so that the other garbage would temporarily be stopped from coming down.

He would he grab his long handled shovel to proceed to clean out the ashes from the previous days. When incidents occurred, where there was evidence of bones or teeth, word traveled fast. It was probably put out by the janitor himself. It was his job to notify the Chicago Housing Authority and the police when bones and human remains came down the chute. As word got around there would be a large crowd of onlookers huddled together straining their necks just to get a peek at what the janitor had pulled out of the incinerator with this long handled shovel. After the police arrived they would slowly don their rubber gloves and look closely into the ashes then they picked through it to remove all of the small fragments, placing them into clear plastic bags and those bags were put into paper bags where they would label them. No one could ever read the labels on the bags. As long as the crowd was quiet they were allowed to stand and watch the police as they worked, as though no one else was there. I was in the crowd of couple of times and had gotten a chance to stand in the front line of the crowd as once again the janitor had found more human bones.

I remember seeing the younger kids who had crawled between the legs of the preoccupied adults and trying to get a chance to see what was going on. Some were too young to understand, but for those that did and who were in the front, I'm sure it would be something that would stay with them for the rest of their lives. I know it did with mine.

I guess if there was anything good to be said about the Dragon it was that its mouth/ door that opened the chute was at least four feet high from-the floor to the handle.

To open and keep it open required more strength than the average small child was capable of. The flames and smoke were usually enough to keep them out of harm's way.

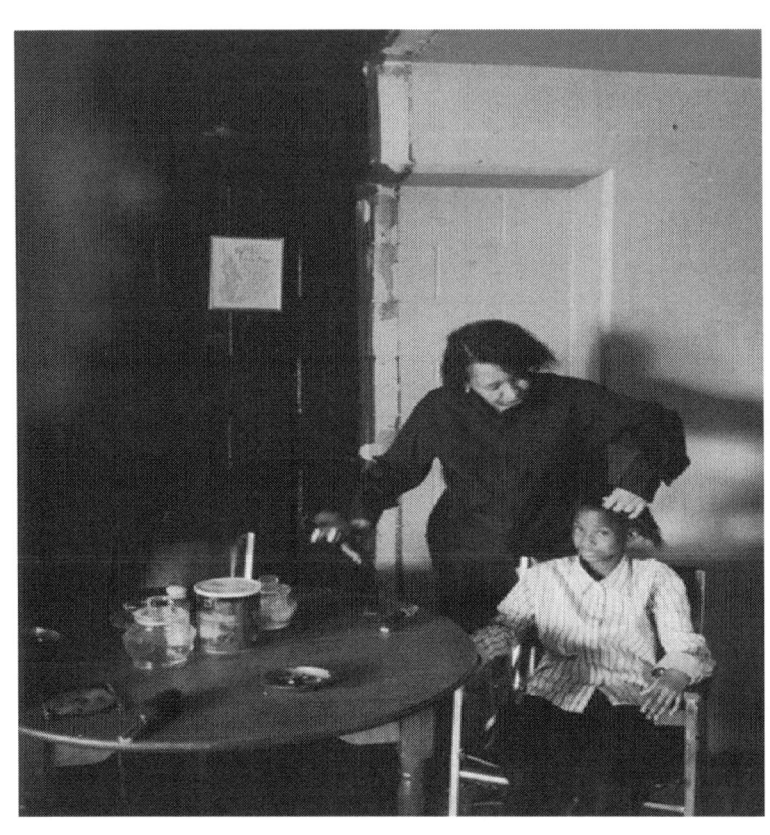

Chapter Nine: Elementary School

My family and I moved into the Robert Taylor Homes and stayed there for 13 years. We first moved into the building, 4845 S. Federal and later to 4950 S State. We stayed there until we moved away completely. I attended the Ludwig Van Beethoven Elementary School. From the end of the asphalt where I stood to get to the school there would be a two block wide open field that everyone would have to cross, to get there. Contrary to what most people believed, kids in the projects started out coming to school every day.

In the winter the cold air would freeze your feet and hands so cold that you couldn't feel any part of your body, even at my age I would feel bad for the other kids who didn't have hats, gloves or even coats. They were the ones who wore windbreakers and walked huddled together to try to fight the wind from the open field. Once inside the teachers would take those kids to the bathroom first to run water on their hands to warm them up then they would dry them off and rubbed them quickly and diligently then they sent them to class. Those of us that had appropriate clothing just hung our coats on the coat rack after placing our mittens and hats inside of each coat sleeve.

It had gotten to a point that there were so many kids that didn't have appropriate clothing for the winter weather that the teachers placed two large barrels filled with hats coats and gloves for the kids that needed them.

One morning I overheard one teacher tell another "That's a crying shame that those kids have to walk to through that open field and in the snow like this". But in the summer going through the field was just as bad.

From that same distance, if you lived in my building where I lived it on 49th Street, once you had started walking, from that point to the field to get to school, the sun beat down on me making my mouth feel like it was full of dirt. I was soaked to the bone so would everyone else from the sweat that poured off of our bodies.

Again, it was the teachers would come to our rescue. I think they really cared about us and what happened to us, and that's why I think that so many of us came. In the summer after crossing the field, we would almost push each other over to get in to the school to feel the cold air that came from the vents on the walls. Everyone would run to find a vent to stand in front of just to feel the cold air. Some of us would get on our knees just to feel the cold air blow on our face which at the time felt like heaven. Where we would stay in front of the vents until the bell rang, which was the signal for everyone to go to class. Sometimes I think the teachers knew how thirsty we were and allowed all of us to get a quick drink at the water cooler before going into the classroom. We would saver every drop as if it would be the last time that we would ever taste it again.

In class they were pretty strict and never allowed us to break the rules. And most of us never tried. But I will always believe that they cared more for us than they lead us to believe. But outside of the class even the teachers broke the rules them by allowing each and every one of us to get some water. And we were all glad that they did. Even though it was very clear that everyone was supposed to be inside the classroom when the bell rang they would allow each and every one of us get a quick sip before shooing us into the classroom. Sometime it would take a minute or two before the bell rang. At other times it would be a minute or two afterwards. She would then put a serious face on and to us class had officially started.

Chapter Ten: The Pledge of Allegiance

After all of our clothing had been put away we would go into the classroom. Everyone would face the board and after placing our hand over our heart we would all say the Pledge of Allegiance. We would stand straight and tall. No one played, whispered or made a sound during that time. The Pledge of Allegiance was something in school to be taken seriously.

At that time being small I didn't know, but later on I learned why it was only said in school. It was the last line of the Pledge of Allegiance that caused so much anger with the black people. It was the last line that said "One nation under God with liberty and justice for all." The grown-ups used to say "not justice the white man meant it for themselves. Jus-us." The Blacks in the projects, felt that the whites who lived and worked a world away from poverty, felt and acted like that line was made just for them.

To the people living in the projects they were made to feel that way by that line, in the Pledge That as poor people, they just sat around all day doing nothing but breeding babies and collecting public aid from the taxes that were taken out of their checks to support them. They also felt that the state enabled them by continuing made it worse by giving them more money as their families grew larger. Whites despised the fact that it allowed them to learn more about how to better misusing the very system that had been put in place to help them. Those were the white's attitudes, "how dare they"? But for everyone who lived in poverty they felt that the system was misusing e very system that had been put in place to try to help them. The claim of misuse was causing a hardship to them, as well as doing a great injustice them because they worked.

The majority that lived in the projects agreed on one thing that the upper crusted white people, "honkeys" as they call them, Those in government used their power to enact any laws and by laws that for the poor even now... Continued to be made and played.

Back at school if you were overweight, you wouldn't last long. Between going back and forth to school, up and down the stairs and, depending on what floor you lived on. If you were out of shape going from one to fourteen flights of stairs, you would feel it possibly having to do it four, or even five times a day, to help your mother go to the Laundromat or the grocery store, and no one ever counted on the elevators to work you were in trouble.

To go to play downstairs, to be able to just come and go at all would leave the skinniest of us gasping for air. There just wasn't any room in the projects for a kid being very fat. In being too fat it made you the target for everyone to pick on. You had to be in shape and you had to try to stay in shape or know how to fight! Most of us had a certain time to be at home when school was over with everyone else, OR ELSE!!!

Chapter Eleven: The Truant Officer

There was only one other person that could scare you worse than your mother could, it was the dreaded Truant officer! When the school became concerned about a kid that had missed too many days at school, that's when you would see him. Sometimes outside of the door you would see the parent talking to him as he wrote on a sheet of paper. Sometimes the parent would leave and he would take that kid gently by the hand and escort him or her back to the classroom but not before speaking briefly with the teacher.

At other times, he would wait for the parent of a kid that wasn't coming on a regular basis to come to school to meet with him to discuss the reason for the child's many absences especially if the parent didn't know that their kid hadn't been coming to class.

The parent would shake hands with the teacher who would call his or her child out. We would all sit in class and snicker to each other because that kid had gotten caught.

If or when they got caught it meant that they would get a timeout in the corner and no recess. Sometimes the truant officer would leave and you would hear the parent take his or her kid to the bathroom, which at that time was right next door to the classroom. The teacher would usually raise her voice when speaking to us to try to drown out the sound. But it usually didn't help and we would here the Whap! Whap! Whap! From the sounds that the belt made as it made a whooshing sound on their skin, followed by a loud cry as that kid made promises of never doing it again and the cursing from the parent making threats of what would happen if they had to come back to the school again.

When they returned to class, usually a boy, they would come back walking very slowly and usually ended up standing next to their desk instead of sitting at it. Everyone at one time or another had seen the results that the dreaded whipping had made by a parent. On the playground the boys would show the others what the whippings looked like. Seeing what those whippings could do usually kept everyone in line.

When it was lunch time, the bell would ring, On Wednesday at lunchtime, there would be no reason for the teachers to tell us to walk and not run to get into the line.

We knew that no one would listen. Everyone from the different classrooms would walk as fast as they could to get to the cafeteria. The smell of the food had filled up the air and it smelled so good that you could hardly keep your mind on what the teacher had been saying in class.

The lunchroom butter cookies would be worth crawling across the field for. They would make us lick our lips in anticipation. With the sloppy Joe's we would have mashed potatoes and green peas. Sometimes you would see a teacher speak to the cafeteria lady who would nod her head but say nothing. If you are sitting down and watching you could see her dish out a double portion on that particular child's plate.

The hall monitor handed out the first butter cookies after you finished your lunch. The first two were free but if you wanted an extra one it would cost three cents. For the majority of us at that time that might as well as having been three hundred or even three million. What parents gave kids money back then every day to buy butter cookies with? Years later after having moved out of the projects, I was fortunate enough to acquire the recipe for the lunchroom cookies. After I had my daughter I was able to make them for her and even now she loves them as much as I did then.

At Beethoven School, everyone who finished was transferred for 6th grade to the Overton Elementary School. The school was 4 blocks away on the street named Indiana. Everyone had a huge crush on one particular teacher. He wore a large, shaped afro hairdo, he was very fair skinned and he was tall, thin and always spoke softly and no one ever distracted themselves when he spoke. In fact, we held onto his every word. We would always ask questions so that he would look at us to answer them, day dreaming that one day one of us was going to be his girlfriend. That never happened. Every girl in the school had a crush on that teacher.

He was always professional and polite and probably had girls in every one of his classes that held crushes. He never kidded around and he didn't give any reason for anyone to be able to say that he had said anything that he shouldn't have.

I had freckles across the bridge of my nose, sandy brown and reddish hair and full pink lips none of which made matters good for me at all. Every day I hated to look into the mirror because there wasn't a day that someone at some point was going to remind me of my high yellow color.

Some were bold enough to say that I was one of those albino blacks. There were very few days that my given name was ever called enough to be there if we weren't black. And white people thought that they had it bad! The plus side for me was that my whole family lived there we would probably have caught hell if we had all been my color.

Chapter Twelve: Skin Color

The old saying was, "What doesn't kill you makes you stronger." In the projects the saying was "What doesn't kill you, keeps trying to. So depending on your demographics, both sayings could basically be true. Black people that lived in the projects hated so many things, they definitely hated the people in the white society, they hated their situation, the way they were treated and mistreated. But they also believed in things, good things. GOD, loving their children being able to feed them and no matter how things were they felt blessed at waking up every morning. They also believed in giving a good ass whipping when it was called for.

How some men got their girlfriends pregnant and boys got their daughter's pregnant and wouldn't help, or disappear, or even date the friends of their daughters, there was so much hate that even peoples skin color could cause problems. Being too Dark, or too light or caramel colored. Just Color! Any color! I found that the lighter a person's skin tone was the harder that person would have to prove themselves and that included me.

In living there you became aware that the projects unconsciously approached surviving as anything that took place where you were able to hold your own. That's what made you a survivor. Having endurance, practice, repetition, and having to work through things for yourself and your family. To be able to feed everyone in the middle of the month when the food stamps ran out whatever the situation was, you had to be ready to pull yourself up to meet the challenge. The one thing that the majority of people living there never forgot was to never ever take anything for granted, nothing. Ever. My mother's skin tone was fair as was my stepfather, second sister and both of my brothers, but my youngest sister was darker than anyone in the family. I on the other hand was the lightest and I stood out like a sore thumb.

I always wanted to run away. After hearing all of the names that I was always called, at night I would cry myself to sleep thinking about having to wake up the next day to go through it all over again.

Although the name calling was helping me, at the time I didn't understand how. Later it was that same name calling that helped me to acquire that same tough skin because later there were going to be too many things happening to me that I needed to concentrate on and the cracks were not going to help me to stay alive.

Chapter Thirteen: The Girl Gangs

Girl gangs were rarely spoken in the same context with the boy gangs. There were a lot of them in different buildings and they were as tough as the boys were. The boys carried brass knuckles, switch blades and guns but mostly they used their fist. On the other hand, the girls used anything. They used razor blades, bats, knives, not to mention their feet and their fist. You would see it coming when a girl pulled off her earrings or had her face greased down, that was to make it hard for someone to scratch you.

Everything was a go when it came to the girls The male gang members would leave the building and fight other gangs to own turf and to make a name for themselves They would spray paint the area to let others know that they owned that area. They sold weed and got locked up in jail for short periods, but were usually released to the custody of their parents because of their age.

The girls usually fought the other girls who lived in the white buildings down on Forty-Seventh Street. Later I found out that the girls' initiation was just as horrific as the boy gangs.

On the second to the last day at Overton School my life altering experience, unbeknownst to me, had started to be set in motion. In school as with any school, if you listened and did your homework you got your grades. You either passed with good grades, you passed with the minimum that would allow you to pass on to the next grade or you didn't pass to the next grade at all.

I was going to pass with good grades! I couldn't wait! Summer was here and soon, so would be my freedom!

Sometimes the girls from the gang came to school to make appearances and to keep the truant officer off of their backs and having to deal with their parents but not enough that once you went into the school you would have to worry about them.

They spent most of their days outside smoking cigarettes and drinking or not being around the school at all. I had made friends with one of the sisters of one of the gang members. She wasn't part of the gang and they didn't pressure her. She was really smart in school and I found out that we had a lot of things

38

that we had in common.

The girl gang members didn't like me and I could tell when I would see one or a couple of them walking together, they would just roll their eyes at me and give me dirty looks. I didn't know what I had done to any of them hell, what it boiled down to they just didn't. I hadn't done a thing and it didn't matter. They had set their sights on me and had made other plans that I never dreamed of and they were all just for me.

On the second to last day of school I stood in line waiting for the bell to ring to enter the school to which I would soon be saying goodbye. After the bell rang I started to walk into the building. A gang member I had noticed had been leaning on the fence. She was watching me as she inhaled on the cigarette deeply and let the smoke rings waft out of her mouth and the rest flow slowly through her nostrils. I tried my best to keep looking forward to prevent having to make any eye contact with her.

She finished the cigarette and flicked the butt into the grass, continued to walk towards the entrance to the school. As she passed me, without any hesitation, she turned and slapped me across the face so hard that the tears immediately jumped out of my eyes. As I turned to look around to see what the other kids were doing, it surprised me that no one had said anything. In fact no one had responded at all. They had just stood in their places, paralyzed with fear, trying to pretend that they hadn't seen what had just happened.

In the meanwhile, she had entered the building and continued to walk down the corridor; she turned her head towards me, smiled, and disappeared into her classroom. Within a minute, she was gone. No one in the projects had ever warned me that this was about the time that gang members had started to make their mark to determine which kids were going to be the ones who were either fortunate enough to be left alone, or would end up being the ones that were going to be harassed. I had become the latter. My face was still burning as I continued to hold it as I entered my classroom, but not before watching to see which classroom she had gone into at the end of the hall. I sat down at my desk but only for a moment. In fact, as the teacher spoke, I couldn't even concentrate on what he was trying to explain.

The teacher was standing with his back turned towards us writing what we were going to discuss in class that day. I barely heard a word that had been spoken. I raised my hand and as he turned to answer I told him that I needed to leave... Now!

I didn't even wait for an answer nor did I turn in the homework from our previous assignment. I just walked out. My mind was reeling, I was afraid of what was to come, I was afraid that It could get even nastier later on. I had been right.

It had not been my brain that had warned me it was a gut feeling and gut feelings were usually not wrong, but as I walked down the hall with her handprint on my face, it didn't matter anymore. After I had made my way down to the end of the hall I looked into the classroom through the glass panel. The teacher was busily writing on the front board the day's assignment, as all teachers were probably doing at that time.

I placed my hand on the doorknob and turned it quickly, but quietly. As it opened I glanced around the room to see where the girl gang member sat. She was sitting at her desk with her back toward the blackboard talking and laughing with two other girls. I walked over to her, at about the same time as the teacher said something to me to the effect of if she could help help me.

I didn't remember exactly, but what I did remember was just as the girl turned around to see what the teacher was saying, my fist was meeting her face like a head on collision. She wore her hair in an afro. I remember digging my hand deep into it to reach her scalp, at the same time I pulled her head all of the way back, where she was able to look straight up into my face.

If I had pulled her head back even a couple of inches further I would have snapped her neck. The teacher was now standing in the middle of the floor but she knew all about this particular girl and knew that she was nothing but trouble. Every teacher knew that girl gangs were trouble and tried as hard as they could to ignore them or pretend that they weren't there. I slapped her as hard across the face as she had done to me. Then I turned her head to the other side and slapped her again. Then I pulled her by her hair and threw her to the ground desk and all. I kicked the desk to the side. While straddling her I

40

leaned down close enough to kiss her and I whispered, "Take that back to your leader and be sure to tell her who did it." Then I hit her with my fist and said, "If I had to, no matter what price that I would have to pay, "I would get each and every one of them one by one when they least expected it."

They needed to start making plans to kill me, or leave me the fuck alone!" With that I let her hair go but I never shifted my gaze. I wanted her to know that I was not going to be the one that was gonna be messed with. I un-straddled her and walked out of her class room, without looking back. As I walked the long hall back to my classroom my knees were shaking, my hands were hurting and shaking, and my mind was reeling.

All I could think of was what I had told her, for them to start making plans to kill me, which is exactly what I felt, they were going to do. My first thought was, were they gonna riddle me with bullets to make me an example for the next person who had thought the way that I had, or were they going to shoot me just once through the head. As I reached my classroom a tear rolled down my cheek. Just one. I thought to myself, "It really didn't matter now did it? I wouldn't need tears later, *because dead was dead.*

Chapter Fourteen: Here We Go!

The girl gang member must have left school early because I didn't see her walking through the halls or leaning on any of the lockers with her girl followers. When the class lined up to go to the cafeteria for lunch, she wasn't there. I started to get a bad feeling. Trouble was going to be coming my way soon and there wasn't a thing that I would be able to do about it. As the day went on everyone talked about only having only one more day of school. I became more involved in what was going on inside instead of what may have been waiting outside. Then something changed, kids started whispering, and I overheard one girl say, "It's gonna be a fight after we get out." The teacher in the last period class was telling everyone to be quiet much more than she had before.

She gave me this look, like she was trying to tell me something with her eyes, that she would take me away if she could, but I knew that she couldn't help me. Most of the teachers were lucky to get out and away from school each day without having anything done to their cars, like having their tires slashed, keyed, or broken into. Or they might have been verbally threatened or assaulted. Knowing that no one would really listen to them and they knew that they would have to return to teach at the school. For them, it would be at their best interest to just turn their heads and pretend that nothing ever happened. No one messed with the kids in the projects.

Buy then I knew that she had left the school and had returned with the other members of her gang. Just the thought of it, and I became instantly sick. I knew that fight would be with me. What I had said earlier to Corkey was a reflex from the slap. I really hadn't expected to react the way I did. It just happened. Now I was going to have to pay for that reaction--possibly with my life-- I picked up my books to leave class.

There wasn't anything else that I could do. As I came out everyone parted themselves on either side of the fence like they do for the kings and queens coming through. Kids that usually went home straight after school were now milling around and watching quietly and waiting. My only friend, Diane came out of the

school to walk home with me. I told her when we ate
lunch together what had happened. But word had spread
through the whole school like fire and she already
knew. I told her I just lost it I didn't stop to
think about what might happen later. When the girl
slapped me I just had lost it.

After school, by the time we had gotten to
Wabash, we knew the gang where behind us. At first
they were laughing with each other then they started
making remarks about my skin color especially about my
freckles.

Then someone stepped on the back of my shoe,
causing me to literally step out of it but not before
falling and having my papers fly all over the place.
As I bent down to try to pick them up before they all
blew away, I was able to get a better look at who they
were and how many of there were. Diane's sister was in
the gang and she made her walk away from me because of
what was going to happen. As I stood up they were no
longer behind me now they were all around me in a
circle that I wouldn't be able to get out of.

Bay-Bay was leader of this gang. Although Corky
was the fastest and she was Bay-Bay's right hand girl.
Now that the gang was there, Corkey was the first to
look at me and laugh. It was Corky's right hand that
threw a sucker punch with so much speed and accuracy
that not only did it catch me off guard, but the power
from it knocked me off my feet and the wind out of me
at the same time. Then someone punched me in the eye,
and I truly saw stars and dots from my now rapidly
swelling eye. I tried to get on my feet and
felt a kick straight to my stomach. Then two of the
other girls stood me up and held my arms out to my
sides, BAY-Bay hit me with everything that she had.
All of the girls cheered while she threw punch after
punch. Then she turned around to walk away but instead
of doing so she took her arm back as far as she could
and hit me in the jaw. My face reacted by giving up a
prize for her trouble…My tooth.

As I was still being held the gang took turns
working on my face and body. After a while I didn't
feel a thing, no pain at all. I was the example to
others of what would happen if one of their girls was
ever touch by anyone. The beating seemed to go on for
hours, though it probably lasted fifteen minutes at
best. As the two girls dropped me to the ground each
one that passed by me kicked me as hard in my head,

knees, legs, whatever part of my body that they could reach.. Diane's sister, who was in the gang pulled her away as they left.

All that I could think of was that it was over. I laid face down on the ground. At first I didn't think that I could even move. As I tried to move my head blood came from both of my lips and nose. I lay on the ground on my stomach with my face turned to the side I could feel a clot forming where my lower lip had been almost split in half. The last girl was laughing, but before she walked away she bent down over me and spit on the side of my face. As she caught up with the others she hollered back, "You better be glad we didn't slit your throat bitch." I could hear them giving each other high-fives and laughing about what they had done to me.

After lying on the ground where they had left me, blood from my nose started to form a stream as it started to go into the cracks in the concrete. All I wanted to do was sleep. Just to try to escape the pain. I didn't want to walk, I just wanted to sleep. Then I felt a pair of arms. One pair around my waist the other pair was holding my arms around their necks. It was one of the girls from my building and her brother. Her name was Brenda too.

I don't know or remember if I walked or they carried me. I ended up on the fifth floor. She didn't ask what happened to me. Everyone already knew.

After she cleaned me up, I realized that it was almost time for my mother to come home from work. I staggered up to my apartment which was up five more flights. I thought I was going to pass out. I don't know why I thought that she wouldn't notice. She did.

My mom kept me home for a whole week, after my begging her not to take me to the hospital. She didn't but not before grounding me and taking away all of my privileges, which wasn't bad because that only meant I couldn't watch television or go outside after school.

Going to the hospital would only make it worse. Everyone would see that I had sutures and bandages I just couldn't let that happen. The one good thing about it all was that school, was. Out!

I stayed in the house for over a week. Before and after work she placed a towel around my chest and made me keep it like that every day because it hurt so much to exhale, she kept saying that my top and bottom lip had needed stitches but I still refused to let her take me to the hospital. My stomach felt as though I had been run over by a truck. I couldn't chew, I didn't want to eat I just wanted to stay in bed.

My eyes were the worst and they took the longest time to heal. They were swollen and bruised, and both were blood red. I also had a huge knot that had started to grow over my right eye. I had missed Mohammed Ali coming to the opening of the hotdog stand that had been put up at the end of the parking lot in his honor, but it looked like he had gotten mad because I had missed the opening, he had come straight to my house instead and taken his anger out on me. For weeks my family ate everything that used frozen vegetables. We had them in soups, stews, side dishes, you name it, we ate it because we were poor, there were no steaks, and the frozen vegetables were handy and had to make do. The freezer froze them my face melted them. In fact I felt that I wore more frozen food on my face than the jolly green giant. It was the time of the year that everyone had waited for. I looked like a zombie on lockdown so it didn't matter.

Chapter Fifteen: Boy Gangs

I probably was the happiest person in the projects, just because I was alive to be there for the summer. It could have been worse, and if it had been, I wouldn't be writing this memoir. The second best thing was that for three months I wouldn't have to worry about the girls in the gang coming for me again. Until school started back. One day as I came out of the stairwell to sit on the benches in the front of the building, one of the gang members said something that I never forgot.

He laughed and pointed at my face and said, "You show got fucked up!" He kept laughing as he walked back to join the others who were leaning on the fence. The second one walked over to where I was sitting. I had my head down, trying to think. Why was I still sitting there and letting them make fun of me.

The last one walked over and lifted my chin up with one finger shook his head from side to side, " Tsk, tsk, tsk, yella girl, you got seconds when they served kick ass stew." As he turned around to walk away, I noticed that none of the others were laughing anymore. He hollered out to them, "Com on yall, lets git this shit started."

Chapter Sixteen: Tommy

At that time I didn't really know who Tommy was let alone that he was the leader of the gang in our building. He was leaning on the fence watching the other gang members slap box with each other and he was watching me. I wished I could have been invisible. I felt stupid. As he slap boxed he hollered out to me, "High yella, yu beta take yo head outta yo ass and start watching so they don't kill yo ass next time." And that's how I got that name. It had been given to me by Tommy.

"Didn't nobody eva teach you how to fight?" I thought to myself "Now that was a brilliant question wasn't it?" No one had uttered a word when he was standing in front of me; no one said anything when he walked away. They got together to pretend to fight. Sometimes they fought each other just so they could be ready for any action that came up. Or until Tommy decided that he wanted to do something else. But before they left that day, Tommy wanted me to see him in action. I noticed that the members of his gang always referred to him as Lil-Tommy. He called out to one of the other members. Tommy put his fists up, he kept them close. Always keeping one fist up to guard his face whenever he threw a punch. If the punch was blocked, he would pull his arm back and quickly bring both arms up again for protection.

It was similar to watching him and his gang appeared as though they were training for a boxing match. His gang members were good. Tommy was better. He stood facing in my direction. One of his gang members had his back to me. Tommy would glance quickly at me to make sure I was watching him as he would bob and weave.

When he got one of the gang members up against the fence he would literally pummel him to the point that they would holler "OK, OK, Tommy you got me man I'm through." His point was to teach them how to react, and me. Eventually when a blow was coming they would get it or they would get beaten until they did. What I remembered about the gang members was that the majority of them were muscular. Being buffed was what we call it today.

I could see the muscles in their stomachs. The muscles in their arms looked as If they had been lifting weights. Their necks and legs were like football player. When Tommy would do a move on one of them he would do something to get my attention, like call on another member so That I could take notice. When he would get a member on the side I would watch closely. In fact everything that he did that revolved around fighting I had watched closely. But I had secretly hoped that I would never have to use them, but knowing soon that I would have to when I went back to school so I made sure to pay close attention to every move that he made.

Tommy had one of the gang members in front of him. He put his hands together and hit him with his elbow in the lower part of his back. But before the gang member fell Tommy was so quick that he was able to clasp his hands around his neck, bending him forward, and as he did so, brought his knee up hard into his face and as soon as he let him go he fell to the ground face down hard. When he got up the blood was coming from his nose like water. The look that he gave Tommy was one that could kill but the thought of it quickly made him lose that look.

He just put the bottom of his tee-shirt to his nose and extended his hand, palm out to give and receive a high five from his leader, Tommy. I watched as Tommy said nothing but made sure that we made eye contact. And we held it for what seemed like a very long time. To Tommy it just reinforced his leadership among them to maintain the respect that he deserved from them. So there would be no doubt as to where he stood. In Lil-Tommy's gang he was the leader. He issued the orders of what would happen, when it would happen and to whom it would happen, if it would involve fighting or perhaps who would possibly die. Or wish that they were already dead.

And whenever he and the others tired of sparring they would get cans of spray paint and spray their names and the gang that they represented, which was The Gangster Disciples. Every place that wasn't already marked by them they did it on the outsides of the building, on the doors of the elevators, the laundry room doors, the walls in the hallways and everything in between. Tommy had a lot of members in his gang and most, if not all had either been called their street names from having been used by their families.

Even relatives would call them by their street

names when they came around. No one ever called them by their given names that I knew of. I wouldn't find out their given names until much, much later. K.C was his first lieutenant, Emmett was his second lieutenant, and Roy was the back up for Emmett. I only knew the street names of some of the other members. Cisco, T-bone, Marky Mark, Mad Dog, Andrew, Out of Town, Blade. I never paid that much attention to the others. They were considered foot soldiers. Tommy had a tattoo. Not that I ever remember seeing it up close on him even when his shirt was off. In fact the only member that I did remember seeing one on was T-Bone. He had one on his arm that said mom. All gangs represented themselves and their affiliations by the colors that they wore. Everyone wore afro. The boys and the girls. That was the style at that time. The High school colors were black and red. Tommy and his gang wore the same colors to represent our area.

Tommy was known for the way he used his fists to fight but he wasn't above occasionally using a pair of brass knuckles when fighting rival gangs. I had gotten to know and had started dating one of the members of his gang; his name was Mark. The people that knew him called him "Markey Mark." He was actually a part time member because he came up to Chicago from Los Angeles.

During the summer but returned to LA when school started, so he was accepted. Mark had told me that Tommy and the gang carried guns, .9mm and a gun made of the hinges from the top parts of the door in the hallways. They called them zip guns. They also had shotguns called sawed offs. Most carried 38s. Only Tommy, K.C. and Emmett knew where the shotguns were kept. Mark told me that although he didn't know for sure that there was something about one person who he wouldn't name that wasn't right.

He told me that he couldn't put his finger on it, but it was something that each time he saw that person he felt it. I remembered how his facial expression changed when he looked at me. I could see the anger in his eyes that no one in the group had noticed. He said that if Tommy found out that anyone in his gang was a snitch they would pay In the worst way. One day as Mark and I stood downstairs talking Oswald walked by. I saw the way Mark looked at him as Oswald walked by on his way towards the bus stop which was north on the corner across from our building which was 49th street. After He got on the bus with Mark and

49

I went upstairs I started to wonder why he looked at
Oswald the way he did. I wondered if he felt that it
could have been Oswald.

Oswald had just returned to stay with his mom
for the summer too. He had been doing that for a
couple of years that I knew of. I don't think anyone
knew where he lived when he wasn't with her. At first
he would hang around with Tommy and his gang but I
never saw him have a lot of interaction with them.
Then I started thinking about what Mark had said about
him that he had changed and he acted like he didn't
really want to hang out with Tommy and the gang
anymore.

Mark later told me that Oswald would start using
excuses, that his mom would want him to go to visit
his other relatives since he wasn't going to be up
here for long and when he did come back he wouldn't
let them know that he was there. Every time one of
Tommy's boys came and asked for him they were told
that he wasn't there. But I knew that he was there
because we lived on the same floor.

He would look at me in an odd way when he saw me
looking at him when he went into his house. When Mark
came to see me one day I told him that I had seen
Oswald go into his house but and was told that he
wasn't there when one the gang members had been told
that he wasn't home. Mark left immediately to tell
Tommy so he could see what they would be told when
they asked for him.

One of the gang members returned and knocked on
Oswald's door. Mark and I saw Oswald's mother shake
her head again to say that he wasn't there. Mark and
I stood together pretending to look over the fence. As
the member started on his way back he looked at Mark
and nodded. When Tommy came back with the gang and
knocked on Oswald's door he pretended that he had just
gotten home. Now Mark knew what it was that made him
uneasy about Oswald. He came back and told me that
Tommy was not going to do anything right then. They
were going to start watching him very closely. Later
Oswald came to my house asking to see my sister but I
told him the same thing that his mother had told the
gang that she wasn't there. So! Oswald had a crush on
my sister!
After Oswald left I noticed that Mark was looking
differently instead of looking at me he was looking
down at the ground and slowly turned his head away so

that I couldn't see his face. I asked him what was wrong and for a moment he said nothing, then he took my hand and faced me. He told me that he, Tommy and his whole gang had seen me the day that I had taken that beating from the girls in the gang that day. My eyes grew as large as saucers, as my mouth dropped, I yanked my hand away from his to leave.

I couldn't believe that he, having seen me almost get killed had the nerve to say to me that he liked me like what he had told me was no big thing. I shook my head not wanting to hear what he had said and as I started to walk away. He grabbed my hand, In doing so he pulled it so hard that I literally fell backwards onto the ground I was lucky that he caught me because it would have been a hard fall and I would have really hurt myself badly because it had happened so fast. He pulled me close and hugged me and as he buried his face into the side of my neck told me how sorry that he was, but there was nothing at the time that he could do because it was the rule: boy gangs did not get involved in girl gang fights or vise, versa unless the leader decided it was necessary. Tommy didn't know me at the time; he didn't know anything about me so he felt that it was none of his gang's business. I just put my head on his shoulder and started to cry harder as he hugged me. He told me that he didn't agree with most of the things that the gang did or said. Sometimes when he came to Chicago he really didn't want to be involved with them, he really didn't want to be a part of what they did and that he just wanted to get out, but he explained that it was twice as hard to get out as it was to get in.

Sometimes in trying to get out you may have been able to live through the beating. But if you were unlucky enough to have been one of the members who knew too much about them and what they did, the beatings would be all the more merciless. Sometimes enough to kill you and even if you lived through the beating it wouldn't matter because they were going to kill you anyway.

Killing would be better because it would have been quicker. He spoke of having seen it happen to another gang member and it wasn't pretty. In fact no one ever saw that
gang member again but the dragon did and it wasn't talked about after it happened. Tommy had a way of making things happen and no one would say anything.

51

That's what Tommy used the bar and the handcuffs that were locked on it were for. The laundry room on the sixteenth floor, everyone knew not to go near the sixteenth floor because if you did it meant one of two things. Sex, a beat down, or death. The decision to kill someone was always Tommy's. There were only a few that were willing or able to take a bullet and live to be able to completely leave. Mark said that he would be willing to take the beat down for me but it would have been useless because if they didn't kill him he wouldn't ever be able to come back to the building to see me again. I stood up and without looking back and walked away.

There were members of Tommy's gang who had older brothers who belonged to the quote "Real Gangs." The older men were the ones that involved real violence. It was the type of violence that made the news. They had the original organizational ranks, the up and coming gangs copied the military organization. It was said that Tommy's gang was mostly involved in property and petty theft, and the domestic abuse. Most of the violence involved rival gang members. And there was the violence that involved their girlfriends, and family.

Within the gang, any dispute between gang members was allowed to settle between themselves only when given permission by the leader. It would have had to have been something that had been definitely deemed necessary to do to get the matter settled, So if anything happened whoever the dispute involved wouldn't affect their not covering that particular members back in whatever dangerous activity that may have turned up.

Chapter Seventeen: The Real Gangsters

The Black P. Stones wrote graffiti on the wall and everywhere else to identify their ownership of turf. Turf meant territory. All gangs agreed on one saying which was made popular by Huey Newton, who was one of the leaders of The Black Panther Nation. The gangs referred to him as "The Brotha." His saying became infamous "flowed through the trigger connected to the barrel of a gun."

Another so called brotha, (Bill) Malik Shabazz referred to the white man as "honkey" along with the rest of their kind, who he called "The United Snakes of Amurderer." Malik Shabazz was a notorious gang banger known all over Chicago, and even other states. He was a drug dealer and a drug user.

"After being elected marshal and getting accepted into The Nation of Islam, he left after Muhammed's death due to his difference of opinion in how it was caused. The party was satisfied that Muhammed had died of natural causes. The Party of The Black P. Stone Nation felt that he had been assassinated. The individual gangs united under one organization. The Black P. Stone Nation. Other gangs followed, those were The Black Gangster Disciples. The two organizations controlled much of the drug trade, and later became rivals. When the leaders went to jail or prison there would always be others to do for them on the outside of prison what they could not do while incarcerated. New members felt that gang identification was needed so that gang members could be distinguished as friend from foe. That carried down through each generation of gangs.

# # #

It was said that in prison no one was allowed to wear belts or shoes with strings, to prevent strangulation of rival gangs and to prevent men feeling suicidal from being unable to act out on their plan. Because they were unable to wear belts, their pants fell of off their waist. The skinnier ones had pants that fell three fourths of the way down their body, which made them walk like penguins because there was no other way for them to maneuver their legs to try to carry their trays of food or for any other activity that required the use of both hands.

Does that ring a bell with the fashion of the men today? In the prison population, much like today, prison gangs had their own rules and symbols. Gangs who were affiliated with the Gangsta Disciples wore their clothes to the left side along with the caps, bandana and left pant leg rolled half way up. The Black P. Stones did the opposite. Back in the mid-sixties and early seventies, the minimum number of street gangs had at least fifty individual gangs. These men *were pros. They were ruthless, they cared nothing about nothing. They had nothing to lose and if they were going to do something that paid off, they had everything to gain. The one thing that the Pimps and the older gang members shared was the types of cars that they drove. They both drove Cadillac Eldorado's and Deville's. But most people of the people who lived in the projects whose families were lucky drove old Chevy caprices, station wagons and impalas.*

# # #

Some of those were the brothers of the boys that were in Tommy's gang. Even though Tommy was a gang leader, the more violent Gang members considered his gang as shorties. I would hear the older gang members give the shorties a slap to the hands as a welcoming sign. They used the same sign to greet their own members. Those gangs were almost never seen. And the less you knew about them, the better.

Chapter Eighteen: THE WA WHO BA MAN

In the better neighborhoods, where the white people in the middle class lived, on television, the Good Humor Man drove a white truck that always played a jingle through the speakers on his truck. The Good Humor Man wore a white hat, shirt, pants and white shiny shoes. On TV he would have a big smile and he was always very, very polite as he greeted the parents with their children.

In the projects when the Good Humor Man's truck came around everyone who saw the truck or heard its jingle would shout "the WA WHO BA man's here! He was called that because it was the only treat on his truck that the mothers would give enough money to buy. You could hear kids from everywhere begging their mothers to let them have money for a WA WHO Ba! They would hug their mother's waist saying, "pleeeeze mom! Let me git sum-um from the Good Humor Truck!"

After wearing their mother's down with their continuous whining they would get their wish. I guess the mothers remembered how they were as kids when the Good Humor Truck came around. Even Tommy and his boys would come to the truck sometimes, but usually they just paid some of the kids to get their frozen treats for them. At first The Good Humor Man didn't come around the projects often. I dunno, I thought that maybe he was making his rounds somewhere else. But when he came it would usually be in the early afternoon. When you would get to his truck, you could see that he seemed equally as happy to see the kids as they did to see him. He sold popsicles, push-ups, ice cream bars, and the works. But the cheapest dessert that most of the kids could afford was the WA who Ba.

The WA Who Ba was almost like a dream sickle but without the ice cream. The inside was almost like a Popsicle that came in assorted flavors. Mine favorite was the raspberry kind. It was the only treat that cost seven cents. Since it was the cheapest price and sold by THE WA WHO BA MAN, that's what everyone named it, and then started to call him. "The WA Who Ba man. A couple of times some of us older kids would see him before the little ones did because we would be downstairs playing softball.

He wouldn't open up the serving window until he heard the sound of the little kids call for a WA WHO

BA, then he would raise the window and signal for the kids to come quickly, smiling as he shouted "hurry up kids, I can't wait too long I've got other places to go" That would make the kids run with all of their might. I remember getting to the truck once where I was the first in line. He completely ignored me. He seemed lost in thought as he waited for the younger kids to arrive. As I looked at him, he didn't look like the mild mannered happy go lucky Good Humor Man that was on TV.

To me he looked like some dirty old man that if you saw him on the street you would run away. *Fast!* .There was something different about the WA Who Ba man; there was something about him besides his looks that just wasn't right. His clothes were just like the man on the TV but what he had that the Good Humor Man on TV didn't have was, a long apron with a towel draped over the strings that tied the apron together. Unlike on TV where there were different drivers in the trucks. I noticed that he was the only one who always came to our neighborhood. And not only that, this WA WHO BA MAN came more often than the others. Sometime as some of us made our way towards the truck we would see a little girl or boy coming out of the door of the truck skipping away. Sometimes holding two WA WHO BA's and other times the kids would have their WA Who Ba's and the money that their mother's had given them to buy it with. Sometimes holding two WA WHO BA's and other times the kids would have their WA Who Ba's and the money that their mother's had given them to buy it with.

We would just shrug our shoulders hoping we might get lucky enough to get a free bar and keep our money too! Sometimes when he would open the window we would notice that his face would be red and sweaty.

He would be wiping off one hand onto the towel that draped over the apron strings as he used the other to raise the serving window, and then he would wipe both hands on the towel. Again everyone got what they came for and he would wave and drive away. One Friday as the jingle of the bells began, I remember standing next to a mother and heard her say, "Na he gone have to stop coming round heah so much, hell, he's making me go broke". As usual kids came running from everywhere, Instead of keeping the window closed as he usually did. I walked up first expecting to be served right away because the window was up, but this

time The WA Who Ba Man was so interested in getting
one of the kids into his truck that instead of having
left the window closed as he always did. He slipped.
He forgot to keep it down.

After letting one little boy inside of his
truck, he sat him on his lap and gave him Popsicle to
lick. As the little one giggled in delight, He put his
hand under the apron. The little boy started laughing
and squirming but continued licking on the WA WHO BA.
The man started breathing hard and sweating, and then
he let the little boy go out the door. What he didn't
know was that his disgusting act was going to catch up
with him one day, and that day was it. He didn't
notice that one of Tommy's boys, "T-BONE" was standing
by the truck waiting to get a WA WHO BA too and had
seen just as I had what he was doing with the kids. T-
BONE stood at the window long enough to see him take
his hand from under the apron, as he stood up to wipe
the wetness from his hands.

When the WA Who Ba man went to collect some
money from another little girl, T-BONE quickly grabbed
him by his shirt. The WA Who Ba man struggled to try
to keep from being pulled out through the window, one
of the other gang members who had been standing by the
building watching the truck saw T-BONE hitting the
man, who was then trying to fight back. As the second
one reached the truck, T-Bone told him what The WA Who
Ba man was doing to the little kids as he pointed to
one of the little boys holding two ice cream
sandwiches as he happily skipped away.

A long line of the other kids were already
following behind him. He looked like he was from the
fairy tale called, "The Pied Piper." T-BONE made a
loud whistle and within seconds there were at least
ten more gang members at the truck. The WA Who Ba man
tried to hold on to stay in the safety of the truck,
but he was no match for what was in store for him, in
fact in his haste, he hadn't even closed or locked the
trucks door. So all they had to do was step up into
the truck, He was fighting for his life but he didn't
have a chance. A few kicked him and instead of pulling
him off of the bus, The gang members hoisted him up
and threw him through the serving window of the truck
onto the ground where they started to beat him in the
face, they kicked and stomped him, and then others
from the gang came with bats and ropes. They wrapped
the rope around his neck and held it tight where he

couldn't turn his head and continued to beat him until
he stopped struggling.

The blood was coming from his mouth, nose and
ears when they picked him up and threw him back into
his truck. But not before passing out everything that
he had inside. Every barrel was emptied of its
contents and then threw them out on the ground. As he
lay on the ground, a couple of the gang lifted him up
and slammed his body back onto
the ground. All of the small kids that were standing
around the truck, and even the older ones, including
me just stood there frozen in place.

The WA Who BA man was a bloody mess. The little
kids didn't understand what was happening, but my
friends and I did. I know it was what he was doing
to the smaller kids. The one gang member "T-BONE" who
was as tall as a tree turned around to face us, sweat
was pouring off of his body and I had never seen
anyone look so mad. He yelled "none of yawl beta not
go near any of dem trucks wid-out sum one olda dan
yawl again or I'm gonna come and beat yo ass! Not less
it's yo mamma, yo brotha, yo olda sista, I on give a
damn! Jus don't let me catch yu down hea by yo self"!

"He ain't no Good Humor Man, ain't shit funny
about what he do. None of the little ones knew what he
was talking about. We gonna watch them trucks every
time dey comes around here."

"He's The WA WHO BA MAN don't fo git what I said
then he pointed at the truck. Piece of shits what he
is. He ain't even gone be dat now" As I grew older I
understood why they did what they did to The WA WHO BA
MAN. As an adult, every time I flash back to that day
I think of The WA WHO BA Man.

He actually had three names. It was the last
name that got him killed. To some he was the Good
Humor Man, to the little kids he was The WA WHO BA
MAN, to the adults and to others in the projects he
was a pedophile.

A man who preyed and tried to molest little
children and what better way to conceal it than to use
his ice cream truck. The Good Humor truck sat where
it had originally parked for three days. No one went
near it. On the fourth day there came the blaring of
sirens from lots of police, shortly afterward the
ambulance drove up. As they were transferring the body
to the ambulance an arm dropped out from under the
sheet. It looked black. The ambulance drivers quickly

put it back under the sheet and whisked the body away. As they did all you hear as the ambulance pulled away was clapping! It sounded as though everyone in the whole building was clapping. It was the sort of cheering that you would hear when you would watch a baseball game on television.

Shortly afterwards the media broke the news that they had found the body of a Good Humor Man. The media portrayed him as though he was a genuinely sweet family man who was loved by all. They said he was a good friend who would help anyone who needed it. He attended church regularly, and made it known that he loved people regardless of their skin color. The media spoke of how he would go into the worst neighborhoods to try to sell popsicles and ice cream at a loss to himself just to give cold treats to the poor that would have otherwise gone without.

The news media kept repeated over and over what a horrific killing it had been. That it had been a senseless killing done to a very good man. That the people in the projects acted like animals having such little regard for human life, that they left him in his truck after they had killed him. No one has the decency to even call for someone to come to check on a Good Humor Truck that had been sitting by the curb for four days. He may have been a well-mannered man, a good father and loving friend He probably did go to church on a regular basis.

He loved people, but he loved children even more, but the people of the projects really knew why he loved the children so much. Once again the animals in the projects had killed a white man without provocation. Yes he was a man who had only tried to help. He helped himself through the innocence of children. Goodbye Good Humor Man, Goodbye WA WHO BA MAN, Goodbye pedophile. You will never be forgotten.

Chapter Nineteen:
Visitors, Look Outs, and the Breezeway

In the projects every building had lookouts. The gangs knew when someone was there that hadn't been there before or just didn't belong as soon as they walked near or into the buildings. Visitors were grilled on what their business was for being there, or who they had come to see. Once the information was given it was always double checked for truthfulness. If they were there to visit a relative of friend they would not be considered a threat. Usually the person they said that they came to visit was asked and if they said yes it would be okay. But someone had to vouch for them.

If the person was a male and had to come to live with a relative they would be sized up for possible indoctrination into the gang. In the projects everyone in their building knew everyone. No one would venture into a building where they didn't know anyone they could be robbed, killed or both. In buildings where there were girl gangs it would be the same as the boys.

It was not just about being someone to rob. The gangs also protected the families that lived there. If someone was fighting someone from another building there would be no hesitation of the gang getting involved. The tunnels were also referred to as the breezeways. They were located right around the corner from the janitor's room. It could be used as an entrance to go through the building.

Sometimes the wind gusts were so strong that mothers would hold on tightly to their little ones to keep them from almost being blown away. The mailboxes were also located there. For a while in nineteen-sixty four, the mail stopped being delivered because people would grab the postman's bag and run away with all of the mail. People had to go to the post office to get their checks. That became a problem and an inconvenience because the women had to dress and take their little ones and walk to get them. In the summer it was not as much as a problem but in the winter it was hard. After that happened for a while on the first of the month Tommy and his gang would walk with the mailman so that he could put the public aid stamps and checks into the mail boxes.

After he finished closing and locking all of the

boxes, two gang members would escort him back to his truck. They could have robbed him but there were too many women and babies including their families that depended on those stamps to eat and to pay their bills. Children were important. You would always hear a mother when talking about their child speak of them continuing to go to school to make something of themselves to get out of this dump that held them and everyone else prisoner. What they meant was the same for their children is the same thing now that we want for our children today. Because no matter where they lived, the children would always be our future. Whether we lived to see that future or not. Just because they weren't educated, it didn't mean that they didn't have hopes and dreams for their children.

With a better education they could get a good job, learn what to do and what not to do and most of all, to get out of the hell hole to give them a better life than they had had. One that had trapped them and kept them as prisoners with no chance of getting out. But mothers in the projects and everywhere else realized that their babies would grow up and become teenagers and they knew that with teenagers came raging hormones. White girls got pregnant, but they were sent away to live with a relative or their family had enough money to let them have abortions and although at that time they were considered illegal there was always someone who knew someone that would do it. My mother worked downtown with a lot of white women and although they wouldn't talk to her she would hear them talking and saying how disgusted they were that their daughter had gotten pregnant and what they were going to have to do about it. Blacks couldn't afford those luxuries so they had their children and were stigmatized for it.

The mothers living in the projects had been teens themselves and they remembered no matter what their mother's had warned them about, especially about getting pregnant but it had fallen on deaf ears. Their girls felt that they could sneak and not get caught but they had. They felt that the boy loved them and would be a good father, but he wasn't and he usually left as soon as he found out that the girl had become pregnant. Although they still had high hopes for their daughters, but in their hearts most knew that it was be an uphill struggle at best.

There were a lot of girls who had real
relationships, they dated boys who really cared about
them, it didn't stop them from sneaking around having
sex with someone who would but they did otherwise
treat the girl they were dating well. Sometimes when I
was downstairs sitting on the bench I would overhear
them talking about which collage they were planning to
attend. They were already in their senior year and
felt strongly about it. I knew of one family that had
four boys and all of them went off to college. Now
remember I am speaking of my building only. I don't
want anyone from other buildings to feel that there
were none in theirs. It was probably the same in a lot
of others, but as I will repeat, I can't write about
what I don't know. There were a lot of girls that got
pregnant. Some were as young as twelve years old. No
one spoke of abstinence or not to have sex because
they could get pregnant. No one told the twelve year
old that she should still be playing rope or
hopscotch. The mothers knew little because some had
dropped out of school for that very reason, No one
told them that had been too young, to do those things.
And the teachers at school certainly didn't care.

It wasn't their problem. Some of the older girls
who had sex were literally lucky, and would get away
without getting pregnant for a year or two, but in not
having it to happen they continued to hand down the
myths and told them to their younger sisters who they
knew were having sex. When asked the majority had
never even seen the private parts of their boyfriends
they just did the act in the dark and brag about his
prowess form its thickness and length, but never about
using protection.

There were some girls that didn't plan to get
pregnant; no one ever did but they were tired of the
responsibility of always being put in charge by their
mothers to care for their younger siblings. They were
either too afraid to ask their mom to take them for
birth control then their mothers would know that they
were having sex. They would be put on punishment
indefinitely, whipped, forbidden to leave the house or
not allowed to have any company at all. It never
worked because when the mother went to the store they
would either let the boy in, or sneak out. Where there
was a will, and there was, there would always be a
way.

Sometimes they would have sex in the hallways on

a floor where the light had been broken out. Most of the time the pressure from the boy was too great, some gave in rather than take the chance and lose him to someone else. And then be labeled as a tease to all of the other boys which made her ostracized by all. Once she became pregnant or her growing belly began to show, they would then tell their mothers. Not knowing that their mothers already knew. Mothers have that instinct and they are usually always the first to know.

What their daughters didn't know was how much they had hurt their mothers and themselves. She wasn't old enough to take care of herself let alone a new baby, the responsibility of changing a diaper, heating a bottle burping getting up even if it was in the middle of the night and they were sleepy. It was something they had not thought of, but now had to learn quickly. Having little to no education, some were not even old enough for a job. And the chance of getting a job even if it were in housekeeping, her chances would be little to none.

She wouldn't even have been considered for one. It would have been given to a white person immediately rather than her. Her understanding of what discrimination was incomprehensible because she had never ventured out into what was considered the white man's world. The thought of being turned down for a job to her had no meaning. After having tried unsuccessfully in her own environment without getting one, She decided that she would have better luck on the outside of it.

Once downtown she was referred to names that she didn't understand a number of times. She wasn't used to the treatment or names that she was called or the mean faces of the people who looked down their noses at her. As if she had rolled around on the ground in the alley.

Or that she was no better than the rats that ran in it. By the end of the day, usually broken down to tears and in spirit she went home having given up because no one would even look at a black girl, for a job when there was a possibility that there was a white one that wanted it.

No one even gave her chance. Especially after reviewing her application which showed where she lived. She was invisible. She was treated just as badly as the men who went looking for jobs. She never got a chance, because she didn't have a chance. Her rejection threshold was nowhere as strong as the men who had talked about how it was. Sadly the only resort for her was to stay with their mothers and siblings and the extended family emerged.

Each girl having made the mistake thinking that it would be different and that it wouldn't happen to them. Sometimes the older sister's luck ran out and she too would end up living in the same apartment. If she or another sibling had two or more of their own, then the CHA would give them an apartment of their own, usually in an apartment in the same building but never on the same floor. Perpetuating a new generation all over again. When a mother that had three or possibly four daughters if each got pregnant no one ever really left. Mothers became grandmothers to many. Nothing ever changed.

Chapter Twenty: Brenda, Candy and Me

After The beating that I took from the girl gang, I remembered that it was a girl named Brenda and her brother that had helped me to get back to the building. She had also been in a few of my classes at school. She had helped to clean up my face that night. Although she wasn't in a gang and they never seemed to bother her. I had thanked her some time ago for what she had done for me.

One day I was sitting on the brick banister by myself near the school. She and another girl that I had seen around but didn't know personally came over and asked if Id mind if they sat with me. I was shocked that they wanted to. Me! Of all people! Trying not to sound desperate I said, "Sure".

So they sat on the stoop and the other sat down on the next stair. The first thing she said was, "Let's just not talk about it ok?"

I said," okay"

Brenda asked, "Why you over here by yourself?"

"I always sit over here by myself."

"Well, you don't have to if you don't want to. You can hang out with us."

The other girl spoke up "Since she's ignorant I'll tell you my name myself. I'm Candy"

Brenda started laughing "sorry, this is Candy the butthead. She's the one who gives most of the parties here in the building." My first though was why her mother allowed her to have parties every weekend.

But I figured that if that was something that they wanted me to know they would have told me. Brenda was my height but she was heavier than me, with a medium dark complexion. And she wore her hair in a short ponytail although I had seen her wearing an afro with a head band.

Candy, on the other hand, was shorter than both of us. Her skin was more of a caramel color and she wore her hair in an afro with a patch of copper in the front. The color was made from a mixture of peroxide mixed with ammonia. She had a chip on one of her front teeth that looked kinda cool when she smiled.

The cool thing was that neither of them was involved in the girl gangs. I found out from them that they had been close for years and so were their mothers with each other. It seemed that everyone knew

Candy maybe it was because she had lived in that building for a long time.

We started to hang out so much together that summer that people started referring to us as the three musketeers. We would sit by the school and smoke cigarettes, tell corny jokes and laugh like crazy at them. We did things that girls did. There was a grocery store that was all the way up near Prairie, under the L-tracks, a mile from where we lived.

Just for the hell of it we would walk all the way up there sometimes just to buy apples. We used to say that that store had the largest crunchiest apples we had ever seen for a quarter. Sometimes we would walk further east to Martin Luther King Drive.

On the west side of the street was the movie theater called "the Met." Which was short for Metropolitan Theater. We would look at the pictures to see what movie would be playing for the weekend. Sometimes the action on the street was more exciting than that being played at the movies.

Chapter Twenty-One:
Blaxploitation Movies

The 70s were an era within itself. For blacks it was the movies where emotions ran high. Black movie stars who played pimps and drove Electra 225's with sunroof tops and diamond shapes on the backs of their tinted windows even had what they called, "gangsta white walls on the tires some had fake TV antennas in the back. Others drove Cadillac Eldorados and Devilles, but most people of the projects who were lucky enough to drive drove old Chevy Caprices, station wagons, and Impalas. Some people felt that blacks had finally had a chance to make it to the big screen, that the black race had finally been accepted in Hollywood. The Black actors and actresses had the chance to be the center of attention. There were other blacks who were disgusted at the way things were taking shape. They felt that the actors and actresses were there to be exploited.

Something to looked and laughed at. The whites knew the black actors and actresses were going to really make a profit for them. They knew that blacks were going to find ways of getting money to go to see their own people at the movies. They knew blacks were tired of seeing white only shows. Most shows didn't reflect anything about black people or how they lived at all.

Occasionally there were movies where blacks would portray an occasional maid or chauffer. At one time they put a black actress, whose name was Diane Carroll, in a show called "Julia, whose series ran from 1968-1971. It stared a black actress but she was only that in color. The series could have easily been portrayed by any white actress because none of the situations ever really happened in real life as they made it seem on television. But there was one program that we all were able to identify with. It was called, "Soul Train." This, for teenagers like us was the most popular show of them all.

Then, a film came out that just about every poor black audience could identify with. The movie was called, "Cooley High". The writer of this movie, (Eric Monte) based it on his own experiences where he had grown up the Cabrini-Green housing projects in Chicago. That movie made blacks feel that much more superior in to our southern cousins. That movie took the most realistic look at teen life here in Chicago then any movie of that time. So did the TV show, called, GOOD TIMES and SOUL TRAIN. There were a few more television programs but it's been a long time and I don't remember them all. Later as time passed came the other movies which featured black actors and actresses, "Shaft," "Coffy," "Scream, Blacula, Scream," "Super Fly," and the list went on and on. One movie after another, but hey, we loved them all! Most put blacks in the lime light but they were portrayed as pimps, prostitutes, Drug dealers, and thieves.

The directors flipped the script and in putting Blacks in the lime light, and by exploiting them, they made millions, now they had it both ways for maximum effect blacks could go to the movies and see blacks acting or maybe go and see white movies and get to watch them as well on television. Or do both! Lucky us!

Chapter Twenty-Two: Pimps, Prostitutes and Peddlers

It was early evening as we started to walk back home. The air was as hot and muggy then as it had been that morning. Older men and even some younger ones had started to gather, bringing their boxes to sit on. Some of the others on the ground near a building to keep from sitting in the burning sun. They would shoot dice and drink from bottles of alcohol that they had placed in paper bags, and had twisted the bags around the necks of the bottle so that the police wouldn't see.

After getting drunk they would start cursing at each other and argue amongst themselves but mostly it was just the alcohol that did the talking for them. On the side of the street that we were walking, it was a little more serious. There were alleys that were separated by the curbs in the street.

When we looked down the alleys we could sometimes hear the sounds of the prostitutes screaming, crying, begging and pleading to not be whipped or beaten again.

We could see the pimps dragging them by their hair, clothes or their bodies. And they didn't seem to care who saw them, except maybe the police. Every now and then a man or teenage boy would walk up and tell them to ease up on the beatings. Then you would hear the pimp say "You need to stay yo ass outta this. "This bitch is my property, I do what I wonna do to her, when I wanna." He would just shake his head and walk away. The pimp would turn back to the prostitute that he had been beating on and tell her "Go somewhere and fix your make-up."

And that she had better have his money that night or her beating would be worse. Then He would straighten up his cheap suit and put his walking cane over his arm and strut out of the alley onto the street. The way the women looked always made us stare. Because of the way they would dress, and walk in their platform shoes with the shorts up to their butt cheeks, and the fish-net stockings and wild colored short skirts. They also wore low cut braless blouses their large afros and outrages make-up. They would walk up and down the streets pretending that they didn't look any different than anyone else. They would stand near the curbs of the street and say, "Hey baby, want me to sho yu a good time?" Another would say, "Come on baby, I'll give yu a good price," or "Come on, and after I finish wit yu you'll keep on commin back! Cause I'll keep you cumming." Then she would laugh with the other girls who walked further down on the same side but within earshot of what had been said.

Sometimes a car would pull up and you would see one lean inside the window. A moment later she would get into it and disappear. As we continued to walk towards home we would pass a car and see the woman get out of the car wearing a big grin adjusting her clothes and when she looked at us she gave her left breast a slight lift, which was to let you know that she had made out good. Then she would give us a little wink and smile as she walked away.

Chapter Twenty -Three:—Respect

The one thing that I noticed while I lived in the building was that the gang members had respect for their mothers. If you stood close enough to hear a mother speak to her son, whether he was a gang member or not, he always answered question with, "Yes, mam," or "No, mam." Mothers were someone who all gang members gave the respect. No matter that most of the things their boys did were against the law, most mothers were both mother and father. And they did their best. The teenage boys were the men of the house. The first of the month when everyone got their food stamps it would be the gang members helping their families who were trying to haul their shopping buggies from the first to the fifteenth floor or in between-because remember, the elevators seldom worked.

Usually, this took multiple trips until all of the food was brought up to their apartments. Sometimes when they finished taking their own groceries up, if their fellow gang members needed help, they would carry bags of food without being asked. It looked like a massive expressway with so many families going up and down the stairs, passing and re-passing each other as they went up and down to bring up supplies.

After a while people started to make jokes with each other and laughing, as they continuously passed each other in the halls carrying the bags. On the first of the month, everyone was in a good mood because everyone got a chance to eat each meal until they were full. It was a good thing. When people needed help like that everyone pitched in, gang-bangers and all.

After dinner the kids would come outside holding a bag of potato chips, some had popcorn, and others had candy. The first of the month was a good time. It was good for everyone.

Chapter Twenty-Four: The Confrontation

My brothers and I continued to go into our pre-teen years. They, like most boys went through what was supposed to be a growth spurt instead my brothers went through it in leaps and bounds and neither wanted to be involved with Tommy's gang. They just wanted to be able to go out and have fun. But what they wanted was not as easy as they thought it was going to be.

My brother that was just under me had found friends and had started drinking and at home be began to get out of control. My stepdad was what one would now be referred to as a functional alcoholic. He never drank in front of us and he was always good to my mother he treated us like we were his own kids.

He was a carpenter by trade who went to work every morning and came home every evening. He would give my mother almost all of his money except the little things that he would buy for himself. His little (taste) which alcohol was called, gas for the car and money for a carton of cigarettes. At night after dinner my mom would sit on the bed with his face in her lap and she would use the tweezers to pull out the ingrown hairs from his face. Yuck!

One day my brother had been drinking more than usual and by the time my step-dad walked in the door he heard my brother mouthing off to my mother that he was a man and wasn't going to be doing any chores or anything else anymore. Then my brother turned his wrath towards our step-dad telling him that he wasn't going to do what he was told anymore unless he wanted to. With that, he turned around and walked towards the bathroom. My stepdad followed him. The argument, if it could be called that was so short that it was over before any of us could blink our eyes.

My mother was standing at the back of the hall in the door of their bedroom; the four of us were in the second bedroom, which was shared by my two brothers. My stepdad said "what! "You a man now? So I'm supposed to do what? Let you try and kick my ass?" My brother had started sticking out his chest showing off.

He started to try to stare him down to try to intimidate him daring him to touch him. Because my brother was as tall as him he felt that by saying that it would make him stand down. My stepdad said, "So I'm supposed to do what?" My brother made the mistake of giving our stepdad the middle finger at the same time he answered "you can do what you wanna do. In fact, you can go to hell!" bad move! Both he and my stepdad were standing near the bathroom door. In that instant without even rearing back he hit my brother so hard in his chest that he fell backwards into the toilet of course neither of my brothers ever let the seat down when they came out. After falling into the toilet the medicine cabinet came crashing down on him!

Immediately my brother started screaming "I ain't no man! Please don't hit me no more I was just playing!" He was still sitting in the toilet holding onto my stepdads fist as he said it! My stepdad let his fist fly right into my brother's chest again. Before turning around to walk away he told my brother "you better get better than that if you gonna say something like that to me again, cause next time I'm gonna break your damn neck".

With that he turned around and walked towards the bedroom calling to my mom saying, "Baby, get the tweezers I'm ready so that you can pluck my face". He had bowed legs and was skinny and he couldn't imagine how funny he looked as he walked back to their bedroom. It was almost a year before the rest of us stopped teasing my older brother.

My younger brother would start by saying "I'm a man; I'll do what I want. Both my sisters and I would laugh so loud and so long that our stomachs would be hurting. Then my other sister would make her voice deep and say "I'm sorry I ain't no man! Please don't hit me no more!" again we would end up on our knees laughing.

We were doing it one day when my mom caught us and trying her hardest not to smile said, "Now that's enough! Let it alone." We stopped saying it while she was watching us but as we walked away we would all clutch our chest just like my brother had done. Even after we became adults we never let him live it down. When he would talk about it he would laugh and say, "Dad kicked my ass with one hand, and he was high at that! Even now I tell people, Shit! My old man knocked my ass into the toilet with one hand; As long as he lived I never got that drunk again When it came to my old man I ain't ever considered myself the man I thought I was to him since!" All of us would roll in laughter. But in his teenage days my brother continued to drink more with the crowd that he was hanging out

73

with and had starting cutting classes and smoking cigarettes.

And although he didn't notice it, it was soon to be inevitable that he had started catching the eye of the last person in the world that he wanted to be associated with. Tommy and his gang. Mark, the boy that I liked had warned me to tell my brother to get himself together because if he didn't it wouldn't be long before Tommy would be after him. I didn't do too well as growth was concerned but I was more athletic than both of my brothers were. I loved softball and football. The girls in the building also played basketball, softball, and touch football against the boys but there were only a few that were exceptional enough to keep up with them to make hook shots or score baskets. Softball was my favorite.

One day since the boys had beaten us badly in basketball, the girls decided that we would play softball against them. We had a secret. The girls that batted well, or could catch well were put in outfield. I was one of them. It was kinda cool that day so most of us were in light sweat shirts and jeans. I usually wore my favorite, sweatshirt which was a dark grey.

Because my skin was light and the color of the sweatshirt was grey most of the girls gave me a compliment saying that I didn't look half bad when I wore it so of course I wore it as much as possible. When it was our turn at bat we played what was called shoot the pitcher. When they pitched the ball if you were good you could aim the bat just right and shoot the pitcher and watch him fall to his knees, then roll and rock because we did it because we knew that we could. On a good day every one of the boys left holding their family jewels. We were very proud of our accomplish. For us it made a statement: don't *mess with the girls when it came to softball.* As we got better, more and more people started to join which made it that much more interesting. It got to be so good that people started making bets on who would win. Tommy and his gang never played with us, they didn't really bother the young boys but they did keep an eye out for the chance to be taught as they called it. As with all good things those growth spurts brought out the worst in Tommy's gang.

One day while downstairs I saw Tommy standing in front of his mother. All of a sudden there came this loud sound. Slap! The inside of her open hand went right across his face. He never said a word, never even looked up. Then I heard her say at the top of her voice "think about raising yo hand towards me so I can shoot chu!" He kept his head down as she walked away. Tommy's mother was very nice looking and kind to all of the kids. But when she got mad at Tommy, his brothers, or friends, it wouldn't be hard to see that she had a helluva meant streak in her and when she spoke in that tone she meant every word she said.

She was kind short and chunky and she refused to wear her false teeth, which made her whole face light up when she smiled. She wore a neat short afro that showed years of stress by the salt and pepper coloring of her hair. After she slapped Tommy she lowered her voice as she finished what she had to say. Then she turned and walked toward the parking lot where a car that had some other people in it was waiting for her without even looking back. Tommy rubbed his jaw then walked towards the playground where the other members of his gang were leaning on the monkey bars. No one would dare say a thing about his mother slapping him; in fact no one acknowledged it at all. No one in his gang would be bold enough or stupid enough.

Tommy, in his own way, by spiral fighting with the other gang members, was showing me the basics without the gang really having paid any attention as to what he was really doing. For the short time that I sat on the benches, and had watched him teach it was really just enough to keep me from getting busted up again by the girls in the gang. Never in a million years did I ever expect to have to use it on one of his own gang members. But that day was coming. And it was going to happen sooner than I thought.

Chapter Twenty-Five:
Stand and Fight or Fold and Die

One day after walking up the ten flights of stairs to my floor, as I came out of the stairwell the first person that I saw was Tommy and then I saw his gang. He barely acknowledged me as I looked at him. Suddenly the distraction that I heard was loud and clear. One of the gang members named Roy, who I hated the most for bullying younger boys was holding the screen door to my house and kicking the door. It was a stupid act since everyone in the projects knew that the doors were made with steel. He was mouthing off at the top of his lungs cursing and screaming like a madman.

He wanted his presence to be known. It was. Now the windows were of a different matter completely glass and one kick or if anything were to be thrown through them they would be able to get into our apartment.

I guess that's why I've always slept where the television could be seen just for the glare to be able to see if someone would try to come in through the window. After Roy got tired, I took the house key from around my neck and quickly opened the door fearing that they would knock me down and come inside. But as I looked out of the window they were calmly passing a cigarette around to each other waiting for me to send my brothers out.

I went to my brothers' room fast where I found my younger brother hiding in the closet I wanted to know what they had done to the gang to make them so angry. Then I looked at my other brother's face.

My younger brother came out of the closet and sat on the bed and started rocking back and forth with his arms crossed around his body. I moved over and gently lifted my other brother's chin and saw that one of his eyes was swollen completely shut. That would have happened only if the gang had tried to recruit them and they had refused. Someone had hit him in the mouth and his bottom lip had split and the blood was running down onto his tee-shirt. He even had blood coming from a cut to his eyebrow and nose. They had worked him over before letting him get away. My younger brother had sat quietly as I had looked at my brother's face.

Before I could even ask he blurted out that they

76

said it was our initiation time. He said, "I got away. My other brother must have been drinking and couldn't out run them. He had been worked over before having gotten a chance to finally get away. My younger brother said that Tommy's boys had chased them from school all the way home and now they're here to git them. He looked at me and asked a question that I didn't have an answer for.

What was I gonna do? I didn't know myself but I wasn't going to tell him that. I hated these buildings, they were like traps. No back door and nowhere to run. There were only two choices, to fly which wasn't gonna happen or the most obvious one, to go back to the front door. My family and I were like mice in a cage. And for a moment I didn't know how I was going to do it, but what I did know was that Tommy's gang was not going to get them.

It never crossed my mind that I wasn't going to have a chance in hell trying to fight them or what the outcome would be. But now it had come down to what I would have to do. Either stand and fight for them or fold and die trying to save them. If I did die it wouldn't have happened because I didn't try. Because If I was going to die someone was gonna go with me. For that I was sure. I was the oldest and my mom depended on me to take care of my brothers and sisters. She and my step-dad were working hard every day to try to get us out of the projects. And I wanted to get out, and that day I couldn't have wanted it more.

I thought to myself, "If I fold they were gonna take my brother's and finish their initiation and kill me anyway for thinking that I could do something to protect them. I went to the room where my two sisters were sitting on the bed holding each other and I leaned over and gave each one a kiss on their forehead. Then I went into my brothers room and did the same but my younger brother kept saying, "Don't go, stay here they'll go away."

I told him, "But you know they'll be back." kissed them both on the forehead and told them that I loved them. Then I went to my sisters room, and did and said the same. I went back to my brother's room and told my youngest brother to follow me, and that as soon as I was out of the door to run behind me lock it, and to stay in their rooms with the door closed no matter what they heard, to not open their bedroom doors. My brother started to cry as I walked to the door. I didn't look because I was afraid that I would start cry.

I told them to stay in their rooms. If the gang beat me to a pulp my brothers wouldn't hear me cry out from being beaten. As I walked out of the house I heard the door being locked behind me. Good. At least he had done as I told them to do. Roy was the first to speak when he noticed that my brothers weren't behind me. He passed his cigarette to another gang member Cisco, who was standing beside him.

"Where day at?"

"They ain't coming out, you can't have-um."

Tommy stood leaning on the fence away from his gang, smoking a cigarette, blowing smoke rings that floated into the air.

Roy, keeping his eyes on me said to the other members who were standing behind him "Hey man! Look at this! Now ain't this a bitch! Look at the big bad sista trying to protect her brothas now ain't that sweet." He started making kissy sounds with his lips and making little circles while standing on his tiptoes to act like a girl. All of the gang members were laughing so hard that they were stumbling over each other. Everyone except Tommy and Mark. As quickly as the laughter started it stopped. I could see a circle forming around me to make sure that there would be no place for me to run to and no place to go. Tommy hadn't moved from his spot. "Yella girl didn't you just git yo ass kicked by them girls? I know --Damn well-- you can't possibly be even thinking of fighting me, Hell naw."

Now I'm gonna give yu one mo chance to git yo yella ass in there and bring them out, fo I git mad and kick yo ass and do it myself." He was really starting to get mad. Roy was starting to get serious he had quit trying to be funny. I had been looking down at the ground for most of the time that he spoke, but with my head down I could see each side out of the corner of my eyes as I wondered if they were all going to jump on me at the same time or what their intentions were.

Mark was standing behind Cisco. I had only glimpsed him for a moment when I had first come out from the house. He had dropped his head and was looking down at the ground. Tommy was standing there but there was nothing he was going to do. Inside I was shaking like a leaf I thought that my legs were going to give out. I was afraid now more than I had been when I had taken the beating from the girl gang. But they had caught me by surprise. Now I was standing here in front of a gang member who, just to show how bad he was, was going to try and beat the life out of me. I didn't have a choice; there was no way that my brothers would have had a chance trying to fight him. I told him, "You'll have to do just that, go through me to get-um.".

I took one last look at Tommy, who didn't acknowledge me at all. I looked at Roy and brought my hands up and made them into a fist. At first he looked surprised, then a grin came across his face and I knew that he was going to really like what he was going to do. The last thing that he said was, "This is going to be one for the books, Bitch." He threw the first punch to the right side of my jaw so fast that I didn't even see it coming. The pain raced up to my brain, registered in it and exploded! The punch turned my head around so hard that I thought he had broken my neck. Immediately a tear flowed down my cheek as my face hit the wire on the fence.
The cut that was on my eyebrow from the girl fight had not completely healed and it opened up like a person opening their mouth to scream.

If I could have registered the pain on a scale from one to ten, with ten being the highest mine registered a twenty. My newly opened eyebrow yielded a gush of new blood which started to stream down into my eye and onto my sweat shirt. I was familiar with the jaw pain and knew that any punch to the face after that was not going to be felt it would then be just my body's response to the blow. Wherever I was hit my face responded in a tear or a swelling. Roy laughed so the gang could hear him and said, "You crying already bitch? Dis gone be fun cause its gone be too easy."

I pulled myself up by using the holes in the fence and looked over towards Tommy; his head had turned away as he spoke to one of his gang members. Then a light bulb went off in my head! Now I knew why Tommy wasn't watching me he was disgusted with me for not using the moves that he had secretly shown me to protect myself. Now I was in the same situation as I was before but if I didn't get it together Roy was going to kill me! Roy threw another punch towards my face again this time I held my fist up and blocked it!

I stepped up using my hands the way that Tommy had shown me and moved the way I had been shown making every punch connect to its mark. I saw Tommy step up to the front of the circle, after doing that he didn't move again. None of the gang members interfered. In my mind I could hear Tommy's voice; right jab, right jab to the same time don't let him up, then left jab to the stomach and when he bends down use both yo elbows on his back. As Roy bent over, I intertwined my arms and brought both of my elbows down as hard as I could on his back. As he laid there I kicked him again and again, the last blow came when he sat up. I lifted his face and got the best shot that I was ever going to get and I took advantage of it. He slumped over towards the ground with two swollen eye and bloody nose. His mouth was bleeding at the corners and blood trickled down his chin and now he was sporting a busted lip. *Now I'm even for what you did to my brother.* I knew what the other members in the gang were thinking, because some of the moves that I made had only been used by Tommy. But no one dared to say a word to question him. I glanced in the crowd for Tommy. He did a quick smile and nodded, then quickly looked away. He was proud of me!

The next thing that I saw was another member barreling through the crowd. It was Andrew. He and Roy were close in the gang and he was going to do to me what Roy hadn't. I was finished, I didn't think that I had anything left; He grabbed me by the hair and threw me against the wall. He did it so hard that I felt the back of my head when it hit the brick wall. He hit me in the stomach and immediately I threw up. Tommy's gang was laughing Tommy and Mark were not

As I went on all fours, he pulled me up by my hair and hit me with as much force as he could to my mouth, then he kicked me. I rolled over on the ground into my own vomit holding my stomach the kick made my body go haywire instead. As he prepared to kick me in the face I heard Tommy say to him "Not her face". By then Roy was up on his feet but it was another member, K.C., who pushed him back.

Andrew was about to hit me again but suddenly the crowd parted. My stepdad had gotten off the elevator and I think that he saw Andrew when he hit me. He must have sprinted down the ramp because Andrew didn't have time to make his connecting punch. He grabbed Andrew by the collar of his tee-shirt and lifted him up by his neck completely off of the ground. Everything went completely quiet. So quiet that for one moment, while living in the projects, you could have heard a pin drop. Andrews's eyes looked as though they were going to pop because of the way that he was being held. He was pinned to the wall and he was running out of air. Tommy only looked at what was happening once as though he hadn't noticed what had happened at all and shifted his gaze away. K.C. and Emmitt remained quiet; they were all waiting to see how the ending was going to play itself out. He knew that I knew the rules. T-Bone kept looking at Tommy waiting for him to give him the word to get my step-dad so he could get in the fight. Tommy said nothing and continued to ignore his gaze. He directed his eyes back on what was going on. Tommy was there for one reason to make sure that the fight was fair. It would be one on one no matter what.

No one was going to be allowed to break that rule. Again in my mind I was grateful because of what had happened with me, Andrew, T-Bone ,and some of the others would have made short work of me and Tommy would have never known.

Chapter Twenty-Six: The Unspoken Law

Thank you Lord for that extra moment I had made it once again on borrowed time. I was barely able to catch my breath. Slowly I got back on my feet and once again I put my fist up and took my stance. If you grew up in the projects you quickly learned of the unspoken laws that were. You learned them and you memorized them.

I struggled to take my stance. Then suddenly it dawned on me that I was about to let one of those unspoken laws be broken. The first law was if or when a fight started you were not allowed to let your parent interfere-*ever*. My parents didn't even know that this law existed I knew my step-dad didn't. And because they didn't know that the law existed they wouldn't have known when they had broken one. Sometimes if a fight did break out and a parent intervened if it was their child no matter what the consequence would be from them that child had better do his or her best to break away from them and to continue with the fight. Because that child should have known better.

The parents didn't know that by interfering and trying to break up a fight that they were only making it worse. They were setting the whole family up for retribution that sometimes was so severe that their only recourse would be to move to another building or risk getting killed by staying. I didn't know how I was going to continue fighting. I was running on empty. I felt like I had given my all in the fight with Roy. But now I had to finish the one with Andrew so I started saying to myself, "If I don't stand and fight you'll fold (give up) and die."

What I said next made everyone, including my step-dad look at me as though I had seen a ghost. The consequences of the unspoken law would happen if he stepped in. It wasn't because of what I said I think it was how I said it. I didn't scream out or speak as though I was out of breath which I was, I spoke in a voice that was barely a whisper and the tone was now a command. I said to my step-dad, "Let him go." Even Tommy's eyes showed surprise.

My step-dad looked directly into my and hesitated but slowly let him slide down the wall. He didn't know about the retribution that would follow otherwise. In the projects you had to be able to hold your own. After being let go Andrew looked back at my step- dad and gave him a threatening look before shifting his gaze towards me. My step-dad returned the same look at him as he passed by and went into the house, but somehow I knew that he was close even though he was inside. Andrew walked over to me and without hesitating hit me in the face. That hit knocked me from my knees and took me straight to the ground where I fell flat on my face. One of the gang members, Cisco, shouted, "Way to go Drew, knock dat bitch out!"

Mark came out from behind the circle and walked over to me. He whispered in my ear, "Stay down babe, just stay down. He's really trying to kill you-just don't try to get up. Let it go." My face was a bloody mess but he had hit me in it anyway. I could barely make out Mark's face as he whispered in my ear. He had his hand on my back trying to make me stay down. T-Bone grabbed his arm immediately and pulled him back saying "What's yo problem? Don't let me have to give the same thing to you!"

Tommy spoke up "Botha yawl stay out of it." No one said anything afterwards. Mark stepped back into the crowd I had turned over on my back and laid there. Andrew walked over and stood looking down at me. He was laughing at the way I looked. That was it! I turned to my left side and kicked him as hard as I could behind his knees. As he buckled and fell, I rolled over and straddled him sending blow after blow to each side of his face. With the last hit to his face I rolled off, I was spent. I could barely breathe let alone try to move. I just stayed there lying on my side with my eyes closed. I thought it was only a moment but then I heard the sounds of feet walking away.

I was barely able to open my left eye or turn my head in the direction of the sounds. Tommy looked at me for a second he gave another half-smile then he started walking towards the stairwell. The other gang members helped Andrew up and they all followed him disappearing down the stairs. I could hear their footsteps as they were walked down. Andrew had it harder because T-Bone had grabbed him by the back of his shirt while He was still lying on his back and drug him buy his collar down the stairs. I could hear him begging out of pain for T-Bone to let him go. I knew being drug down those concrete stairs was going to do some damage to his back. But then I thought to myself, "Why should I give a rat's ass? I was hoping that T-Bone carried him that way all the way down to the first floor by the scuff of his shirt."

I was swallowing blood. It was coming out of my mouth and nose but in my mind I was screaming, "I made it!" but the only thing that I could do was lay in the spot where I had fallen for what seemed like forever. Every part of my body had started screaming in pain again but my arm made the pain feel like bolts of lightning shooting up and down it. The rule was since I had won they had to leave my brothers alone. No one could take out any retribution in any form on me or my family. It was to be followed to the letter that was also in the code of the unspoken law. I knew that my step-dad had been watching the fight from behind the kitchen curtains all of the time and I know he wanted to come and help me but he also knew that I would have hollered out for him if I couldn't handle the beating anymore.

But he had no idea of what was on the line. As I heard the door open I tried to crawl towards it but my body wasn't having any part of that. It had done all it could do for me. It could do no more. It was at that moment that I felt my step-dad lift me up.

He gently laid me down on the couch and had my brothers and sisters to bring him wet and dry towels to help clean me up. They were all standing around me. I could hear them crying and asking our step-dad if I was going to be okay. He didn't answer they did as they were told and brought the towels. The wet ones to wipe my face and he used the dry ones to stop the bleeding. He touched my shoulder which was hanging from the side of the couch.

He said something but I didn't know if I was sure of what he said, I didn't care or remember. Something about my shoulder being pulled out of its socket. I was so tired and beat up that whatever he said didn't seem to matter because I was becoming too incoherent I kept saying, "Not to the hospital dad please, please don't take me there. I was lying on my back on the couch. Then I heard him tell my brothers to put the towel into my mouth. He said, "Ok now this is going to hurt but don't move." All of a sudden I felt him pull my arm forward and the pain made me pass out. My shoulder had been popped out of its socket and he had popped it back in place. When I did open my eyes I was in bed with the covers pulled up and there was a towel over my face. I lay with my eyes closed as he picked me up to take me to the bedroom I could hear him talking to me as he carried me but the pain was so bad that I just kept my eyes closed. Then I heard the door open, and knew that my mother was home. My dad walked her straight to their bedroom and closed the door.

After a while I heard the sound of her slippers coming down the hall. They stopped at my brother's room; she was in there for a while. I knew she was looking at my brother's face and checking to see if there were any other bruises on his body. Again I heard their sound this time they stopped at our door. My sisters were sitting on their bed. She turned on the light and walked over to where I lay. She sat down next to me on the bed. I could barely open my eye but I see her face close to mine looking at me. I knew that I was a bloody mess. I felt her hand gently turn my head from one side then to the other. Then she pulled the covers down and saw that I was still wearing the clothes that I had fought in. She rose from the bed and walked out of the room. I could hear the sound of the pots, pans and plates being moved about in the kitchen. She called my brothers and sisters to the kitchen table to eat.

As I lay in bed my mouth felt as though I had gone to the dentist and received too much numbing medicine in it before they pull your teeth. It felt as though it was hanging down and I couldn't stop the drool that was coming from the corner of my mouth so I had to let it slide down the side of mouth. Again I heard the sound of her slippers as she came back into the room. I heard her whisper, "Why do you keep getting into fights with the boys in that gang and jeopardizing everyone in this house? You're going to get us all killed one of these days." She left the room again and I heard water running in the bathtub. I prayed that she was running bathroom water for herself and not me.

I tried to move my neck but the pain was like I was being hit all over again and I couldn't even feel my jaw. When I touched it the pain shot up into my head like lightening. I just lay in bed trying to stay still by not moving any part of my body. Afterwards it was time for everyone to take their bath. I thought that because of the way I looked and that my mom had seen me and knew about my arm she would leave me alone for the night but I was wrong. She came back into the room and gently helped me off the bed and walked me to the bathroom. She sat me on the toilet lid and helped me take off my clothes.

Each time I moved it felt like my body was going to break in half as she helped me she told me how the water would take away some of the pain. After she left I sat I could soak my body, which by now had started to throb all over. I held my stomach as I eased into the warm water. Everything hurt, just like it did when the girl gang had jumped me.

That was nothing to compare with this, this was much worse. As I let the water run I tried to stretch out my legs but it was no use the pain made feel almost impossible, it was if they wouldn't stretch out. I could only hold them close to my chest to try to ease the pain that was kicking in my stomach like it was trying to break out. I turned off the water and rested my forehead on my bent knees, and then I wrapped my arms around them to make myself as small as I could. The last time I did that I was lying on my side after Roy had kicked me. The tears started running from my eyes and then I just cried. I sat there in the tub and sobbed so long that I ran out of tears.

With my head down I asked myself, "Why do I keep getting into this shit? It's not fair just because I'm the oldest wasn't supposed to mean that I had to keep getting fighting!"

I made a fist and hit the water as hard as I could. "*I hate this! It's not fair! She put me in charge of my brothers and sisters; this was the result of doing that.*" I did what I had to do; I thought that she would have appreciated that." I got out of the tub. My eyes were red and swollen again everyone would hear about this. I started crying again, but this time not out loud.

My brother had a split lip and because I had won the fight he wouldn't get another one, at least from them. But what did I get? Nothing: nothing but getting busted up again.

My Mother didn't even realize what was happening when she wasn't home. She didn't think about the responsibility that she had heaped on my shoulders when she put me in charge. *And I hated it!*

I looked in the mirror; I looked like I had just

stepped out of a boxing ring and lost. Although I had been in a boxing ring I hadn't lost I had won. Some big deal that turned out to be. My mom had started turning off the lights in our house and soon it became quiet. After a while I sat up on my bed and looked out of the window. I saw the moon. It was completely round and it looked so close. It looked as though I could reach out and touch it silly, but I didn't care. All alone what I had been thinking I started to whisper out loud.

"Star light, star bright, first star I see tonight. I wish I may, I wish I might get the wish I wish tonight." My wish was that we could move out of the projects so that I could stop having to fight.

I was tired of it. I felt that no one really liked me I was only added into a   group when there was no one else available. I was tired of getting into fights that weren't really mine and I was really mad at my brothers for not sticking up for me and telling our mom what had really happened. That I had been fighting for them! As I sat in bed with my back against the wall I just closed my eyes, dropped my head and shook it.

I looked out of the window one more time and said, "Forget it. It wasn't going to stop and I was gonna lose sooner or later. Sooner or later someone was going to kill me." Girls don't fight boys, especially not gang members. The word about that fight was going to spread all around the buildings and every bad-ass gangbanger was going to want to have a piece of me just to see how bad I really was.

It was a no win lots of pain and no gain spot to be in and there wasn't a damn thing that I could do, especially now. I eased down under the covers, knowing that I wasn't going to sleep. I was too worried what the next day was going to bring. In the darkness I saw a shadow and a small dull light coming from a flashlight circling around the room.

As the figure came closer I could see that it was my step-dad. He paused for a moment and moved closer to my bed and sat down and stroked my cheek. I knew that he felt the wetness of my tears as he did so and gave me a hug. As he did, he whispered to me how proud of me he had been for doing what I did. He told me that my brother had tip toed in his and my mom's room and without waking her had told him and he in turn told her what had really happened. He laughed

87

quietly as he held my head next to his shoulder and told me how good that I was and how well I had kicked those two gang members' asses.

He added that I looked like Muhammed Ali and that he couldn't wait to go to work to tell his friends how his baby had whipped the shit out of two so-called gang bangers. With that he kissed my forehead, turned and as quickly as he came into the room was gone. I pulled the sheet up to my aching chin. It was painful the whole time that he held me but I was grateful for it anyway.

I mumbled softly, thanks to him but he was gone so my words went to no one that would even hear me. I guess I just wanted someone to notice not what I had done, but why. And that I hadn't gone to look for trouble but sometimes being in charge, it was trouble that somehow found me. What my mother didn't know earlier was why trouble had found me. Not directly, but indirectly because I had stepped up to the plate for my brothers, for being in a fight where I had no choice but to stand and fight or fold and die. I guess somehow I was glad that I had been in the right place at the right time and that I had locked the door behind me. As I laid there it was my last thought before drifting off into a fitful sleep. It had been one long hell of a day.

When I woke up the next morning there was a five dollar bill under my pillow. Every bone in my face felt as though it had been broken, the one and only thing that I could muster was a weak smile and there was nothing that I could think of that made me want to even remotely do that. In the projects the last thing you would expect to hear would be that you would be able to fight and still be able to live there for any length of time. Let alone have your life be uneventful. But the one consolation that I did have was in knowing that this time I wouldn't be the only one trying to heal from the pain that I took from that fight. There would be two others nursing their wounds too.

Now Tommy had two of his own gang members that would be looked at by others and teased, "Who opened up that can of kick-ass on yawl man? Yawl look like yawl had double portions of that kick-ass stew too! girl whooped yall punk asses." Everything else on me was too sore to acknowledge the little joke that my brain had whispered to me, but I got it, and it made

88

me smile although weak it felt better on the inside then it looked I'm sure on the outside than anything else. To this very day I still have that grey sweatshirt and I can vividly remember the specific fight that I had worn it in, so many years ago. Amazingly for a while that's the way it turned out for me, uneventful. Tommy kept his word. He and his gang didn't harass my brothers and there was no retribution against me or anyone in my family. Outside of that nothing changed. The pop, pop, pop from the gunfire going on in the building and around could still be heard at night. Sometimes I would watch the TV screen lost in thought and wasn't aware that the shows had gone off.

My mind was in another place. It was always in another place. Usually wondering what the next day would bring. I would lay there in front of that TV until the picture of the Indian came on followed by the star spangled banner that let you know that every station was going off the air. Even then I would lay on the couch unable to fall into a sleep.

I had seen Roy and Andrew from time to time they usually gave me a look as though they wanted to shoot me or give me to the dragon. But as long they completely ignored me it was fine with me. The previous year my mother had been adamant about my not going to any parties in the building but I think that my stepdad was slowly wearing her down. He reminded her of how well I took care of my brothers and sisters, and that I always did my homework and most importantly I had taken of my brother and sisters and with the exception of having gotten into that last fight I had been pretty good. I didn't even get pregnant! that although my mother never said anything about it to me, I'm sure with all of the girls she saw with poked out bellies when she came and left for work it had probably been the thing that she had worried most about for me.

A few days later as my mom and dad sat at the kitchen table I heard him tell her that I had always did good by my brothers and sisters, I always did my chores and made dinner when she asked me and that that should count for something. Then he reminded her of why I had been in that fight. He said, "Hell, I would have given her a party, you something. You ain't going to be able to keep locking her up because when you do let her out, she's gonna go buck wild and you know it." After getting out of school that year, my mom gave in and let me go to my first party. You weren't there, I saw the hits that she took, you just saw the aftermath, hell I wondered to myself if I could have taken so many hits and not gone crying to **my** parents!"

My mom sighed, and I heard her tell him that she was going to apologize to me and if things continued without anything else happening and if I asked to go to a party as much as she wouldn't like it she would let me go. I felt happy but not like a whoopee type happy because I had started my mornings by taking every moment at a time.

Chapter Twenty-Seven: Social Services

They were the Social Workers. They came to the buildings in twos' to try to sneak in without being seen as though they were coming to visit someone they knew so they wouldn't be noticed. Their intention was to try to give the unannounced knock at the door so they could search the apartments to try to catch any males that were not documented inside. The 1970's federal legislation ruled that women could only receive welfare if they did not live with spouses or partners. They were supposed to search a certain number each day. They would document what they did or did not find after tearing the apartments apart. They were the social service workers.

These women felt that because they had been given a trickle of power that had dribbled down from The Chicago Housing Authority, it made them qualified to determine if the conditions in the apartments that they checked were to their satisfaction. They had the power to determine if a family could stay, or had to leave just by the look that was given to them.

For that reason, knowing that there would be no other place to go and live most of the women just kept their heads down when the social workers did their job. Their attitudes towards their own people were mean, nasty, sarcastic and superficial. They would say things like "I know you got a man in here, one day I'm gonna catch you and then you and these crumb snatchers will be out on the street." Or try to trick them by telling the women just tell us where he is. Does he hit you? If you tell us we can get him arrested and make him take care of his kids. That rouse never worked and when it didn't they would get nasty again and give them the warning that they would be back and add the nasty threat that when they did come they better not get caught because if they did they would be thrown out before the day was over. The one thing that they didn't know was that no matter how hard they tried; people in the building knew that they were there as soon as they came up the walkway. Once in the building, a whistle from anyone who had seen them would alert people which floor they were on and whether they were coming up or down everyone that had a phone would start calling who they knew, those that didn't have a phone sent their kids door to door and soon everyone knew where they were and once they went into an apartment all of the men that were there would have a chance to leave.

The workers would document on what they had or hadn't found because never found anything. They seemed to want to keep the poor the way they were as long as they could continue to be poor, hapless, and hopeless. So the documentation although wrong was the same. The black women were written down as before unmarried; they were the heads of their households with whatever number of children that were stated that they had. My mother and step-dad had jobs so they could not come into our apartment. I'm sure the social workers hated not being able to evict as many people as they had wanted to but not half as much as my parents and they people who had to go through it did. It was sad to know that people were trapped because no one wanted to rent to them. Even though my parents paid rent we were no different than they others in the eyes of the Chicago Housing Authority.

For some of the other families it was too much. I would see some of the kids that I knew helping their parents and others that were there, probably relatives helping them pack their belongings to put into old trucks, into the trunks and the roofs of their cars.

Sometimes there would be one extra, sometimes two that sat near the sidewalk, with the doors opened so that the items could be placed into it carefully to prevent any damage from happening to it. The mothers who were friends of some of her neighbors had told them that they were moving back south, where they would at least have the chance to have something to show for their hard work or have to hide their men or fear every day for their lives and those of their children having been shot or inducted into the gangs. They were tired of bowing their heads down and having to listen to the way they were talked to and having to be talked down on at the public aid office like dogs. All they wanted was something to call their own.

The most important thing to them was that they wouldn't have to live like caged animals. There was no arguing with that. Every point made was a valid one. Everyone wished them well, some cried as they held them as they said their last good-byes and watched their friends drive away. Hoping that one day they would be the ones doing the same and hugging their friends as they said good-bye.

93

For those females who moved away it was a new beginning, one that soon I hoped my family and I would have. Once the Chicago Housing Authority let the people who worked for them have bits of power they gloated. So did others who were thrown little pieces of clout with the ability to intimidate others. And the ones who got those jobs and the clout that came with it loved it. They were the CHA'S eyes and ears. Like good dogs that brought back papers filled with information, they were rewarded with the bones that made Higher ups at the Chicago Housing Authority were happy, the social workers were happy. They got promotions, a little bit more in their paycheck and they became that much more vicious to the people in the buildings, but always loyal to their employers. They became happy little dogs eating larger scraps from the larger bones that were given to them.

Although most of the people who worked for the CHA were very educated they were book smart but didn't act like they were very street smart. Because if they had been smart, they would have realized that they were putting their lives at stake every time they entered any of the buildings. Since no males were noted on their census it didn't mean that men weren't somewhere in the building or around them and even if they saw them around them there was nothing that they could do or say because they couldn't prove that they were ones that lived there or that they were visiting. It didn't seem to occur to them that they cared that they were hated by everyone. They didn't have to be so heartless where their own people were concerned. They didn't ever think that they could have just as easily ended up in the dragon and no one in The Chicago Housing Authority would have been the wiser.

It was this supposedly accurate documentation from the census that became written up as the statistics which were all wrong. That social service continued to write that the women were illiterate may have been true to an extent but no one who lived in the projects was stupid. The truth of the matter was that the Chicago Housing Authority was ruthless for the rules that they enacted.

It was the law enacted in that the us congress enacted that supposedly no men were allowed to live in an apartments but we all knew that there were men who fathered children and took the chance to live there to be a part of the family. They left but came back the moment the social workers left. They were in their family's lives and no, they didn't just beat women and take their money on the 1st of the month as was often stated. Not all of them slept with every woman that they could But After becoming an adult I found out that that bill had been passed by congress CHA were more than happy to follow the law.

The statistics assumed that the women were without men so that became the assumption became then became what the people that didn't live there assumed. Everyone that lived in the projects wasn't as stupid as the Chicago Housing Authority thought that they were. But throughout the buildings I'm sure there were others with the same situations and thoughts going on. There were so many women with children to care for the public aid allotment and stamps were not considered as income from a source that had little to no odds in been expected to be paid back.

# # #

Flash forward:

Now as an adult looking through my mind's eye at situations that occurred back then, the how and ways of how politics were played, as a kid I wouldn't have been able to comprehend any part of what was going on. Coming up I was as clueless about things that started one day and the next week it had be stopped as the adults that lived there. As an adult and looking back at how it had been it was nothing less than pathetic. Even if I had been able to understand, the situation would have been the same.

Chapter Twenty-Eight:
What Went Undocumented

What wasn't documented and couldn't have been documented was that men who lived with their girlfriends did go out to work. Not in any of the nine to five jobs, those were out of reach unless they got lucky enough to get janitorial jobs and even they were few and far between. The jobs they got paid the minimum wage almost next to nothing. What helped more was their ability to hustle, beg for something, anything they could do they would do. I never asked my neighbor where the men hid their clothing when the social services came to an apartment where one of the men lived. My friend just hunched her shoulders and said "they probably just keep they clothes in a large laundry bag and got someone to take them to somebody's else's house before the social services got to their apartment. Bags were passed around all over the building until the social workers were gone.

In the mornings I would see men with makeshift wooden boxes stuffed with rags, brushes, and shoe polish usually black, white, and brown waiting for the bus, If it would stop, I was told that they would take the 1 downtown and go everywhere, around the corners of the tall office buildings downtown where some of the white men in expensive suits would stop and get their shoes shined on their lunch breaks. It had nothing to do with low self-esteem that allowed these men to subject themselves to have to shine people's shoes;

It was the instinct to survive after the allotment of food stamps had run out. Some of the men would go door to door selling products.

Some became well known they were products were very popular and the men that went door to door to try to sell them became known as the fuller brush man. They and only they in their hearts but sometimes spoke with hoarseness in their voices as they recalled the rejections they would receive during any given day or week and the degrading names that were referred to them while the white men sat next to each other getting their shoes shined. It had nothing to do with low self-esteem that allowed them to subject themselves to have to shine men's shoes; it was the instinct to survive after the allotment of food stamps had run out to know that they had to do something to keep on living. They sold newspapers on the corners, socks on the 1-platforms, towels between cars on the streets and other things that they though would help them and their families.

There was one place that they could always get work, but they would have to race to get ahead of the other men who were also vying for that same job. It was called, Maxwell Street. If they could get there fast enough they would get to work for the day. It was back breaking work. Loading and unloading the heavy boxes off of the trucks and then carrying those boxes to the back of the store. Maxwell Street was also known by another name, Jew Town. The food carts sold pork chops, polish sausage, and hot dogs all smothered in cooked onions heaped on top with catsup, mustard and anything else that they had. The onions and food could be smelled from blocks away. The few times that I went there I would even see police cars parked alongside of the sidewalks which clearly displayed no stopping, standing or, parking because if vehicles did so as the sign said it would be towed at the owner's expense. But then again, the sign referred to everyone except the police. The police could park anywhere they wanted, and could do anything that they wanted and there was nothing that anyone could say or do about it. Sometimes when they ordered their food, they would park right in the middle of the street and eat it. Men that were hired to sweep in front of the owners' shops would be forced to sweep around their cars until they decided to move.

In Jew Town, the owners would hire some of the men to put jewelry chains into their pockets or they would try to get them to get people to buy movies that were mostly rated-X for adults. Some would get a little extra if they could steer customers into the store and the customer made a purchase. In Jew Town everyone knew to haggle with the store owner to try to get them to come down on the prices of the merchandise that he sold. Everyone also knew that the chains that the men sold were not pure gold; neither were the watches or other jewelry that they sold but a lot of the older boys would buy them anyway. They did make quite a few sales because women wanted to look nice when they went out and everyone knew that nobody was able to afford anything that was really gold. Most people knew that the owners had put the price of his merchandise up so that when you had haggled with him, even when he sold you the merchandise he still made a hefty profit.

It didn't matter when people went to Jew Town they knew what they could afford and they would spend that and not a nickel more. I had gone there with a friend and immediately after walking in the alley amongst the vendors I wanted to get out as soon as I could.

My relatives had warned me to put my money up because the area was known to have a lot of pick pockets. They were and who were very good at what they did, men who knew the trade and knew it well. One minute a person would have their wallet, the next minute you would hear him cry out, "Somebody's got my wallet!" And of course, there was nothing that anyone could do. The pick pocket was long gone. I didn't like the idea of someone constantly getting so close to my face and say, "Want to make a deal? I'll sell this item to you for little or nothing." And when the men flashed their coats open I never knew if they had merchandise in them or were going to expose themselves to me.

That never happened I told my friend about it she had come to Jew Town a number of times. She said, "Girl get real, they trying to sell yu som-um to make a little money, they ain't thinking bout yu." I would see the working men's face grimace from the strain of unloading box after box from the truck as they carried them on their backs. After doing that kind of work all day they would keep a little of the money that they had made for themselves and give the rest to their old ladies (girlfriends).

What began with a sometimes fruitless job search, the demeaning and degrading insults from the white people on the streets, the bus drivers, and the subway drivers and last but not least our policemen, whose car logos displayed a logo that said, "We serve and protect, but what really meant that they served themselves and the other whites and protected them as well.

Black men were called niggas when no one was around, back then it was always the other way around guilty until proven innocent. They would throw them in their cars for anything or nothing. Soliciting or standing around, but if the men were soliciting in Jew Town they never bothered them. In fact they always completely ignored them. As if while they were there, they didn't exist at all.

When they did haul them away to the police station, the person arrested was let go the next day. They wouldn't even give them a court date; they didn't because they hadn't charged them with anything. If it was possible they, our ever present police officers should have been locked up for the harassment and cruelty that they doled out just for the hell of it.

Whenever they stopped black men, adults would say that they would call it probable cause; the man was literally thrown up against the back of the car and told to spread their legs and to place their hands on the trunk of their cars.

They would frisk them, go through their pockets, and after having not found anything, they would push them onto the curb and drive away. If a man asked what he had done their reply would be "because you might have robbed someone, or that they felt the need to and that they could because they were the police." They could hassle anyone at any time. Their badge and gun allowed them to do so. When any of the men that had worked and had not returned home that evening, chances were that they had been arrested and taken to the police station. The men knew that the ones that did not return that evening had been picked up by the police for one thing or another. They would go to the man's house to tell his girlfriend or send one of the older kids to go tell their momma that their dad was busted as usual for nothing. That was nothing for the kids even the littlest ones knew where daddy was if he didn't come home. Once arrested if there were no charges he would be turned loose the next morning. But if he was taken in with any valuables or money it was never given back to them. It was always something about court cost but no one ever left with a receipt. They would have done back breaking work all day for nothing. And there was nothing they could do and there was no one to tell.

One day when I was in the Walgreens I found myself standing behind a policeman and his partner. They were laughing and one of them joked, I guess I'll go and arrest one and lock him up. While he laughed, his partner, in between laughs said, "Hell, we don't need to lock them up just look at where they live, they're already locked up." With that, they laughed even harder, falling all over each other like what they had said was a big joke. Then one poked the other on the arm and said "stop talking like that, we have a

little lady standing behind us." As the other officer
looked back at me he started laughing even harder.
They paid for their merchandise and left, still
laughing at what they had said. In the eyes of the
black people it was nothing new. The whites felt like
the poor blacks who lived where they were there
because it was what they all deserved.

Everyone just ignored what most of the whites
said. Even the men who had worked so hard only to lose
everything they had worked for. Some of the others men
from the building would give him a couple of their
dollars to get by for the next week. There was no
reason to cry over something that wasn't going to be
able to be replaced. After everything that the men had
endured during the week and the problems that the moms
had to endure with the babies and their siblings by
the time Friday rolled around there was only one
question in the air.

Chapter Twenty-Nine: Where Da Party's At?

The parties were called quarter parties because that was the price that was always paid for admission to get into one. In the projects Friday and Saturday were the partying nights and there wasn't a building standing that didn't have at least two going on back to back. You could go from one to the next or if you were comfortable where you were you stayed there. You could always tell where the party was just by the loudness of the music that was being played, and the laughter that could be heard from the bottom of the building to the top. All of Candy's party themes were based on the previous weeks Soul Train shows. You couldn't find anyone on Saturday afternoons when Soul Train came on. To us that show was the hippest show in the world. As soon as The show would start there The psychedelic train which was the shows logo would go "TOOT TOOT, It's SOULLLL TRAINNN," Don Cornelius was the host. At the beginning of the show he would say, "It's all gonna be a stone gas honey," For those that didn't have a T.V. they would surely be found at someone else's house that did. The start of all of the parties would be the appearance of people as they arrived on the porch to come to the party to show off.

Those who could hustle up on a little money to buy new shiny bell-bottom outfits with the psychedelic shirts that they wore opened down the chest and the guy usually wore one of the Jew-town Fake gold chains. Those that couldn't buy outfits always knew of someone: a relative, sister, brother or friend that had something that they could borrow and wear for that special night. The party would start just as the sun went down so that people could line up on either side of the wall while the songs blasted and did their best to imitate the soul train dancers. They would dance guys would do half splits and girls would giggle and shake their hips as they came down what was known as, "The soul train line." aisle. The line would continue until it either got dark or when everyone had had their chance to show off what they had seen on the previous show. The first thing that you would notice would be the hair. The larger the afro, the cooler the look and your hair styles weren't complete without the large black afro picks that were always worn in the back of the head.

New flared bell bottoms. Psychedelic shirts, platform shoes, and the dark pimp glasses for the boys, mini- skirts, culottes and let's not forget the infamous hot pants and laced up platform boots and platform shoes, or see-through blouses. Some of the dance moves were really funny. I never got in the line; I didn't even wear an afro. My hair had such a reddish brown color that along with my freckles and big pink lips, I looked more like Bozo the clown than a soul train dancer so I just wore a pony tail which I held in place with a bobby pin. The stomping from the people along the sides of the line parties made the table that held the record player seem like it was moving. Sometimes the crowd would even let the little kids come through to do their own dance interpretations of the dances. Every now and then even an adult or two would come through holding a bottle of beer in one hand and popping their fingers with the others.

The record player had the volume turned all of the way up, and it trembled as James Brown screamed "I feel good don Na non Na non Na no Na!" Followed by songs by Aretha Franklin, The Temptations, Chi-Lites, The Spinners, Earth Wind and Fire, and more that I would need a whole page for to list. The majority of the time it was Candy who held the parties. Her mother was usually around during the week but she was never around on the weekends.

Although most parties were only supposed to cost a quarter, most of the people that attended gave twice that amount or whatever they had. Some even gave her a dollar or two because they knew what her situation at home was like. Now I understood why neither of them had mentioned it

Most of the people who came were regulars. Those that came didn't have that much money but everyone usually came to Candy's parties on the weekend. Because most people knew that by the second week of the month her family was usually down to almost nothing. No food for her or her brothers or sisters, no money for pampers, nothing. Her mother drank heavily and by the second week of the month she had sold all of the family's food stamps. By the third week she was seen only sporadically. Sometimes there was nothing in the house to eat at all. She gave them it every week. Everyone who came to the parties or knew Candy knew what went on with her family. So when her party was over Brenda would keep the money so that when Candy's mother would leave, she would let Brenda take money out of the jar to buy the kids food and milk. Candy had four younger brothers and sisters that she would always have to take care of when her mother left.

I didn't know how old they were but the youngest was walking, still wearing pampers, and drinking milk from a bottle. And just as she had told me when I met her Candy proved to me that she really did have a sweet tooth. She was always munching on licorice sticks, peppermints, Now and Laters, Nutchews and anything else that was sweet. Outside of drinking Boone's Farm from the jug, Wild Irish Rose wine, White Port and beer, there was nothing in the world that Candy liked more. Without the help of the people in the projects knew that without their help Candy and her family would have been in dire straits. Sometimes Candy would leave her siblings with her next door neighbor and would go to the grocery store to get food and whatever they needed. She was very careful to keep it hidden so that her mother wouldn't find it.

Sometimes when her mother came home on Monday morning Candy would let her little brother wear a disposable diaper and keep it on after he soiled it. When her mother walked into the house she would smell the·soiled diaper and give Candy money with orders go to the store to get more, always with the reminder of coming straight back. It was cunning on Candy's part; it was a way for her and her siblings to live. It was dishonest, but it became more about survival than anything else for her siblings and her. After my mom allowed me to have a later curfew, I started going to Candy's parties. I came to Candy's party because she asked me if I could help her to get the snacks out and get the decorations for the party together. I think she was glad for me to be there as I thought I would be. We removed the light bulbs and put in black lights, we plugged in the lava lamp added a strobe light and hooked it into the ceiling.

Brenda would end up knocking on the door and the three of us would set up one large table add the chips, popcorn, tuna fish and crackers, a small bowel of candy and two pitchers of Kool-Aid. Candy would have her Boonsfarm, cans of beer and other wine in the refrigerator and would take it out just before the first group of people arrived. Kool-Aid was a requirement for any party you could get away without the other things, food, snacks and munchies but you couldn't forget the Kool-Aid.

Before the party started Candy would feed her brothers and sisters their dinner, making sure that they were all full, give them a bath, and afterwards took the youngest one and placed him in a clean pamper. They were all placed in one room laying them in different positions on the queen size mattress that lay on the floor. As I watched her taking time with each one of them she was so gentle with them, giving each one the same amount of time before putting a sheet over them and giving each one a kiss on the forehead. She was the oldest she did what she had to do to make sure that they were safe. We were both the oldest and although we didn't want it, we had the same responsibilities. To make sure that our siblings were safe. I just had a little on my plate to get it done then she did.

As she turned off the light and close the door I never heard any of them cry they seemed to be used to it they were already tucked in and were already falling asleep. As people started knocking on the screen it that was the queue, time to get the party started. I asked her if she wanted me to check in on them from time to time. She smiled at me and said, "Naw, they alright they used to it dey know I'm here."

As the people came in some were already dancing to the 45 vinyl records that played songs from popular artist such as; Eddie Kendricks, Marvin Gaye, James Brown, Aretha Franklin, Diana Ross and the Supremes, everyone would get their partners and do dances like the bump, the funky chicken, the penguin, the bop and every other dance that was popular at that time. There were also The Chi-Lites, The Temptations, Earth Wind and Fire, The Ohio Players, The Jackson Five. The songs went on and on. The lights were on, but dim but that didn't stop the boys from trying to imitate James Brown's dance steps and the girls try to imitate Diana and The Supremes. Most of the records were Candy's but sometimes she would tell other people who were going to attend which records to bring.

Everyone danced to songs like; Kung-Fu Fighting, Disco Inferno and believe it or not there were a couple of white artists, that were songs that everyone played. Benny and the Jets, by Elton John. And Cisco Kid, by War. Just as Candy started to turn the black lights on Candy's youngest brother came out of the back room rubbing his eyes, still appearing to be half asleep.

He was wearing his little tee shirt and a pamper that made him look as cute to me as his walk was more like a waddle. He continued to move forward through the crowd holding his empty bottle out for milk.

There were so many people in the room, but it didn't seem to bother him at all. He went through, around and I even saw him crawl under some girls, who looked startled when they first felt him tug on their skirt tails. But once they saw who it was they casually went back to their conversations not missing a beat and even picking up where they had left off. He pulled one girls skirt and spoke as though he were standing next to Candy and said, "I want some milk." One of the boys sitting on the couch holding his girlfriend took his arm from around her and got up from the couch, picked him up and walked over to the kitchen. He sat him on the counter and opened the refrigerator and pulled out the gallon of milk and poured enough into the bottle to fill it up.

I watched as he carried him over to the couch where he and his girlfriend were sitting and handed the toddler to his girl. She promptly reached out for him and placed him on her lap. She rocked him gently while he drank the milk from his bottle. I guess I watched closely because for one it was the first party that I had attended second I felt uncomfortable for a strange people to be holding Candy's younger brother without her even knowing that he had gotten up and had been given milk by someone other than her.

By the time he had finished his bottle the girl had gently rocked him back to sleep. She handed him over to her boyfriend, who gently took him and carried him back to the room. I watched him place him back on the mattress next to his sister and slowly close the door as he came out. It was if he was the little boy's father but that's how it was; everyone looked after each other's kids as family. That's just how it was there were no pedophiles in the building that I had been aware of. In the projects word traveled fast about anyone and anything if anyone had been known to be one everyone would know.

No one had ever been afraid to leave their children with anyone else. And for certain, he would have been lynched, and then fed to the dragon. There

105

were no pedophiles before The WA Who Ba Man and his Good Humor truck came around the Projects, and there weren't any Good Humor trucks seen near the projects afterwards. Candy stopped drinking her wine and walked over to the wall and dimmed the light in the kitchen and turned on the black lights and lava lights that were placed on tables around the room. That was the queue for the slow-dancing to start. I heard knocking on the door and realized that there were going to be late comers so one again I took my place at the door.

After the tuna, chips and crackers were gone the party became a BYOB (bring your own booze) and if you wanted it would become a bring your own food too but it was okay everyone knew how it was that's why if you wanted something to snack on you knew to get there while there was something there. Everyone knew that by the third week of the month what was going on with the food. There wasn't going to be any no matter how early you got there so you either ate before the party or went out and got something to eat while the take outs were still open. At the parties everyone smoked pot. It was one of the highs of the times the other was the alcohol, otherwise known as oil.

I had tried it a couple of times but I didn't like the feeling that it gave me it made me feel like I was on a carousel. I became dizzy I couldn't speak clearly I ended up stumbling and it made me feel like throwing up.

A lot of the guys would do shotguns, which was where someone put the marijuana joint fire first in their mouth backwards, then they would blow the smoke out of the joint and whoever was on the receiving end would   inhale as much as they could. They did so much that they would end up backing away, trying their best to not cough. All that tried to inhale it and hold in the smoke. Most could not.

Sometimes some of the people that attended brought hash to smoke; it was usually brought by that person's relative or a close friend. The guys usually smoking it but none of the girls tried it none that that I remembered. Usually when someone tried something new they would come out afterwards and tell what it did to them and how it made them feel. I never heard any of the girls talk about it. We had all heard about acid. Hollywood stars and uppity white kids did it. On television when they had a commercial about drugs they would say, "This is your brain. Then they would show a skillet on a stove with an egg frying in it. As the egg fried it   would say, "This is your brain on drugs." To show the harmful e to function if they were effect on not just the brain but the body as well. Most of the time the white kids who did LSD or PCP would usually overdose, died, or went crazy.

I didn't know anyone who had tried acid, Candy and Brenda said that they didn't know anyone that had tried it either. If anyone would know it would have been them. Candy knew more people than Brenda and no one had ever approached either of them.

It was an expensive drug and since no one had the money to even think about buying it why dwell on it? There were too many ways to have fun. When they showed the white college kids on campus they referred to it as an acid trip. And when they showed someone who had done acid they looked like they weren't coming back to planet earth again. They would talk about things no one could see or hear and use all sorts of stupid words when they were trying to describe what they saw when they were high. Those were the ones who were referred to as the vegetables, the hippy's.

At the party's if I wasn't standing at the door collecting the entrance fee, I would stay around for a short time and then usually go home. Some of the boys would make what I called lite conversation that didn't amount to anything and it was usually short, I felt that it was just to show the others that I was accepted and okay to talk to. Some would bring me a drink or one of the few snacks since I was at the door and they knew that I wouldn't be able to leave until Candy or Brenda came to relieve me. But usually when they did I refused, both Brenda and Candy had boyfriends who were there and I thought it was better that they spent time with them. If Mark were out with Tommy and his gang I was usually without anyone. And I was without anyone because of Tommy and his gang most of the time. I had fought well and won, I had proven myself.

But I was still yella girl and most if not all of the guys were too embarrassed to dance with me. I just made them to uncomfortable. Usually as the party got underway, the lines became long quickly, and I had to make sure that people were paying their quarters to get in. Since most were regulars; they knew what to expect if they didn't get there early and usually it was no big deal. This night it was completely different. As I was collecting the quarters, one of the boys in the middle of the line shouted, "Hurry up albino nigga!" His words caught me off guard. Tears sprang up into my eyes as I stood there watching him but still I collecting the money as it was put into the jug of quarters. I did my best to ignore him.

All of a sudden, without missing a beat, some boys that were behind and in front of him turned around pushed him sown the stairwell into the corner and worked him over. Then I heard him scream as they physically threw him down the concrete stairs he screamed out "Don't thow me down the stairs man! I was only playing wit er!" They threw him down there stairs anyway; I heard his body hit the railing. They came back to the door dancing and doing the bop with the girls they had brought and acted as though nothing had happened. One boy said as he dropped his quarter in the jug and said "sorry bout that yella girl problem solved." He paid for his girl along with the boys who beat him and their girls and half danced, half walked into the door that lead to the party. So did the others who had beaten up the loudmouth. They paid for themselves and their dates and apologized for what the boy had called me and they went into the party as though nothing had happened.

The last one who beat the boy paid for himself and his girl and took her by the hand and twirled her into the room. They didn't want me as their girl but they weren't going to let anyone else disrespect me either. They called it being dissed.

Candy must have been nearby because as soon as she heard the boy screaming she one of the regulars told her what had happened but that the situation had been taken care of. Candy knew what he meant by it she had given too many parties not to. There was always a fight about something going on but as long as they took it outside of her house she didn't care. None of the people at the party knew that it was my first time being at a party but Candy knew and she knew that I wasn't going to just let it go. I felt that now would be the perfect time. she came to the door and took the jug out of my hand and told me not to worry because he would never get into any of her party's again then she turned on the light in the kitchen and shouted, "Na if somebody else wanna be a bad ass or got some-u um day one to say, den come try it on me!" of course no one said anything. A lot of the people that were inside

108

didn't know what she was talking about. Only the boys that had been involved and they told her that some of the other people that had come from parties at other places said that he had been thrown out of those parties too because of his mouth but no one had remembered seeing him before and nothing was said because no one knew if he had relatives living at the ones he was at or not.

With the exception of what had happened to him in our building that night was proof enough that no one knew him here, but maybe he didn't have to say what he said to me anywhere else because how many people were as light as me? In a lot of the other buildings, where he had been thrown out probably for talking crazy, it was night and everyone's mind was on having a good time he had been lucky.

Damned lucky because if it wasn't for those few exceptions he could have been found **dead.** Candy told the others if he even tried to come back there again for them to take care of him. Then she came over to me and told me to forget about it and to go and enjoy myself and to go in the refrigerator and get myself a beer. Beer or not how could I forget about what he had called me? I would have expected Tommy or one of his gang to have called me a name like that but they never did.

The name that I had been called that night had been completely new and I thought I had heard them all.

I eased my way through the sea of bodies to try to get to the bathroom feeling that a beer was the last thing that I wanted. No one thought anything of it and had gone back to their partying. The girls giggled as the boys hugged them close trying to slide their hand between her legs. There were couples standing close against the walls kissing, others were in the corners doing the same. Some boys got lucky and were able to get the girl to part her thighs after a few drinks. Others were trying harder to get there themselves.

Girls giggled and you could see some who were being explored by the boy whose hand had succeeded to get to her magical place as she held her head back and no longer tried to keep her legs clinched tight. Some were even exploring the boys and after a while they would leave the party. As the night wore on more and more girls left with their boys they came with. They would lead their girls by the hand outside of the house and would disappear for a long time. Once they had paid to get in and left they were allowed to get back in without having to pay twice.

I could see what was happening but it wasn't like I hadn't seen it before. At night, if you walked down the hallway stairs you would always end up stepping over a couple who for the moment you had temporarily interrupted. No biggie. In my mind the sting from the name that I had been called cut through me like a knife. I finally made it to the bathroom. I knocked on the door, when no one answered I rushed in and closed the door not bothering to notice if it had completely closed or not.

As I looked at myself in the mirror and thought to myself, "Who do you think you're kidding? You'll never fit in. "Never." I held my head over the sink and started to cry. It was nothing but a name. A stupid name I said, "Let it go." Only I couldn't. I didn't care about what people said about sticks and stones. They were wrong about the words. The words did hurt, just as bad if not worse.

Chapter Thirty: Rafael Tries To Fly

Everyone knew Jason and Ralph but no one ever called them by their real names. Jason was known as Rafael because of his afro. It wasn't kinky like ours. He was mixed; He was half black, half Puerto Rican. His afro was the largest, softest, and darkest that I had ever seen or felt.

Ralph was called Good and Plenty but most people just called him Goody. He was slim with bright eyes and long eyelashes and had lips that always seem to have a little smirk to them and he had a dimple on both side of his jaw. Rafael lived in the white building across 51st street.

Goody lived in the building to the left of ours. Both were allowed to move about out building freely, mainly because both of their brothers were inmates with two of Tommy's gang members' brothers who were also locked up.

That made them not quite but almost family in the building with neither considered to have been a threat. Goody was much more outgoing then Rafael. Neither was in Tommy's gang but both spoke with the members whenever they were around. Goody was what was called, a ladies man. He flirted openly and without hesitation and knew what girl belonged to whom and which girl was free game.

Rafael was every girl's dream. He was thin but not skinny; he had thick dark eyebrows and long eyelashes his voice was soft; when he spoke it was barely above a whisper and had a smile that lit up a room wherever he was. But he was not a ladies man. Although I'm sure he could have had his pick of any girl that he wanted. I never saw him flirt with anyone. He was just considered everyone's friend. He danced any record, fast or slow with any girl that wanted to join him. He had no problems with the guys when he danced with their girls he just wasn't that type. Goody on the other hand, could not dance with girls as freely as Rafael. He would try to feel on his partners behind or breast while dancing, and even tried to press his body against them.

So with him one would be taking a chance in letting their girl dance with him unless they didn't really care that much about them then they would let Goody dance as many records with them as he wanted while they went off to get hit off of a joint. And the guys didn't let their girls dance any of the slow records with him for that exact reason.

Goody was soft spoken too, but he was always waiting for an opportunity to move in on anyone's girl. He was cunning like a fox. While I was in the bathroom, I turned on the cold water to wash my face so when I came out people wouldn't know that I had been crying. Not that anyone would have noticed because the lights were turned down and everyone was doing their own thing. As I turned off the water I heard a gentle knock at the door, I told them that I would be right out. I don't know how Rafael knew that I was washing my face instead of relieving myself. He stuck his head halfway in the door. As he saw my face he opened the door all of the way.

Candy or Brenda must have told him of the earlier incident when I had been called that name. Rafael was caring like that; he cared for everyone who came in contact with him.

Like a big-brother or a boyfriend, he pulled me by the arm to the dance floor I didn't resist. He never asked me what was wrong and I didn't bother to tell. Once we got on the dance floor every one watched as we danced to six records straight. Some were fast the others were slow. On the slow records he held me close and looked into my eyes and smiled. He wanted everyone to see that he wasn't embarrassed to dance with me.

By then I had forgotten about the name that I had been called earlier and now I couldn't stop smiling. I was shaking on the inside because everyone's eyes were on us, looking at him I was excited and for just that short time developed a school girl crush on him although I knew he was doing it to be kind and the thought never crossed his mind, to me to it was just the two of us on the dance floor. When the seventh record started a guy came up and whispered something into Rafael's ear and headed back towards the door. Before leaving with the two guys he looked back at me, winked and said, "Save the last dance for me." With a big grin I nodded my head yes to let him know that I would. And I planned to, if it was the last thing that I did that night. After dancing with him, No one could say anything that could hurt my feelings again that night. He had swept me off my feet and I was in heaven. I was the only girl that he had danced with before he left. But Death had come back to our building. He had an appointment with someone that night, and he had planned to do his job.

An hour passed and Rafael still hadn't returned to the party. Thirty more minutes passed, then Goody told people he was leaving. He was going to look for Rafael because they were supposed to go to another party after leaving this one. It got later and later and my curfew time had come. Goody and Rafael hadn't returned so I let Candy know that I it was time for me to go. For once I wished that night that I could have stayed I even thought about staying pass my time but I had just been given permission to go to a party and I definitely didn't want to lose it. I was hanging onto Rafael's promise to dance with me two more times as he promised. But he didn't come back. I thought to myself that I wasn't going to get my last dance after all.

Disappointed at myself for believing that he would come back just to dance with me I left. When I got home I took a bath and went to bed but I had been too excited to sleep. I looked out my bedroom window remembering that I had danced with the finest looking boy at the party. And everyone saw that he had danced with me.

The next morning after my mother went to work there was knocking, almost a banging sound at my door. Candy had tears in her eyes and asked if I could come out on the porch. I nodded my head and closed the door behind me to see what she wanted. Then she told me what had happened after I left. She told me that Goody left and was trying to decide which way he should go to look for Rafael, up the stairs or down. Couples that were still in the hall had told him that he had gone upstairs with two other guys. There was a couple having sex on the fourteenth floor and the guy glanced up for a second, pointed up and continued with what he was doing. There were only two more floors left. Candy said that Goody stuck his head out of the stairway to look down the ramp to see if he could see Rafael and the guys he had left with. He found Rafael but at the same time saw the guys and heard them laughing as they ducked into the hallway. He could hear them laughing from the echo going down the stairs. As he looked hard under the dull light he saw Rafael standing on the top of the fence laughing and mumbling something about being able to fly. Candy said that Goody had told her that he had tried to run over to try to grab his friend's leg to keep him from falling but before he could, Rafael stretched out his arms laughing as he did so, saying he was gonna fly.

Goody had told Candy that just before he stepped off the top of the fence he seemed to reach out for something and then did a swan dive straight down to the pavement below. Goody ran back down the stairs, stepping on couples as he did so to get back to the party.

"Rafael just jumped off the fence!" He ran into Candy's house screaming what he had just seen. The music so high and the lights were so dimmed that no one even knew that he was there. She said the next thing she knew; Goody had ripped the record off of the record player and turned on the kitchen light. He started screaming over and over that Rafael was dead and how he had seen him jump over the fence. Candy said at first everyone though Goody was joking around, talking shit but when they saw the look on his face, that he was crying and screaming the same thing over and over again, they started to really pay attention to what he was saying. Looking at him she said that she could see that he wasn't playing at all. She said as people started running out of her house, A lot of them were looking over the fence just to make sure Goody wasn't lying, but they couldn't see anything because it was too dark.

But they heard the voices of the men that had been sitting on the benches drinking wine as they hollered up, "Yall betta git down here its som-body dead laying here." They knew what Goody had been saying all along was true.

No one wanted to believe that it was really Rafael's body down there but everyone felt that they had to go down and see for themselves. They started splitting up. Groups of people started running down each side of the stairways. Candy was crying as she said that one boy had said, "If Goody's ass had lied he was gonna beat him til he wished he was dead." But by then he knew better. He like the others just didn't want to believe that it was true.

Candy said that once she got down the stairs that there were too many people already around the circle and that she literally had to fight her way through the crowd to see for herself. Some people started saying that maybe the guys he was with had given him something that made him think that he could

114

fly but he couldn't and he didn't. He fell like a rock
from fourteen stories above, and was probably dead
before he hit the pavement.

Everyone called him Snookie; He never bothered
anyone he would just come and sit with the regulars on
the bench and drink wine and talk crap about the
things they were going to do in the future or one
reason or another as to why they weren't doing what
they said they were going to do. One would say as soon
as they got hooked up with a certain person they were
going to be made in the shade. They always sat on the
bench talking about the things that they had done back
in the day. Maybe they had done some of the things
that they said but the way they were then, they
weren't in any shape to do anything other than what
they always did sit out with their wine and tell lies
to each other. Snookie swore that he and the rest of
the men had all heard the sound of Feather Heads bones
break when his body hit the ground.

When they saw the body they ran over to him.
Candy said that they told the crowd that he made a
gurgling sound that lasted not even a second and then
stopped as the blood flowed all over the ground and
into the patched of grass and dirt where he lay.
Snookie had pulled off his tee shirt as fast as he
could, balled it up and placed it under Rafael's head.
As he lifted up his head to put the shirt under it the
back of his skull seemed to come apart and brains were
spilling out. Snookie and the other men didn't know
Rafael. But what they did know was that whosoever body
it was, was as dead as dead could be in every sense of
the word.

Snookie and the other men from the bench kept
telling people in the crowd to stand back to give him
some air. He and the other men couldn't stop
themselves from telling him to hold on. Snookie
cradled Rafael's body telling him that help was
coming. But just looking at the body it was clear that
everyone knew that Rafael was already dead.

One of the boys from the crowd ran over to an
apartment on the first floor and banged on the door
until someone opened it. As they let him in he told
them what had happened and why he needed to use the
phone so badly to call the police. He even pointed to
the place where Rafael's body lay to prove that he was
telling them the true. One of the boys that lived in
the apartment saw the crowd and walked over to see for

himself. He saw Rafael and came back to his house shaking his head as the tears ran down to his chin. One of his family members had already made the call to the police.

The men told the group that they had seen two guys run through the breezeway laughing loudly going towards the parking lot right just as Rafaels body hit the pavement. Several of the guys in the crowd ran through the breezeway to see if they could see them. But the parking lot was empty. And whoever it was would have been long gone by then. But Snookie never got over the experience of having held Rafael's broken body. Some months after Rafael's death some people said that Snookie's memories became too much for him to handle. His memories turned into nightmares and after that, he lost his mind. Snookie was found in an alley in the latter part of the summer. He had drunk himself to death.

No one had noticed that Death had made its rounds and had moved back into our building. He had not been in my building for quite a while Two months if I remembered correctly.

He had been in plenty of other places for plenty of people that needed to be touched by him. He was thorough. That was his job to be in the right place at the right time. Not a minute early and not a minute late. He had probably been waiting for Rafael all day. He knew that he had business to attend to in our building that night.

For some I guess, like the old people who were ready to die or were dying from other reasons that had caused them to give up hope. And the constant feeling that they had become a burden to their family, they had simply lost the fight and their dignity and where ready to go, death gave them the touch that they welcomed to put them out of their misery. It was then that I wondered if Rafael had seen death when it reached out and touched him to welcome him to his new home. As Candy continued to tell me in detail what had happened my eyes watered up and the tears ran down my face. Before I realized it I was crying so hard that I was shaking. Sitting on the pavement Candy and I held each other tightly as we both cried.

Brenda came down to tell me but saw that Candy was already there. I could tell that she hadn't slept either. Her eyes had bags under them and they were bloodshot. We were all crying because we, like the others, didn't want to believe it was true. Not Rafael of all people. But it had been true because both Candy and Brenda had seen his body. They both said that they had never seen anything like it and that they would remember it for the rest of their lives. Everyone had a sad look on their faces because he had been everyone's friend. When the police finally got there, they had an unconcerned look on their faces. Although there was nothing that they could do, it was obvious to all that they could have cared less. One of the men from the crowd was very upset. He screamed out, "What happened to yall? I called yall over an hour ago; yall ain't but a block away!" Candy said the police officers completely ignored him. One policeman fished around in his shirt pocket and finally brought out a pen and a note pad. Nothing that he asked required any detail in which to answer. He had asked if anyone had seen what happened or if anyone knew if he had jumped or was pushed. No one knew the answer to his questions, not even Goody.

The other policeman had been holding the flashlight for him as he wrote. Candy said that the officer holding the flashlight walked over and shined the light on Rafael just as the ambulance drove up. The policeman who was doing the writing pulled the ambulance driver to the side, away from where the crowd stood and spoke to him in a very low voice. Candy said that every now and then the first ambulance driver would glance over in the direction of the crowd and then shift his gaze away towards his partner who was coming from the ambulance holding a body bag. They seemed more concerned with their own safety by trying to hurry up and get away from the building more than anything else. After all, they were all white and everyone knew that if it hadn't been their job they wouldn't have cared if he had lain there until his body had started to rot.

The body bag was one that almost everyone in the projects was familiar with. The ambulance drivers and the policeman walked over to where Rafael laid. The ambulance driver passed his flashlight onto Rafael's body from head to toe.
 Brenda said that's when she and everyone else got a chance to get a good look and was able to see just how badly broken Rafael's body really was. As the policeman held the flashlight on them, the two ambulance drivers bent over to pick up the body.

Everybody watched the ambulance driver who was bending over his body. He looked at what was under Rafael's head and without showing any emotion, took the tee-shirt that Snookie had put under his head had been under his head and kicked it to the side. Snookie who saw him do it became so angry that he started to charge the ambulance driver. One screamed, "You wouldn't be treat-in his body like dat if dat was yo brotha would chew white man?"Candy said the policemen immediately put his flashlight towards the crowd but this time he had his hand on the butt of his gun. Then he shouted out, "Anyone out here got a problem with how we do our job, file a report!" the policeman returned the flashlight on the two ambulance drivers while they bent over to pick up Rafael's body.

In the darkness someone from in back of the officer cleared their throat, possibly to get everyone's attention. He had gotten it because Candy said when they looked behind him everyone and was surprised to see that the he had secretly called for other policemen on his walkie-talkie to come to the building as backup for him, his partner, and the ambulance drivers.

She said she guessed the policeman had gotten scared for the remark that he had made to the large crowd that stood before him. Candy said "about ten more policemen had driven up, gotten out of their cars and stood behind the first policeman. And what was so bad about it was that nobody in the crowd saw them drive up or had even seen them walk up the pavement.

As everyone's eyes adjusted to the darkness, and then have to re-adjust to the flashlights you could see that the arriving policemen were making sure that their fellow officers were protected. None of them said a word then Brenda chimed in that they all had their guns out. Not pointed at anyone but they them out where they could be seen.

Candy cried even harder as she told me how the policeman backed up the paddy wagon close enough to where the ambulance drivers stood and got out and opened the doors for them.

The ambulance drivers hoisted Rafael's body up to put it into the body bag like he was a rag-doll and in doing so, his head dropped back and some of his brains fell out on the ground. His arms had twisted backwards and his elbows were facing towards the front instead of the back of his body. They just threw his arms across the top of his body. Then they zipped it up and dumped his body inside of the paddy wagon like he was a dead animal. After they had finished, the policeman who had arrived first, put his fingers on the front of his hat as though he was going to tip it, said thanks and walked away.

With that memory, Candy was crying so hard that Brenda and I had to hold her because she had stopped hugging me and had started to just slide down to the ground. I sat on the ground next to her with my arm around her shoulders to comfort her as much as I could. Rafael had danced with me and had made me feel more special than Mark ever had. He had danced the last dance with me. I would always remember his smile, how he held me, and had whispered in my ear not to pay attention to the others. He said he would always be glad to dance with me. If I needed a partner to just let him know.

The police had only wanted statistics. He was a male, he was black, he had been drinking, and he was dead. They didn't even ask where he lived.

In his memory, for those who knew him personally and those that knew of him, there were no parties in any of the buildings for two weeks. Especially in the first white building where he had lived across fifty-First Street.

The buildings were quiet as everyone thought of Rafael and how he died trying to fly.

Chapter Thirty-One: Time to Pay the Piper

It was late at night a couple of weeks after Rafeal's death; I was lying on the couch having another restless night. The couch had become my second bed after my family had gone to sleep. I knew my step-dad could handle any problem that would have come up while he was there but I just felt better being close to the window opposite to where the couch sat.

It had been a long time that I had had a full night's sleep but the couch seemed to be the place that was able to at least make myself feel better. I could see any shadows that walked pass our window at night. It was on this night that I heard a soft tapping at first on the window and then the door. I was glad that I had my pajamas on instead of my night shirt. I had looked through both front windows and wasn't able to see who it was. I tip toed with my bare feet over to the door and opened it. There was a figure standing in the night I could see his shadow, but I couldn't tell who it was until I heard the voice and when I did I immediately recognized it as belonging to Cisco, one of Tommy's foot soldiers. I thought quickly, I hadn't been in any arguments with anyone since the fight with Roy. All he said was, "Tommy wants you."

It didn't matter now I knew what I was being called for. It was time to pay the piper. The piper was Tommy and it was my time to pay him for teaching me what I needed to know to protect myself in a fight and from anyone else that threatened my safety. I should have known something like that always comes with a price.

Now it was my time to pay. As I sat on the couch attempting to put on my house shoes, both of my hands were trembling. I knew that if he wanted me to try to steal something he would have had one of his gang members to tell me earlier while the stores were open.

With it being so late I figured that there was nothing else that he would want or anything that I had unless it was to have sex. I hadn't started having sex yet and I guess the only reason why that was no one wanted me in that way. When I came out Cisco said nothing else he just turned and walked in the direction of where the elevator was. Which meant that I was to follow him. I walked behind him without asking any questions.

I knew that he and none of the other gang members liked me for what had happened when I had fought with Roy and Andrew. We waited for the elevator and when it came, Cisco got on and I followed him quickly inside. We took the elevator to the sixteenth floor. No one lived up there so Tommy had taken it for his own to use it as he pleased. Once the door opened the whole floor seemed to be completely dark but it really wasn't, the lights had been broken out in certain places except the one light directly in front of the elevator but it was very dimly lit. Cisco walked me to the laundry room, banged on the door twice before pushing me inside. He looked at me with a big grin and turned and let the door slam as he took his place outside of it for Tommy's privacy.

Once inside, I was barely able to make out the figure, but as my eyes adjusted it wasn't long before I realized who it was.

Sitting on an old dirty mattress was Tommy. I watched but could barely see him but as he lit it I could see him a little I could see the ash from the cigarette as he offered it to me one but I refused. He stood quietly for a minute and all that I could hear was the stillness of the night and him exhaling the smoke from the cigarette. After doing so a couple of times, he took the flash light and shined it into my eyes. It blinded me instantly. As I put my arm across my face to block the light, I heard him give a short laugh. He said to me, "Yu no why yu here?" He moved the light away from my eyes. I wasn't able to see him; The only thing that I could see were spots that seemed to twinkle as I blinked my eyes. I answered him, "Yea I know why." He stood up and placed his hands behind the waist of his pants as he did I started to unbutton the top of my pajamas. There were two flashlights, but he had only one on. The other one sat on a make shift cigarette stand. He walked over to the other flash light and when he turned it on I could see anger in his face.

No. I take that back he wasn't angry it was more than that. He was pissed! He shouted, "*Hell naw! Shit naw!* He stopped talking for a minute and just looked at me. Then he started smiling and shaking his head left to right like he couldn't believe it. "Look yella girl, I don't need yo ass fo dat and I definitely ont won it from *you*! "I kin have any bitch any time and any place I won't." "I got plenty of asses for the asking or *takin!*" I asked him, "Then what did you want me for?" He took his hands from behind the back of his waist. He something out and handed it handed it to me. I looked at it and back at him then I did a double take. It was a book! He looked at the book, then at me. "I won't yu to teach me ta read an yu beta not fuckin tell nobody". "Yu heah me?"

"Yeah, I hear you."

"My boy outside thinks I'm in heah getting it on wif yu, I own care what he thinks." Then he got up off of the old smelly mattress that he had been sitting on and kicked the door. I heard Cisco standing guard outside laughing.

He must have thought that Tommy was roughing me up first before he raped me. Slowly I looked down at the book. The book's title was called, Fun with Dick and Jane. As he handed it to me he looked at me and gave me a little smile. "I lifted it from one of ma boys' kid brothas. "He won't miss it no way he ont hardly go to school anyhow."

He went back and sat on the dirty mattress and motioned with his hand for me to join him by patting a place for me to sit next to him. I walked over to the mattress sat down and opened the book up to the first page. We were like two little kids in a dimly lit classroom we both held each side of the book. He looked down at the book as I read the first page. Then I asked him to read the next page. He tried as hard as he could, but even a book that would be easy enough for a first grader to sail through like a breeze was giving him trouble. I could see the anger in his eyes and then disappointment on his face.

In his frustration, out of the corner of my eye, I could see him as he began to reach towards his shirt sleeve to get a cigarette.

I continued to read and without looking at him I moved my hand toward his and placed it back to hold his side of the book.

I never looked at his face so I didn't see his reaction to what I had done but by him placing his hand there I knew that I had moved a step forward with him. To get him past his frustration I closed the book. I asked him if he knew the letters in the alphabet. He put his head down, hesitated like a little boy and finally said "naw, I can say-um but I cain't write-um."

"Well, how do you write your name?"

"I don't have nothin that I need to write my name fo, and If I do my old girl(OG) reads it to me and signs what needs to be signed."

I told him what I planned to do, to read half of the book then we were going to start to do things with the alphabet. I could tell that he didn't like the way I was doing it because he immediately looked disgusted and bored and reached for the box of cigarettes again took one out of the pack and lit it. Then he got up from the mattress and went to the door. He leaned on it putting one foot against the door and resumed blowing smoke rings in the direction of the other flashlight.

I stood up and walked towards him. I took the cigarette from between his fingers and threw it on the floor and stamped it out with my foot. He looked down at the cigarette on the floor and then up at me. "What yu do dat fo yu stupid bitch? You know who I am? Jus cause I asked yu to do som-um fo me don't let it go to yo head." For some reason it scared me, and then it didn't. He was a gang leader who always had his way; no one ever said no to him. Because he didn't get things to go his way he, in his own way was throwing a temper tantrum.

He pinned me against the door and got close to my face and before I could blink he hit the door with his fist with such force that if it *had* been my face the punch would have killed me. I was shaking inside but I wasn't going to let him know. I looked him in the eye and told him that he was still going to have to learn to read and write the alphabet, make words and everything else before he could be able to read and understand what a book was saying. His anger got the best of him this time. "Get the fuck out! I got dis far, so I'll stay like I am!" I tried to tell him that he couldn't do one without the other. If he couldn't read, know what he was writing, or if it was right or wrong, he would be in the same situation that he started with.

"I'll think about it," He mumbled.

Outside it was time for changing of the guard. Cisco was leaving; Roy announced that he was there for his shift. Tommy heard, but didn't acknowledge him. That was common for Tommy to not answer so no one thought anything of it.

Roy had no idea that I was in the laundry room

with Tommy. The book that Tommy had brought to the laundry room was only a few pages. After all, it was for a child that was just beginning to read. I sat back on the mattress and this time it was me who motioned for Tommy to come and sit beside me. As I read, I pointed to every word and Tommy watched my finger as I pointed at each one so that he could see.

When I read about Spot, I pointed to Spot and did the same thing when it came to Dick, Jane and Sally.

He smiled but stopped quickly when he saw me watching him. We had been in the laundry room for a long time. I finally told Tommy that I had to go so that I wouldn't be missed or caught by my parents. I got him to agree to meet with me three days a week, but he made it clear that we wouldn't meet on any Fridays, Saturday or Sundays. He had said that those were his party days and usually Sundays were for his sobering up days. He said that he would send one of his boys to get me on the day that we would meet, at the same place for our dates.

No wonder I had never had seen him at school! The gang was moving up and increasing in number and he couldn't afford to let them know what his situation was. In a way I felt good that my thoughts on what the payback had all been altogether different. That was going to be another plus for me! A second guarantee that My family and I would be safe now especially since I was going to have even more contact with the leader of their gang. As I opened the door from the laundry room to go to wait for the elevator, Roy, who had been lighting up a cigarette, got a good look at me. I saw the cigarette drop from his lips as the look of anger spread across his face. He was as shocked to see that it had been me in there as I was to see that he was the one that was guarding the door.

Tommy stayed inside the laundry room, and while waiting for the elevator I could smell the marijuana as I came from the room. Roy looked back towards the laundry room then back towards me.

Someone was holding the elevator because it was taking too long for it to come. I decided to take the stairs to go home. As I walked past Roy I could tell that he was still holding the grudge and since Tommy was getting high he felt that it was the perfect opportunity for him to get me back. He grabbed me by the back of my pajama collar threw me to the ground and started wailing on me with his fists. I was only able to let out a soft yell. I thought that Tommy wouldn't be able to hear me I was wrong. Tommy heard the commotion and within a second he grabbed Roy off of me by his neck and hit him hard. Each punch that he gave seemed to be harder and harder. I screamed, "Tommy stop it! You'll kill him!" He looked back at me; his fist was pulled back in midair. He looked at me for a second then he hit him again anyway. As soon as he let Roy go he slid down against the fence with blood pouring out of his nose and the busted lip that Tommy had just given to him. I felt bad for him because I knew that he didn't have a chance in fighting Tommy and second he knew that he couldn't have shown that he was even going to attempt to try to. Not his leader! But it had never left my mind that he was the one who had tried to kill me when we had fought.

Tommy pulled him by his throat him onto the fence. Roy shouted to Tommy that he had hit me because I had disrespecting him by laughing and saying that fucking him was a breeze and that I didn't know what all of the talk was about.

Tommy pulled Roy off of the fence and hit him twice in the face again. Roy had lied and Tommy knew that he had lied. Roy had made it up to justify his hitting me, Tommy said, "Yu think ama fool? She ain't said no shit lack dat cause dat ain't what we was doin in nare. Yu don got yo self-caught in-a lie, an da bad part was yu got caught in nat lie by me. Yu still mad wit yo punk ass cause she beat the shit outta yu." Roy hit me because of the grudge that he still held against me. I had beaten him in front of his gang members and they were never gonna let him live it down. Tommy told Roy, "Care yo ass home we gone talk bout this tomorrow." Roy stumbled to his feet but before he could Tommy, in his same quiet voice he told Roy, yu betta not eva touch huh or even look at a da wrong way I'll tell da rest of um myself ta-marrow.

Roy got up and stumbled towards the stairway at the other end of the hall. Tommy decided to walk me down the stairs himself to make sure that I made it home alright. He lit a joint as we walked down to my floor where he stood by the stairs watching, until I was safely inside of my house.

I tiptoed into the house and went to the bathroom pretending that I had just gotten up to use it. I looked in the mirror and saw the same thing. Handprints seemed to becoming a regular fixture on my face like makeup before it had been a constant flow of tears.

I bent my head down to splash some cold water on my face which took away the sting from the barrage of slaps that Roy had given my face. I looked up in the mirror; instead of having a sad face I had an unemotional one. The thoughts started replaying in my head of how my night had started and how it had ended. I had done two things that not only I but no one other than his mother had probably done. I had said no to Tommy and I had screamed at him to stop hitting Roy.

I think that I was only able to get away with what I had said to Tommy and the way that I had said it was by sheer luck. And if I had, I wasn't going to keep tempting fate, because if I did, I knew that the next time fate might not have be so kind to me. It was trying to warn me not to keep getting cocky.

Everybody had probably heard their mothers say it when talking to someone or about someone that you should never tempt fate. I had, but I wouldn't do it again. Some people said that fate was good, but it never was in the projects. Fate was as bad as death. In fact it seemed that fate was worse than death if that was at all possible.

For the next full Month Tommy and I met in the laundry room. On the days that we agreed to meet Tommy never missed a day. I brought lined paper, the kind that kids used when they were trying to learn to write the alphabet. Which is where we started with, learning to write the alphabet. I would use different ways so that he wouldn't memorize anything. Sometimes I would start at the beginning and go to the middle and have him to finish it, go to the end let him name the last letter, anything that I could think of to make sure that he was actually learning. As Tommy got better with the work I went to the library, got a card and starting bringing books that we could read together. Sometimes I would let him read. Although he stumbled here and there he was able to manage. Then on others I would read. One day I brought a book to the laundry room called, "Three Little Pigs." He was like a kid as I read the story, especially when I got to the part where the little pig had the house made of bricks. As the wolf huffed and puffed he wasn't able to blow the house down. Tommy had been quiet as he usually was when I read.

For some reason, after reading the part where the wolf couldn't blow the house down, he looked at me and in his quiet voice but wearing his trademark emotionless face he said, "Stupid wolf took too much time huffing an puffing tryin to blow da house down, He shudda jus blew dat motha fucka up!" He couldn't help himself he laid back on the mattress laughing so hard that he was holding his stomach and had started wiping his eyes.

It seemed to be forever, before he could stop laughing, then he finally calmed down. I had never heard Tommy laugh; I don't think anyone else had either. After he wiped a few more tears away he got his serious face back and said, "Sorry I coudin't help it took his dumb ass way too long to git dat beacon!" again he rolled in laughter.

As I thought about it and looked at Tommy I started to think about what he had said and I started laughing too. Every time we looked at each other we would just break up in laughter all over again. For Tommy and me it had been a good night.

Chapter Thirty-Two: Deidra's Temper

It had been a couple of days since I had seen Tommy and almost as long since I had seen Deidra. I was on my way back from the grocery store for my mother and had just gotten to the breezeway. I saw Deidra and a couple of the girls who usually hung around with her. Deidra was leaning against the wall lighting a cigarette. I walked up to her I said hi. She immediately stopped leaning on the wall and thumped her cigarette into the grass, got into my face and said, "I heard yu was tha one in the laundry room wit Tommy at night. She started spewing words out before I could say anything. "Dat don't mean fo yu to start goin back in nare when he come back. Dat was me and Tommy's spot til yu started comin round!" As she and the girls stood behind her I walked up to her and stood directly in her face.

I looked at the girls as they had started to move around her and without looking over in their direction I said, "If you don't start no shit there won't be none." They stepped back. I looked back into Deidra's eyes and said, Tommy owns your ass you don't own Tommy! And as far as I'm concerned I don't give a damn what you think! Or hear! You just better not come to me with any kinda shit again."

I told her that I had told Tommy about her having threatened me before he left. Then I said, "That ass kicking must not have been mean enough since I don't see anything broken on you. But the next time and I'm hoping there won't be one, I'm going to handle it myself. And then Tommy will finish up where I left off."

"You have the gall to tell me about me being in your laundry room?" Don't even go there! DON'T GO THERE With Me EVER! "Yeah I got my ass kicked and they did a good goddamn job, but you better believe it won't be by you now, and it damn show won't be by YOU EVER!"

She started to walk away and must have had a second thought because she made a step to walk back towards me. I told her, "Don't do something that you'll be sorry for tomorrow. Don't even think about it." I turned around and walked away without looking back and walked the ten flights up to my house. I was too pissed to bother to look back.

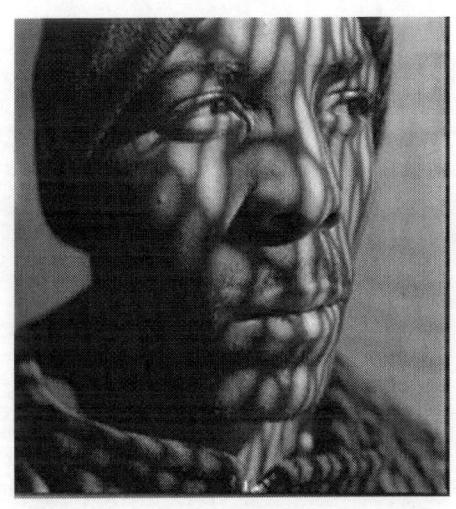

Chapter Thirty-Three: The Mouse That Roared

A couple of nights later Tommy and I met in the laundry room I could tell that he had something more than our reading together on his mind. He told me he didn't feel like reading. He said that he was only going to listen to me read. I told him that was not the agreement but before I could say another word he jumped up and started cursing at me and I had no idea why. At one point he got completely in my face. I didn't know how to react; he was so mad that I could see that he had little drops of spittle on each side in the corners of his mouth. It would be the first time that he would see me react to him in a way that he wasn't used to. I had stood up off the mattress when he first started to call me a bitch. Whatever had set him off had taken him to a level that I'd hoped that I would never be near him when it happened again.

I knew that whatever was causing him to act that way couldn't have had anything to do with me because I hadn't done anything. But whatever it was I wasn't going to let him take it out on me. Every time we read a sentence where he made a mistake he kept calling me a bitch as if it were my fault. He finally sat down on the mattress after he had cooled down, but only a bit. He pointed his finger to the opened book and without paying any attention to me said, "Come own bitch cause I got things to do. I got up off of the mattress and threw the book across the laundry room where it hit the wall and fell down to the floor. And with the most authority that I could muster in my voice I screamed, "You have called me out of my name ever since I've known you and I never said a word back. You *can continue* to call me Yella Girl, everybody does. It doesn't bother me anymore but just to let you know, my name is *Brenda!* If you don't want to learn anymore, okay, but guess who it's gonna hurt? You! That's who. Is it because my skin is this light? Is that the joke? Well you know what? I can't help that but I pay for my color every day! How long Tommy am I gonna pay? As long as I live in our building, until I die? Or until I move?" I was crying so hard that couldn't catch my breath then I picked up the ashtray stand and threw it too.

It ricocheted off the wall hitting the concrete sink before shattered into a million pieces. I turned around and looked into his eyes. Eyes that only saw fire and said, *"I am **Black**, and I'm tired of what I have to go through every day.* But you wouldn't know what I have to go through, do you? Of course you don't because you're Tommy!" Then I picked up the metal stand that had held the ashtray with the last bit of strength that was I had. I'm sure that when I turned around to face him I looked like what my mother used to call women that looked wild and crazy. (Banshees). As kids we all knew that when mothers referred to someone that looked like a banshee she meant a witch or the same thing as my mother had told me. It all depended on who was using either word at that time.

I was breathing so heard that I thought that my chest was going to explode. Then I told him about the encounter that I had with DEIDRA. I screamed "And you ain't gonna do nothing to Deidra because she's your old lady so I'm screwed everytime that I come out of my house! The fight didn't mean anything did it? All it proved was that I didn't take a beat down by your boys. It didn't mean anything else; you were supposed to take care of my family! I won fair and square but I see now it was all for your enjoyment. Still looking at him I just dropped my head and I was almost hoarse. "I've had it Tommy, I'm a girl! I'm not a fighter! You know that and yes you taught me a lot on how to hold my own. But I can barely do that. I can't do it like you I can't take fight after fight or fights with person after person. I know those girls in that gang are gonna be waiting for me when summer break is over and I'll have to prove myself with them again. When does it stop for me? When do I get to have a chance to stop having to prove myself?"

I opened the door and started to run down the ramp as fast as I could, passing Emmett as I did so. Then I heard him call out to Tommy and ask him if he wanted him to bring me back. Just as I neared the stairwell I looked back. I heard Tommy say "Naw, I got summin to take care of. And um only gonna have to use one hand to do it I But I saw that Tommy was walking in the other direction. I didn't know what to think so I continued to run down the stairs as fast as I could. He must have told Emmett to make sure that I made it to my house ok because by the time I opened to screen door I saw a shadow at the other end of the ramp watching me. I put my key into the lock and when I looked back it has disappeared. I had no way of knowing that it was Emmett but I was pretty sure. As I made it safely inside my house sweat was pouring off of me. Not just from the running but from the breaking of the ashtray and last but not least the screaming I had done at Tommy. For everything that I had gone through, including what Deidra had said about my being with him and for the feeling that I knew of what was yet to come. As soon as I locked the door I just stood with my back against it and held my eyes closed for a moment. My heart was still pumping from running down the stairs and the adrenalin rush I had from all of the screaming that I had done at Tommy. When I opened them I could see the shadow and I knew that my step-dad was standing there. I don't know if he knew that it was me sneaking in, or if he thought someone else was trying to. He didn't have the bat that lay against the closet wall. Then I saw him walk towards the light switch and then flipped it on. He walked over to me and turned my face gently from the right to the left.

In a soft voice he looked me in the eye and asked me, "Are you alright? Can you handle this?"

Wiping the sweat from my face, I said, "Yeah dad, I'm alright; I got this,"

"You sure?"

"Yeah, Dad, I'm sure."

Without another word he turned around to walk back to the bedroom but half turned his head and said, "Good." I stood there wondering, "Did he just catch me by accident? Or did he know that I had been sneaking out at night. And if he did, how long has he known?" He never brought it up, and neither did I.

As I tiptoed back to my room my thoughts went back to what had happened back in the laundry room. There was only one reason that he would be going in that direction at that time of night. No one in their right mind, especially the gang members who guarded the door would have dared to have said a word even amongst them. The consequences for saying anything would be too great. Then I thought about Deidra because I knew that that's where Tommy was going. I had a feeling that what Deidra was gonna get from Tommy wasn't gonna be nothing nice.

The next night when I met Tommy in the laundry room I could tell that my telling him about the way he had treated me had made a difference. It shown in the way he spoke to me. Inside I found myself laughing as he asked me if he could still call me Yella Girl. I had gotten over my anger so I told him yeah, that it was okay because everyone called me that anyway. I took the book that I had brought with me and together we read for two hours. There was no anger, no hollering or cursing only our reading. It was a good night.

Chapter Thirty-Four:
The Assault of Tommy's Girl

I saw Deidre the next day sporting the biggest black eye that I thought was possible to have. And believe me I had a lot of experience by having had my share. As was known by everyone Deidra was Tommy's girl lock, stock and barrel. But Tommy belonged to no one and Deidra knew this too. She was also in a gang, one that I didn't know of but that didn't mean anything. There were lots of girl gangs around and it was almost impossible for anyone to know them all. She saw me many times after Tommy gave her the black eye, but she never said another threatening word to me. In fact she started speaking to me, which I thought to be strange. I didn't trust her she made me feel like the toy that the kids would wind up and then a clown would pop out. Although I knew her I was always waiting for the clown to pop out.

I made sure that whenever we were near each other we would always be out in the open where Tommy's gang members could see us. I planned to never let her get me cornered again. Especially without anyone being around.

Because even when she acted as though everything was alright, I knew there wasn't a chance in hell that it was. She was going to try to get me back for telling Tommy what she had said to me. And it would come down to me or her and it certainly wasn't going to be me. Deidra had an older sister named Shannon. She was about eighteen or nineteen and was 5'7 inches in her stocking feet of solid muscle. She had the body of an athlete and the biggest muscles in her calves and arms that I had ever seen on a girl. When she saw me she would always speak to me.

One day when she was walking pass me I asked her, "Why do you speak to me when you know your sister doesn't like me?" Her voice was very soft and she had beautiful white teeth and a smile that made dimples show on the sides of her cheeks when she did that could light up a room. Her eyes were dark as coal and she wore an afro that was large and always neat. Her facial expression never changed when she said, "I ain't got nu-in to do wit what Deidra does. What Deidra does, is what Deidra does, and what Deidra gits, is what Deidra gits." As she spoke I could tell that she hadn't spent much time in school.

As she walked away towards the breezeway she turned put her hand up and sort of rolled her fingers instead of waving as she continued to walk towards the parking lot. I had never seen here much. I told Candy about the short conversation that we had near the breezeway. Candy told me that Shannon had done time on and off in jail for a lot of things. It was said that she had been locked up the last time for almost having beaten a girl to death. Word was she carried a gun, robbed people, the whole nine yards. The women that she hung out with had done hard time in jail.

Candy told me she had seen them a couple of times and they were nothing to play with. She said that most of them looked like men. As I thought of it, the more that I listened to the way that Candy spoke, I could tell that she hadn't spent much time in school either. But there wasn't anything that I didn't like about her or wouldn't do for her if I could. She was a nice person and she was my friend. One of the things about living in the projects were when the boys fought their girlfriends no matter how severe the damage that was done to them the girls mothers seemed to just turn their heads and act as though they had deserved it. It was like it happened, and then it hadn't. I never understood it but then again, I never asked. After listening to how Shannon felt about her own sister it showed me that she felt the same way. Sometimes there would be two girls fighting over the same boy and he would be standing there watching it along with everyone else standing in the crowd laughing.

When the fight was over the one girl that was beaten was left in front of everyone to be humiliated. The boy would leave with the winner, she would become his girl. She would be his and his alone until the time came when he no longer wanted or had any more use for her. The next day the winner would be sitting between the knees of the boy that she had won as he sat on the top of the bench. He would talk to other gang members and almost completely ignore her but she was happy just to be around him. Sometimes the boy would get bored with her too and date someone completely new; never bothering to tell the one that he had that their relationship was over. And that was exactly what Tommy did to Deidra.

T-bone had a cousin who lived on the west side he invited her to visit with him and his family for a while. When she came T-bone introduced her to Tommy and told him that her name was Renee. From that moment on, Deidra no longer existed as far as he was concerned. Tommy thought that Renee was very cute. She had wavy hair that she wore in a afro puff. she wore make-up that he had never seen Deidra wear. To Tommy the eyeliner, mascara, and lipstick that she wore Tommy thought that it made her look very classy. She had a nice smile, was very shapely and there were no marks or bruises on her face or body. She spoke using the correct pronunciation, showing that she was very educated and was definitely not from the projects.

He fell for her immediately and wanted to hurry up to show her off to the members of his gang and, to the people When people in the projects saw how well he treated her, Deidra became the laughing stock of the building. In our building. Never in the time that she and Tommy had been together had he treated her that way. Deidra and her girls came up with a plan. She wasn't going to let Tommy show off his new girl and treat her like garbage. Everyone who saw them together was whispering about him falling hard for T-bone's cousin and that he had dropped Deidra without even saying that it was over.

One of Deidra's girl gang members decided to introduce her to a boy that she knew that lived on a street called "Prairie." He was like most of the boys who lived in the projects. He wasn't interested in a real relationship. Deidra could tell by the way that he acted and by the way he acted it showed that he was really interested in one thing. The only difference with him and the boys in the projects was that he didn't live in them. Everything else about him was the same. But she didn't care. She only wanted him to make Tommy jealous, he wasn't going to be the only one with someone new. Not if she could help it, no matter what it took. Deidra got to know him better his name was Lester and she made sure that they saw each other regularly. She began sneaking over on Prairie all of the time. Tommy didn't notice that she was leaving the building regularly.

He was too involved with getting to know the Renee. But someone else in the gang had started to notice Deidra leaving the building, something that she rarely if ever did. K.C started to follow Deidra, watching her when she left the building, where she went and who she was meeting when she got there. After he had watched her long enough, he decided to tell Tommy what Deidra was doing. Tommy knew that before he and Deidra had started dating Deidra had a thing for K.C but K.C wasn't interested. So when Tommy came along and became involved with her it was no sweat off of his nose because she had started hounding him and following him.

She was always trying to push herself off on him but the more that she did the more he avoided her. Tommy knew that his best friend would never lie to him as K.C told Tommy everything that he had seen and how long it had been happening. Tommy seemed upset but not really. He really didn't care but he felt that she needed to be taught a lesson. She wasn't going to cheat on him and do it out in the open where other people could see.

Although he still wanted Renee, Deidra was still his to do with as he pleased. Tommy decided to set her up. After he was finished with her she would not want to have anyone for a very long time. Deidra belonged to him, but he belonged to no one. He didn't care if the whole building knew that he was messing around on Deidra. Who was going to say anything about it? No matter what he did or who he flirted with Tommy knew that she would always take him back. But this time it was different and he wouldn't allow that.

Deidra had found someone new and Tommy wasn't about to let that happen. Tommy wanted K.C. to meet him by the high school horticulture section. It was a small area that had only one way in and one way out.

Deidra agreed to meet K.C there because she had never really stopped liking him, he just didn't like her. But now she thought that he wanted her and she was happy that he had finally changed his mind about her.

After a short time Deidra let K.C kiss her. She hugged and kissed him back telling him that she had always wanted to be with him. She was about to make the biggest mistake that she could have ever made. Tommy and his gang were right on the other side of the wall. Tommy was able to see everything that they were doing and He couldn't wait for K.C. to give him the signal. Just to see him kissing her almost made him lose it.

He knew that what K.C was doing with Deidra was to let him see that she would have anyone, including him. Tommy and K.C had grown up together in the same building since they were little kids and who were called, "shorties" by the older gangs. Tommy considered K.C. as his brother. Tommy knew that if K.C. was going to betray him he could have done so years ago. K.C started kissing Deidra, gently removing her bra. Then he sat her up on a concrete wall that was attached to the stairs that was used as a flat stoop which doubled as a handrail before the doors there had been locked. K.C gently pulled down Deidra's panties. She had closed her eyes, waiting for their special moment. Mark had told me what had happened up to the point that I been seen before I had accidently walked upon them. K.C was still fondling her as he whistled for Tommy. He walked in right up to Deidra but she hadn't noticed that he was there. But as the other gang members walked in behind him she opened her eyes and immediately knew that she had been tricked. I had gone to the library two blocks over to get books for Tommy and me to read for the next night. And that's how I happened upon the rape.

I was trying to make it home by walking across the gravel next to the school using it as shortcut. I was almost to the opening where the horticulture area was. Then I heard the sound of someone crying. Whoever it was screaming and crying and begging Tommy to let her go. But everyone knew that once inside the courtyard no one would hear her screams unless they were right there. As I listened I knew the sound of the voice. It was Deidra. Begging for Tommy to make them stop. As I walked towards the courtyard I could see that Deidra's head was back, where she could only see who was coming into the horticulture area or up at the sky. From where I stood, I could see that Tommy had already worked her face over. Both of her eyes were swollen and her shirt and bra were off. As I backed away what caught my attention was that the other members of Tommy's gang were standing against the wall with their pants unzipped, talking to each other and calmly waiting their turn to rape her.

They didn't say anything to me because they knew that there was nothing that I could do about it. And I didn't want to be next. Tommy acted as though nothing was happening as he lit a cigarette and blew smoke rings, which he was known to do and never looked at Deidra while it was happening. It was her punishment for cheating on him. He could care less. She needed to be taught a lesson so that she would remember what would happen if she ever even thought about trying to cheat on him again. In that brief moment I saw two of Tommy's boys holding Deidra's legs spread wide open. Another gang member was having sex with her.

And the others that I had seen outside of the wall were going to, too. There wasn't anything that she could do. Then he saw me and ran directly towards me. It only took three large strides before he was in my face. He grabbed my arms and pushed me back so hard that I fell backwards on the ground landing on my side on the white rocks. I felt the sting as the rocks cut through the back of my arms and legs. Tommy had a look on his face like he was going to kill me and yelled *"Get the fuck out of here. NOW!"* the others just pointed at me and started laughing. I was so scared that I started scooting backwards trying to get away as fast as I could. Tommy went back picked up the books and flung them at me like they were boomerangs. I picked them up as quickly as I could, ran across the street to our building up the ten flights of stairs and all without stopping. I think that the shove and threat had something to do with it. By the time I reached my floor I was wheezing so hard that I had to rest my hands on my knees to catch my breath.

Candy had said Tommy had a dark side. It was the side that I had never seen before but saw up close and personal minutes before. He was as cold as ice. And for what he was doing to Deidra he deserved to be punished for it. There was no reason for him to do what he was doing to teach Deidra a lesson; this went far beyond the arm breaking or the black eyes. It was cruel and heartless. It was something that I would never forget. I ran to my room and opened up the window where I could see across the street to where the horticulture entrance was. An hour later, Tommy and his gang came out giving each other high fives. They had finished and were walking towards. Probably to pay a visit to the boy that Deidra had been seeing.

I looked toward the horticulture entrance for what seemed like forever but I never saw Deidra come out. So I ran out of my house and took off up the stairs to where Deidra lived. I banged on the door like someone was after me. Thinking all the while that that's exactly what may be happening to me later after the dust had settled.

Finally Shannon came to the door; she looked at me and said, "Deidra ain't here." At first she was wearing a smile and when she saw that I wasn't wearing one her smile went away. I told her that Deidra needed her help NOW! I didn't bother to try to explain, I didn't have time. I could hear her running down the stairs behind me telling me to wait up, and asking me the whole time what had happened to Deidra. I finally reached the first floor but kept running through the breezeway with her on my heels. As I came to the curb I didn't even look to see if there was any traffic coming. She stopped at the curb and hollered out, "Where are you going?" I looked back for a second. I just screamed, "Come on!" she hesitated for only a second then she was almost on my heels again. She was fast to be where she had been and to have caught up with me so quickly.

As I made the turn into the horticulture area I slowed down and then stopped. I grabbed my knees and bent down because I was breathing harder now than when I had before. I had ran up the ten flights of stairs to get to my house paused a while then up to Deidra's then back down the stairs and over to the horticulture room. I was breathing so hard that I had started wheezing. When Shannon got to the entrance of the courtyard she stopped for a second, there on the concrete stoop was what I knew she was going to see all along. She ran past me and held her sister's head up in her arms.

After I caught my breath and walked over to where Deidra was. Deidra was where Tommy and his gang had left her lying she was only moaning. Blood was coming out like water from between her legs. Shannon looked up at me with anger and tears in her eyes and asked me if I knew who had done that to Deidra. I was afraid because if Tommy found out that it had been me who had brought Shannon to Deidra I didn't know what he would do to me. She put her head down and placed her ear to Deidra's lips as she was trying to tell her sister who had done it. Her voice was soft and so hoarse that I couldn't hear what she said, but I already knew. Then she held Deidra and started crying hard. Deidra had told her how K.C. had set her up. Deidra was now holding her stomach as Shannon put on her side, with her legs closed she slowly pulled her knees up to her chest. Her panties were torn up with blood covering them next to the stoop on the ground. Shannon looked up at me and said trough her clenched teeth, "He's gonna pay for what he did to my sista."

Now I knew: why Tommy had chased me away and had thrown the books at me; the look on her face took the place of any words. I could tell that when she saw him, because she was so angry that she might kill him on the spot. What I saw in her face was pure rage and a want for thorough revenge. Shannon helped her sister to slowly sit up. After a moment both of us put an arm around her waist and held each arm around our own to help her to try to walk.

It wasn't gonna work. Deidra was not going to be able to walk anywhere. Shannon took one of her arms and put it under Deidra's legs and the other behind her back and lifted her up and carried her without any hesitation from the horticulture, across the street towards the building. A girl came out of nowhere and put a shirt around Deidra's lap so no one could see under her skirt. Then she quickly moved away.

When we made it to the building Shannon's boyfriend was leaning against the wall smoking a cigarette. As soon as he saw Shannon walking and holding Deidra he dropped the cigarette to the ground and immediately took her from Shannon. He was asking Shannon what had happened. Shannon ignored him and walked over to me; she hugged me and whispered in my ear thanks and for me not to worry because she was going to handle it from that point on. Luckily for them, the elevator was working that day. While we waited for the elevator, everyone that was downstairs and near the breezeway all came running and asked what had happened to Deidra as we stepped inside the elevator.

Shannon's boyfriend screamed at everyone to get out of the way. As the doors to the elevator opened the four of us got on. I pushed the button to my floor first and then to theirs. It was completely quiet as the four of us rode inside. When the doors opened on my floor I got off-but not before turning to look at Deidra once more, her arms were on her lap and her head down while being held. I told Shannon to take care. As the doors to the elevator closed all I could see was the rage that showed in Shannon's face. Word traveled fast in the projects. As soon as I stepped off the elevator and started to walk down the porch my neighbor ran out of her apartment asking me what had happened to Deidra. I told her what had happened only because I knew that she wouldn't tell anyone. She had never told anyone about the things that we had talked about and I trusted her with this too. Everyone knew that Tommy and Deidra's mother were longtime friends. After seeing Deidra I knew she was going to have to go to the hospital. I went to my bedroom to look out of the window and to see how long it would take for them to bring Deidra out to take her to the hospital. It didn't take long. Within ten minutes, Shannon, her boyfriend who was carrying Deidra, her mother, and Tommy's mother walked quickly to the parking lot. I'm sure everyone downstairs was wondering why if Deidra was hurt and going to the hospital, where was Tommy?

Shannon's boyfriend had an old beater of a car but it ran. After putting Deidra inside, everyone else got in and the beater drove off.

My neighbor and I both knew that the police wouldn't be called. This was a family thing and as Shannon had already told me, she was going to take care of it. With what I had remembered about what Candy had said about her and the way she looked by DuSable's horticulture area I had no doubt that she was going to keep her word. Or at least try to. What Candy had told me might have been here say, when Tommy came back I would see for myself. This was going to something that would be taken care of in the way other things that happened in the projects. By what was known as "Project Justice."

Chapter Thirty-Five: Tit-For-Tat

Candy had once told me that Shannon's temper was as bad if not worse than Tommy's.. She told me that if Shannon had the kind of look that I told her that I had seen on her face it meant that whatever it was that she was going to do was going to be nothing nice. And this time, although Tommy didn't know it, he was going to be on the receiving end of hell's fire. Before two months ago I didn't even know that Deidra even had an older sister. I guess her having been in jail or somewhere else was probably the reason why. By the time all this was over, if she had been in jail she might be going back.

I think that Deidra stayed in the hospital for four days. No one had heard anything about her for that number of days. On the fifth-day, though, there was talk that she had come back home from the hospital.

I went up to her apartment and knocked gently on the door. Her mother opened it. She saw and invited me inside. I started to tell her that I wasn't going to stay but before I could start she had put both arms around me, thanking me for helping her daughter. Her grip was so strong that it felt like she was going to squeeze the life out of me. I asked her how Deidra was and she said, "She's doing better, as well as could be expected right now. Doctor said she's messed up pretty good down there. Had to put a lot of stiches in her. He told me to just give soup and liquids, keep some-um cold on-er down nare and stuff so it won't pain her to much when she goes to the bathroom. He gave her some wipes that have some medicine in-um to keep the stiches from burning so much."

Deidra's mother took me by the hand to Deidra's room. She was sitting propped up on one of those inflatable rings the hospitals gave girls who had had babies to sit on. I could tell that she was hurting pretty bad because I could see the pain was in her face everytime she tried to move. She looked at me with tears in her eyes and said, "Thanks, who wudda knew dat da very person dat I thought wanted dat piece o' shit an I threatened yu foe bee-in wit him is dat same person to save my ass. I'm sorry bout dat, but believe yu me, Tommy gonnna wish he was dead when Shannon gits thu wit him, just wait and see." I told

143

her that I had come to see how she was doing and I
hoped that she would get better. Her mother walked me
to the front door said, "Goodbye and once again,
thanks foe takin care of my baby." I nodded and walked
down the stairs to go home as I walked down I thought
to myself, there's gonna be hell up in this building
when the two of them meet. I would be betting on
Shannon.

Tommy and his gang were just returning to the
building, no one had seen him or his gang for a week,
I didn't think that he or anyone else had a clue as to
what was going to go down. No one even suspected
anything when Shannon walked over to the benches and
had started to talk to the men who usually sat there
at night drinking their wine. No one knew that she had
been sitting there waiting for Tommy the whole time.

As soon as she saw him she got up from the
bench, walked over and said something to him. Her
voice was so soft even the people standing there just
stood looking stupid because nothing was happening.
But I did. What Tommy knew was that Shannon wasn't as
crazy as we thought that she was for wanting to fight
him. And Shannon had a surprise for Tommy and his gang
as well. I didn't see it coming until the day that it
happened. To this day no one would say *if* Tommy saw it
coming or exactly **when** he saw it. As I saw it by the
time the first punch from Shannon came, it had
happened too fast for *even him to react!* It was as
though it happened in slow motion. The first punch hit
his right jaw so hard that you could see the sweat fly
off of his face like rain.

Tommy tried to shake the punch off although it
was clear that he had been dazed. Shannon stood poised
in front of him with her arms at her sides. We all
knew it would be only a second before someone would be
picking her up off the ground or better yet, trying to
get her to the hospital for the beating that Tommy was
going to put on her… *we were wrong! Boy were we wrong!*
Before he could react she had her guard up and came up
with her left hand so far back that people said that
the punch from Mississippi. It hit him on the right
side of his face.

With the speed and accuracy of a venomous snake
coupled with the anger and power of a bull, she took
on a professional fighter's stance. The first and
second blows were to the right and left side of
Tommy's face. Then she wielded a blow to his body.

144

When he bent over, the third blow went to his stomach; the fourth and final one went to his face knocking him out cold. *She was just that fast and she was just that good!* While Shannon and Tommy fought if you could call it that, Tommy's gang had been moving slowly around the crowd formed a circle and had started moving in closer.

Emmett moved towards Shannon, with his fist aimed at the back of her neck. A hand-- a large hand-- grabbed Emmett by the neck. As we all looked around there were at least ten women that looked older than Shannon but twice as tall. In fact, most were as tall as Tommy, who was six feet two inches in his stocking feet.

They were more muscular than anyone could imagine a woman could be. They looked like the amazons that you would see on the cartoons on television. As Tommy's gang stepped up, so did Shannon's. The women dressed the same way as Tommy, with tee-shirts that had one sleeve rolled up to hold their cigarettes, and blue jeans; some wore their hair in a crew cuts. Others wore bandanas wrapped around their heads with the knot to the front.

Each one had quickly and quietly taken a position behind each of Tommy's gang and as if they were acting on a silent command, each woman took each of Tommy's boys and put them in what was known as a Full Nelson. A full Nelson was a position where the person performing it placed their arms up under their opponent's arms and then locked their own fingers behind that opponent's neck. In That position their opponent couldn't move. Now Tommy's boys were now outnumbered, and for the most part, out of luck. One of the women shouted to the crowd, "get the hell out of here dis party's over!" Shannon interrupted, "You! As she pointed to me, you come with us!" The crowd ran as they were told in every direction.

But were still peeping at Shannon's girls from their hiding places. No one was going to even try to get involved or do anything other than what they had been told to do. I followed Shannon as I was told. Shannon and her girls walked a dazed Tommy and his boys still in Full Nelsons, through the breezeway and out to the parking lot. Once there, two of the larger women came and took Tommy's arms and held them out straight. They brought his gang closer so that they could see what was going to happen to their leader,

and them. Shannon pulled a razor blade out of her back
pocket.

She asked Tommy, "Du yu no whut stitches feel
like yu piece-a shit, you really messed up my baby
suster. You acted like you ain't giva shit either, Yu
an deez pieces of shit had a lot o nerve. But guess
what? I on't give a shit either." She took the razor
blade from her shirt pocket. She said, "All yall did
it to huh, na we gone do it to all of yall! and going
very slowly on the right side from his chest, Shannon
pressed and made a straight line down, pausing a
couple of times so that she could watch his face
grimace in pain. Blood started to run down his arm as
it came out of the gash. The further down she went the
more he bled. The women shouted out,
"Turn his ass round so he can sport it on the front
and the back." Quickly they turned him around and
Shannon did the same zig zag marks to his back.
Laughter came from her gang members as one of them
yelled out, "What a punk!" Tommy was tough but not
that tough. He hollered out from the pain. Shannon
laughed even harder and kept slashing him with the
razor anywhere and everywhere that she thought she had
missed in some places when the razor sliced, the skin
opened up immediately. She didn't have to do it two
times. He looked like one of those slaves from our
history class that had been whipped. Shannon said,
"What yu screaming bout punk ass? I on't feel nut-in."

Then they pushed him to the ground. She turned
around to look at him as he was curled up in a ball
and said, "I hope you bleed out and suffa while you
doin it! You piece of shit." Then all of the women
laughingly took each of Tommy's gang members for their
last bit of satisfaction went in their pockets and
took out their switch blades. Two women took and held
each of the gang member's arms as they took turns
cutting long lines down along the sides of their
bodies, laughing out loud among themselves as the gang
member bled.

I asked Shannon if she would stop them from
cutting Mark because he had no part in the raping of
Deidra. I told him that he had told me himself that he
had only did as he had been told by Tommy which was to
hold her legs open. As Shannon watched, she looked as
if their screams made her feel good inside. She didn't
let the women put the razor to them as she had to
Tommy. Again I asked her about not letting them hurt

Mark. Then without even looking at me she said, "Naw." She wanted Tommy and all of his gang to get what they had deserved. They were all responsible for what happened to her sister, and for her, the payback was going to be very sweet. What made it even sweeter was that they had been caught off guard and didn't know what was happening until for them, it had been too late.

But for me it was different to see Mark bleeding. It made me throw up. Shannon called to me, "Come own, and don't git sic." One of the women laughed and said, "This must be huh first time." They all started laughing and pointing at me. Then I heard her ask Shannon who I was. Shannon must have told her. They finished Tommy's gang and left them where they lay. By the time we got to the breezeway the taller woman who wore the bandana around her head said, "Yu a good one, a little scary but yu ok yu did good by Shannon's sista. If you have ANY trouble, just tell Shannon and we'll be back."

One of the women said to Shannon, "I thought you said dis was gonna be a real fight. We could have done nat shit to dem in our sleep or jus two of us kudda came." They all started laughing including Shannon. She didn't seem to have a care in the world. She wasn't worried about Tommy or his gang coming for her later. And later I would learn why. Tommy and his gang had been humiliated in the worst way. Not only had he and his gang been beaten down by a gang of women who were better at fighting than his gang was, but they had taken the beating in front of the largest crowd that I had ever seen, not counting the people who saw it from their porches and back windows. It had come from his own girlfriend's sister.

As it had been said, Shannon was nothing nice. And now the whole building knew that all that had been said about her and the way she could fight was true. If there had been any non-believers in the beginning, there certainly weren't any afterwards. I didn't know how well she could fight, but I knew that she could hold her own.

When Shannon and I had tried to lift Deidra from the stoop, now I know that she had just been being nice to me, She really hadn't needed my help at all. I guess because of having told her where her sister was she let me try to help and hold Deidra up on my side. I had really been more of a hindrance than and help. As much as she had tried I was TOO SLOW she had lost patience with me. Deidra needed help *then!* And she couldn't afford to wait on me. She had scooped up her sister as if she had been as light as a feather and had carried her over to her boyfriend without even breaking a sweat.

But she knew that I had tried my best and If I hadn't come and gotten her, Deidra may have died. Maybe that's why she had hugged me. She knew just what she had planned to do and she did it, and it came off without a hitch. After the way that Shannon's gang had cut Tommy up there was no way that he or his gang could keep from going to the hospital. They would have bled to death. As Shannon's gang was walking away I looked back at Tommy, but he kept his eyes closed. Maybe it was from his embarrassment or maybe it was from the pain. But standing there wasn't doing either one of us any good. So I turned and walked away.

I had seen him in a way that I never knew was possible. He had let his gang rape Deidra to teach her a lesson. And for that action, he and his gang laid bleeding as a payback for it. He deserved it. And I didn't feel sorry for him at all. Mark was on his stomach I was hurt but glad that I couldn't see his face.

As I looked at the ground all I could do was stare at the concrete where there were streams of blood flowing in directions away from the bodies of the gang members. Where they had been laying was next to a sewer well and all of the blood seemed to come together as it flowed into the wells openings. As in all gang fights they would have to nurse each other's wounds or walk away and leave someone else to call the police for a body that they would leave that may not have survived.

Chapter Thirty-Six: All's Quiet in Babylon

As far as Tommy was concerned, in order to keep what was left of his pride and dignity as the gangs' leader, he and his gang were going to have to go underground, to truckish for a while until the talk of the fight had blown over and their wounds had at least started to heal. Although he knew that that would never happen. His skin would never look the same. Not in a million years.

For two weeks straight there had been no sightings of Tommy or his gang. The projects were quieter than they had ever been. That fight would be talked about and remembered as The Fight of The Century. By the end of the second week, Tommy or any of his gang still had not been seen. At first, it had been a good thing. But now everyone had begun to get nervous and jumpy.

No one played in the playground, or hung outside on their porches after dinner. No one knew how Tommy was gonna be when he got back. As some of the men shot dice, others just hung around making small talk. One of the regulars, who sat on the benches drinking with his other friends at night, finally got up the nerve to say what other people were probably thinking all alone, but were too afraid to say out loud. He said, "Man, the shits gonna hit da fan when Tommy comes back!"

Another man sitting on the bench said, "Sho yu right." As the second week rolled around, people seemed to be on pins and needles. Others were waiting for something, anything that would let them know that things could go back to normal gunshots and all. Everyone felt that anyone at any time could become ducks in a row. Days became nights, and night yielded itself again to the sun. And still nothing. Little by little the projects began to stir with activity.

The kids started to play outside, but never from the cover of the building and definitely not near the breezeway.

The music started back at a low volume but never where it could be heard from floor to floor like it used to. By the middle of the Beginning of the third week word got out Candy was having another party.

Tommy's absence had relented to a more lighthearted saying, "Out of sight Out of mind." People seemed to forget what Tommy and his gang was still capable of.

I, on the other hand, had not.

Chapter Thirty-Seven: The Party's Back

Candy's held her party on Friday night. Even then, as soon as it was over she was already preparing for the next one. Once again the music was loud and reached out as it floated into the air in the warm summer night throughout the building. It was the first party held after Tommy and his gang had left the building. There were so many people that it had to be held in two apartments. People were so glad to be able to fraternize and hang out once again that they not only paid the customary admission fee of twenty five cents, they also brought enough snacks and alcohol that even the late arrivals were able to get to share some refreshments and enjoy. An album that had topped the charts and was still there was by a group called, "War." The song that was number one was called, "Cisco Kid Was a Friend of Mine."

It was played all night at the party and from the turn table from the record player. Not to mention that Cisco in Tommy's gang had said that the song had been made especially for him. Before Tommy's fight with Shannon, there had been the two guys, Featherhead and Goody that came and went freely throughout the building but now that Tommy wasn't around more people seemed to be seen around the building. Strangely Oswald wasn't one of them.

After Tommy and his gang disappeared from the area after the fight I started to notice Oswald coming and going from the building more and more. I noticed that as he came and went he had become bolder than before. He had completely stopped looking over his shoulder when he came and left the building.

Maybe he felt less intimidated since Tommy and his gang was gone. He had started staying away for longer periods of time. One day I saw him come into the building with another boy that I hadn't seen before. Brenda, Candy and I were sitting on the bench and as they came into the building I asked Brenda and Candy if either of them had seen the boy that was walking with Oswald before. Both Brenda and Candy shook their heads saying that they hadn't. Out of nowhere Brenda said the very thing that I was thinking. "Something ain't right with him, he acts too sneaky and now he's bringing people to the building. He's up to something just watch and see."

If Tommy and his gang had been there it would have certainly been noticed and Oswald would have been confronted about it, if he had had the nerve to bring someone with him at all. Nothing seemed to bother him now that Tommy wasn't around. I had remembered the day that Oswald had walked by me and Mark and how Mark had said that it was something about Oswald that wasn't right. Now I started to think the same thing too. And like Mark, I couldn't put my finger on it. I let it go and Brenda, Candy and I went back to laughing and talking. But the next time I saw Oswald he was coming into the building with two different boys. As I glanced over at them he looked directly at me as if to let me know that he knew that I was watching him. I felt a shiver go down my back which made me quickly turn away.

Chapter Thirty-Eight:
The Boys Are Back In Town

Candy still had her quarter parties on Saturday nights. She was having them every week instead of every other one because school would be starting soon and the crowd would start to thin out. Since it was Tuesday we had plenty of time to get the party supplies. Brenda and I were going to the store to help buy things to help out. Because we were using our own money which was pretty tight we were only going to be able to buy a few things for the party a little at a time. As always we continued to keep the things that we would buy down to Brenda's house for safe keeping away from her mother. We were both coming through the breeze way from the   Federal side laughing and kidding around.

Just as we crossed the grass we couldn't believe our eyes. At first we just looked at each other without saying a word. Then Brenda said, "Well I'll be damned." There walking up the sidewalk was Tommy's gang. But Tommy wasn't with them. It was K.C who was walking in front of them. After being raped Deidra's mother didn't want her anywhere near the building so she sent her to stay with a relative to rest and continue to stay off of her feet so that she could heal. No one knew where Tommy was and no one dared to ask.

As they walked pass the people in the building you could tell by the looks on their faces that everyone looked as surprised to see them as we were. Everyone who looked at them ended up walking away as if they had seen a ghost. K.C appeared to be in charge now. Shannon was coming out of the breezeway when she saw them.

Brenda or I didn't know what was going to happen. Shannon took her time walking past each one making sure that they knew that she was giving them full eye contact. She made sure that they saw her look at each of their arms. They had no bandages around parts of their arms but where the cuts had been deeper the sutured area was easily seen. They knew that she was looking at their arms but they continued to walk pass her without looking back. And neither did she.

They walked into the breezeway and Brenda and I

continued going on our way to the grocery store as
planned. I said "Oh crap, I guess we're going back to
hell." Brenda said, "Naw not yet, the devil ain't back
yet." There was a concrete wall where the train would
park their load of box cars. They would park it in the
same general spot at night every weekend. Sometimes
while looking out from my bedroom window I would see
all of the gang members standing around the boxcars as
one stood on top of the other's shoulders until there
were three up on the tracks. Then they would crawl on
top of the box cars and pry the doors open, taking any
and everything that they could get their hands on. As
they lifted the goods from the box car they would hand
down the goods to the other gang members. It was done
until the whole car was emptied out. They would take
turns passing their loot from one to the other. They
enlisted other boys to help them take their loot. K.C.
took out a clipboard with paper and started to write
down everything they took. Tommy had originally
started it; now K.C was doing the same thing. He
watched the gang members passing out a lot of things
to people from the train, who had started running to
the wall. They knew that Tommy had always given them
things for free. Then they sold the rest.

From my bedroom window I could see the boxes as
they took radios, boom boxes, and record players and
everything that people could carry. K.C. and the gang
continued to do what Tommy had done before the fight.
K.C knew it would be another thing that people would
look at when it came back to help Tommy regain his
status when he returned. After they had finished
unloading a train, the gang along with some volunteers
from the building carried the rest away to be taken to
the sixteenth floor for inventory.

It was done by orders given out by K.C. It was
weird to me that the boxcars stopped at the same spot
in back of my building every weekend knowing that they
were being robbed. I started thinking that it had to
be done with the help of someone that was working
there and helping the gangs from the inside of the
railroad company. Why else would they put themselves
in a situation by stopping in the same place that they
were constantly getting robbed? I thought to myself
that someone somewhere must have been getting a big
cut for having taken such a chance where if they were
caught they would lose their job and get some serious
jail time.

Chapter Thirty-Nine: The Devil's Back

The beginning of third week everybody in the building knew that Tommy was back. Mark told me what had happened. Tommy spoke to no one but his gang members. As the gang gathered in the laundry room T-Bone asked Tommy if K.C. could be excluded from the discussion. It was as surprising to Tommy as well as K.C. But as Tommy looked into the faces of all of his gang members all nodded with T-Bone in agreement. Tommy knew that something was wrong so he asked K.C. to leave. K.C. was surprised but followed the orders of his leader. Each gang member had their say. Situations were told where K.C. had gotten buck wild after he left. He got loud, cocky, and full of his self and constantly reminded them of his role as being their leader while He was gone.

More than once members of the gang were made to stand down in public in his presence. K.C. humiliated them in front of other members, and although T-Bone wasn't fond of Mark, he spoke up for him, telling Tommy that K.C. had wanted them to vote him out for no reason other than the fact that he didn't live in Chicago. K.C. even implied that Mark was involved in another gang. He had no proof that it was true. They all told Tommy that they wouldn't do it without proof. Then Jesse, one of the gang members who never said much told Tommy how K.C. told him of his plans of taking over since he had been gone so long. Cisco spoke up and said at one point, K.C. went as far to say that he, (Tommy) should be kicked out because he felt the gang was getting soft.

Tommy was angry and disappointed at K.C. but not surprised. Even though he and K.C. went way back K.C.-would have to pay for his actions. He knew that what the gang had said had been true. Now he would have to deal with K.C. in the same way that he had dealt with gang members who had made the mistake of stepping out of line. It was important; he would have to deal with it but not now. There was something more important that he had planned for the gang to do. But he would give K.C the punishment that he deserved.

Mark told me when he got back that while they were on the Westside. The gang split up and stayed with friends and relatives of T-Bones. T-Bone was the only one who had escaped the cutting that Shannon's girls had done to the gang. The friends and relatives of the friends had helped Tommy and had taken them to the hospital there. In the ER they were given stitches. The Doctors and staff asked no questions because they knew that gangs would not tell who had done the damage to them.

While he was healing Tommy was able to see more of T-Bone's cousin, Renee. While he was there she and Tommy became an item. They hung out together more. Tommy found himself really starting to like Renee she wanted to go to places and do different things-most of which, Tommy had never done especially when he was around Deidra. Deidra never wanted do anything except hang around the building. She never asked him to take her anywhere all she wanted to do was lay up with him all day. At first that had been cool but that started to bore him quickly but he felt at that time she would do.

With Renee, he was as excited to be with her as much as she was with him although being a gang leader he tried hard not to show it. Mark said that one night Tommy almost lost his life on the same block where T-Bone's family lived. As Tommy walked Renee back to her house three men walked up to him and flashed their gang sign and asked his affiliation. Tommy pushed Renee behind him so fast and hard that she almost fell. He responded with pride where his loyalty was to, knowing what the possibility of the outcome could be. They could beat him, kill him or both. They chose to beat him as bad as any gang would do to their rivals leaving him on his stomach on the ground bleeding, to deliver the message to his fellow gang members that they had seen on their turf.

That gang owned the streets Tommy and Renee were walking on. While beating Tommy they had ignored Renee, who ran to her house to get T-Bone and his dad. Mark said that T-Bone's mom had started calling friends where some of Tommy's gang was staying. When they got back they found Tommy lying on his back with blood all over his face. They knew that his nose was broken but weren't sure if they had broken his ribs.

T-Bone had helped Tommy to his house while his dad went to the store for him. T-Bone and his dad used an ace bandage and together they wrapped it around his rib cage to help ease the pain. They all knew that there would be no need to call the police; they knew if they had called to tell what had happened they wouldn't come. The police knew that if the beating was

gang related the gang members would never tell who did
it and to them it would just be a waste of their time.

Tommy hadn't completely healed from the beating
that he had taken from Shannon. Now he needed more
time for his body to recover, but he had more things
on his mind than his recovering. Now in the laundry
room Tommy had laid out what had happened to the ones
that weren't on the Westside with them. Tommy told
them everything and why it was so important that they
go back to the Westside. His one and only priority now
was for a payback. No one was going to do that to him
and get away with it. No one was going to live after
making him suffer again. He had gone through the
ultimate humiliation. He had been beaten down twice
within two weeks. Then he let K.C back into the
laundry room to take his punishment.

As Mark and I sat on the porch in front of my
house after telling me what happened he went quiet for
a moment. After taking a deep breath he let it out
slowly and said that he didn't want to kill anyone but
again, he had no choice. He knew that whatever Tommy
had in mind was going to be dangerous because he had
given everyone handguns that night. He looked as sad
as I did as he got up from where we were sitting. He
didn't know if he would be coming back alive Mark told
me that the other gang members didn't seem to care if
they came back alive or not. I jumped up, held him,
and told him that I didn't want him to go. I told him
to tell Tommy what I had seen with Oswald and the boys
he had brought into the building. He kissed me and
held me for a long time before saying that he had to
leave and the time wasn't right. I walked back inside
of my house feeling like my heart was going to break.
I refused dinner; the pit that sat inside of my
stomach left no room for anything else.

All that I wanted to do was to take a bath and
crawl under the covers. After doing so, as I thought
about what was going to happen I ended up crying
myself to sleep. The next night I saw Tommy and the
others walk toward the parking lot but I kept my eyes
on Mark. T-Bone had borrowed his uncle's old truck. I
looked out of my window as they all piled in. A year
ago Tommy and his gang went on the Westside and had
gotten into a bloody fight with a rival gang. He had
lost one member of his gang the first time that they
fought and he had vowed to get even. Now with what had
happened to him it had become personal. Late that

night the gang had returned. Tommy and the gang came back without a loss. Mark had tapped at my door about two o'clock that morning and had told me. I was so happy to see him. I had prayed that he wouldn't get killed and had told him so. He had held me for a long time without saying anything.

When he finally let me go he kissed me on my forehead and walked away. After taking a few steps he half turned his head and said that he was just as glad to be back as I was and then disappeared into the stairwell. The next day I found out that Mark hadn't told me everything. *The Morning News* reported that three gang members had been shot on the West-side. It was stated that one was in critical condition at Mount Sinai Hospital. Back in the building the gang drank beer and watched the television as Tommy beamed with pride as he and T-Bone took credit for the shooting and Emmett took the credit for the one that was in critical condition. They all knew that he wouldn't live long so they counted it as three. What Tommy couldn't have known but would know much later was that they had made a terrible mistake. A mistake that would cost the gang dearly before it was all over.

When I saw Mark again I asked what had really happened that night I wanted to hear it all. Tommy and his gang had partied hard that weekend. They were pleased with what they had done. Mark spoke of how the drunker they got the more they laughed. They even started to re-enact the scenes of how they had ambushed two of the rival members and had stood and laughed as one begged for his life and the last one, being faithful to his gang, used his arm to make his gang sign and even shouted out his alliance as Tommy shot him in the head. Mark admitted to me about having shot his pistol but the gang was so involved in the shootings and with bullets flying everywhere they didn't notice that he had shot his pistol in a completely different directions so that no one would know that he hadn't really participated in helping to gun down at least one of the others gang members. He hadn't been aiming at anything at all. Not getting involved with your fellow members doing something that cool was something that no one tolerated. He knew that if that had been the case that the next time that they went after someone. They would do to him what he had seen them do to another member the previous year.

Get that member in a circle and everyone would

shoot him. So he just pretended to shoot at someone. That night Tommy sent for me. I followed his member to the elevator. It was Cisco, who kept his back to me and didn't look at me at all even as we approached the laundry room. I didn't exist to him either. After the door closed Tommy motioned to me to join him on the mattress. He was so excited that he was like a kid at Christmas. He could barely hold back his enthusiasm. Before I could sit down on the mattress he pushed a brand new book into my hands. Then he took the book away and started to read. He read a whole chapter without making one mistake. I thought that since he was so happy, that now was as good a time as any to ask the question that I had waited for since the fight to do.

I took a deep breath, not knowing if my question was going to ruin his good mood or what the outcome would be. So I gathered as much courage as I could then I asked him how Shannon was able to take him on and win. At first he just looked at me. Immediately in my mind I was saying, "Oh crap, you had to mess things up didn't you? You couldn't leave well enough alone."

He looked at me and with a smirk on his face and with the same soft voice he answered, "Who yu think taught me howda fight? Don let Shannon's looks or huh height fool yu, she cold as ice, ana kill yu in a heartbeat. If I woudda went after huh I'd been havin to look ova my shoulder foever. Them big amazons you saw, ar from da gang she in. If I had tried tu reely fight huh my ass, she woudda cut us in a million pieces. Now gone I'm finished fo da night. With that I got up and walked to the door then I remembered that I still had the book in my hands. I turned to him and asked him if he wanted it back, "naw you keep it, yu da teacha."

With that I opened the door and walked out. As usual he sent a gang member to follow me home. They're following me didn't bother me as much as it had before. The only one that I was still leery of was Roy. Tommy stayed in the laundry room smoking a cigarette. He still had another problem to deal with, K.C. Everyone in the gang was in a good mood after the shooting. K.C knew the gang had told on him coming and that Tommy was going to deal with him no matter how close that they were. And he knew that he deserved it.

Chapter Forty:
Never Make A Deal with the Devil,
He'll cheat ya eva time

Bright was the neighbor and friend who lived next door to me I told her things and felt completely comfortable with her. She was an adult and had six kids of her own. I felt completely comfortable talking to her. She also gave me answers from an adult's point of view because she had lived in the projects years longer than I had. She had four sons and two daughters. The oldest son was nineteen, there one that was my age, the rest were stair steps but not babies. She was the type of mother that every teenage girl wanted because she was so down to earth and so easy to talk to. She had little education, but that didn't matter to me she tried her best to talk to all of the teenage girls including me about the mistakes that she had made when she had been our age to try to prevent us from making them. Because my mother worked so much, after making sure that my chores were done I would always go next door to her house and talk with her.

Sometimes we wouldn't talk about anything in particular but I always learned something new from her whenever I left her. Her mother who lived on the Westside, had come to live with her for a while because she hadn't been feeling well. Bright felt good letting her stay with her until she got better, she would have a better chance of helping her if she needed to go to the hospital right away. I had only seen her mother briefly when I had come over to visit.

She rarely came out of her room whenever Bright had company. I had come over to Bright's house the day after the shootings and together we sat and watched television and listened to what was being said about it. After the news had finished we talked about how senseless it had been because we both knew that it had been Tommy and his gang who had did it. In fact, everyone in the building knew that they had because they had bragged about it and had a party to celebrate. As we talked, Bright's mother came into the front room. It was the first time that I had gotten a chance to see her up close. She was a short heavyset woman with grey and white hair that she wore in a single French braid. She walked with a cane; her legs were very bowed. As she walked every step made her shift her weight from side to side in a rocking motion.

On this particular day she used her cane to guide her to the loveseat in the living room which sat a few feet from the short hallway. As she sat down I could see that her eyes were almost white. Bright smiled as she looked into the direction that her mother sat and said that her mother's eyes at one time had been a beautiful hazel color. But the cataracts had covered them and had taken their beautiful color away along with her sight. Her mother turned her head in Bright's direction, and smiled briefly. She started to twiddle her thumbs as she rocked slightly back and forth. Bright saw me watching her and told me that she had suffered from arthritis in her legs and ankles which caused them to ache when kept in one position for too long.

As the sun became warmer she took her cane and moved to the other side of the loveseat to get closer to the window she smiled as she felt the warmth of the sun on her face. Bright and I continued to talk about the killings and how long Tommy and his gang had thought that they were going to be able to keep getting away with the sort of things that they were doing before getting caught or better yet, killed. Bright's mother turned her head slowly away from the sun toward the direction in which we were sitting. She suddenly started to giggle but soon the giggle turned to a high pitched sound of laughter. It reminded me of Halloween and the sound that witches made when they sat and stirred their pots to make potions.

We both looked over at her at the same time as she suddenly started to laugh. It starled both of us. Her mouth had opened so wide that I was able to see that she had only two teeth in her mouth. But she stopped laughing, the laugh turned into a grin. Her facial expression changed again as the grin slowly disappeared. This time it took on a haunting look. Her mouth turned up at the corners, and then her face went completely blank as every facial expression disappeared as fast as it had appeared. In a soft voice she said, "Dem boys dat do dat killing, days too damn stupid to know dat dey killing days finna come to an end. They dumb and they stupid. They don't know dat day cain't make a deal wif the Devil, cause he'll cheat cha eva time." Afterwards she put her head down, started back to twiddling her thumbs.

   She never said a word after that for the whole time
that I was there. Bright looked at me and looked as
shocked at what her mother had said as I did. It was a
look that made the hair stand up on my neck and goose
bumps that had appeared on my arms. As we left her
house she shrugged her shoulders and shook her head,
"you gotta excuse my momma, she surprised me because
she don't say nothin to company, she usually stays in
her room. What she said shocked me too. But don't
worry about it I'm glad to just have seen her laugh
let alone say anything at all". At that time I felt
that it was definitely time for me to go home. I had
heard other women say a lot of old people could see
things that were going to happen before they did, I
didn't know if it was something about the *way* she had
said it or if it was *what she had said.* That's what
blew me away. She had said it like she knew that
every- thing wasn't going to be alright. Just looking
at her when she said it made the hair on the back of
my neck stand up. All that I was sure of was I had
never met anyone like her before, and I wasn't too
anxious to want to be around anyone like her again.

Chapter Forty-One: K.C's Horrible End

A week after the shootings Tommy was still in a good partying mood so when Candy gave her party although hesitant, I took my place again at the door. Tommy decided to do something that he rarely did. He brought the members of his gang to her party. Candy's apartment was already filled to the limit but a lot of late comers but most of Tommy's gang just went in to share a joint with some of the others at the party but they didn't stay long, just like the others they did the same.

After getting it they would go back on the porch to smoke or drink it. They did that to keep a watch on the members who were inside, especially Tommy. Tommy was inside getting high with one of the boys at the party. I watched from the door as the boy gave Tommy a shotgun that made Tommy shake his head and cough, afterwards he said out loud, "Man dat was some good shit! It's the bess I had in months Next time yu git some like dat let me know!" K.C. was inside by the corner talking to one of the girls. Tommy hollered for him to get him a beer but K.C. couldn't hear him because of the music. So Tommy went to get the beer for himself.

After the girl gave K.C her number he started to make his way back through the crowd to get back to Tommy but as he did I saw someone whisper in his ear, but the room was dark so I couldn't really see him. But I did see K.C shake his head so I didn't think anything else about it. As Tommy came outside K.C. was already on the stairs he shouted to him through the noise that he had a phone call he would be right back.

Tommy nodded and held up his bottle of beer he was drinking from to let K.C. know that he had heard him. K.C ran up the stairs and that was the last time that anyone saw him alive. An hour later I remembered hearing Tommy say, "Damn, what's wif K.C? What call is takin him so long? Don't no phone call take dat long." Just as he finished the sentence there came the sound of a loud of a gun blast, then another one followed the first. Tommy and the members of his gang jumped up. People sitting outside started screaming, "We heard gunshot! We heard gun shot and it was close!" I was afraid so I slowly backed away from the door.

Tommy pointed in both directions to his gang to split up to find out where the sound of the shots had come from. Some went in one direction the others went with him in the other. It wasn't long before the cry came from upstairs. Tommy Come heah! Tommy took off running in the direction of the call up the stairs like he was running for his life. Later Mark told me that they all got to the 16th floor at the same time and stood by the wall waiting for Tommy to come. He said that as Tommy came closer he could see the sweat as it poured off of him. But after seeing that they weren't under attack he slowed down. Mark said no one near the laundry room said anything as Tommy ran up to where they were standing. Their eyes guided him to the body that sat slumped on the floor inside. Tommy just stood there for a moment. He didn't say anything; Mark said for a second he didn't even move, He just stood there.

All of the gang stood and watched as the tears flowed down Tommy's face. Mark put his head down as he told me that whoever pulled the trigger of the shotgun on K.C had done it at point blank range. The cartridge that tore through K.C.'s chest left a gaping hole that went through the wall of the empty apartment next door. The second shot had taken most of K.C.'S face and head off. That cartridge had done the same thing to the wall as the first one had. Afterwards, the shotgun had been placed across K.C's lap as a payback. Mark said that the whole damn thing was so sad. Tommy staggered over to K.C. and cradled his body in his arms. K.C.'s insides were spilling out into his lap. The small part of what was left of it, held the last remnants of just a skull. Brains, scalp and skull pieces were everywhere. The large splatters were on the walls, ceiling, and floor. After calling the police the gang took control of the elevator so that the police would be able to get to the floor to retrieve his body. Getting his body out of the building in the condition that it was in was Tommy's first and only priority. He knew that the ambulance drivers or police wouldn't treat K.C. any different than anyone else. They would not walk up any stairs for any reason at all.

The police came and left with what was left of K.C's body in the infamous black body bag. The police asked the usual questions. Did anyone see the shooting? Could it have been gang related? Who found the body? Where did the victim live? Once again, this was going to be another one for the statistic books.

He was Black, he was male and he was dead. After the police and ambulance drivers left Tommy went into the laundry room and shut the door. Inside he screamed, "Whoever did dis is gonna pay, they all gonna pay!"

The party had broken up after the gunshots had been fired. Tommy and his gang had split up to try to find K.C. Now it was Emmett who had to tell people at the party that K.C was dead. Some of the girls hollered and cried, others held each other and shook their heads. One of the boys had his head down he said, "Man, we just lost another one of our own."

Tommy stayed in the laundry room all night. He had lost the closest person next to him after his mother and he cried like a baby. In fact the gang members didn't know what to do or how to react so most left and told Cisco and Emmett to knock on their door if he needed them.

The next morning Emmett and mark knocked on the laundry room door to check on Tommy. They found him sleeping against the wall that K.C. had been killed. Mark told me that after Emmett woke Tommy up they helped walk him home. As they walked him inside of his house Emmett hugged Tommy's mother as he told her what had happened to K.C. the previous night.

Tommy's mom had known K.C. since they had been shorties. He had been almost like a son to her. She sat down on her couch and shook her head as she started to scream and cry. Saying, "Naw, Naw not my baby! Not K.C." Mark walked Tommy to his room and helped him to get into bed. As soon as Emmett and Mark had woke Tommy to walk him home he had started crying again.

Then he went back to the living room where Emmett sat as Tommy's mom had placed her face on his chest still crying. In the laundry room the gang had come. They brought several buckets of soap, water, brushes and mops, everything they would need clean the walls, ceiling, and floor where several pieces of K.C's brain and skull had sprayed when he was shot. Mark turned his head away from me as he told me how hard the gang had to scrub to get the blood off of the walls and floor. The spray of blood had splattered and made the gray concrete wall look like a large picture that had a grey background, with large blotches splattered on it like the ones we did in art class. Where the artist seemed to just take his brush, dip it in a can of red paint and just whip the brush at the canvass to make large splashes that just seemed to be there. The color didn't' go in any particular direction, it went in every direction. Mark said that if it had been in some fancy person's art gallery it would have sold at an extremely high price because it seemed so real. He said, "It would have sold for even more if someone had found a way to keep the brains and skin from rotting." White people were weird that way they liked real images of death. If they knew that what they were looking at *was real*, that the picture they were looking at had come from an actual killing, the dollar figure that they were willing to pay probably would have had so many zeros behind it that someone like us would have to go to the math teacher for them to tell us exactly how much those zero's added up to. In LA, they would have paid for that much for it. Rich people lived out there and always wanted to have something that was one of a kind. Right after they found him, the blood on the wall was crimson red. And after all, it *was an original.* It was even invisibly signed with K.C.'s own initials.

Chapter Forty-Two: A Repeat of K.C.'s Death

The viewing of K.C.'S body was going to be held in a funeral home that could have easily been mistaken as a small store front. K.C.'S sister and mine had been friends since kindergarten. My sister and K.C's sister had come to the funeral home to meet the family because they had gone earlier. My sister was there to pay her respect to K.C but mainly to be there as support for her best friend. My sister described to me what had happened that day. She said as she and K.C.'S sister entered the funeral home they used one of the double doors which had been left unlocked for the family's entrance and for the flower deliverer. She and K.C.'s family were going to sit in what was called the grieving room, a place where the family could say prayers and console each other in silence before the viewing started.

As my sister walked inside of the funeral home the first thing that she said she noticed was that the whole place was smaller than she had thought it was from looking at it from the outside. While looking around, as she continued to walk towards the door that led to the back room she held on to K.C.'s sister's arm firmly. She also noticed the cleaned but well-worn carpet.

There was only room for twelve pews separated by a narrow aisle that led directly to the front of the room, where K.C lay. They were walking on the right side next to the wall. On the other side, in front of the room behind K.C.'s casket sat a stand where the bible lay. Then there were three steps that led to a small platform, where on the left a large piano sat on the left which could be seen from the corner. Because of the body's condition the viewing would be held with K.C.'S body in a closed casket. It lay on what appeared to be a slightly unsteady stand. To the left of the casket, on the flower stand sat a large round wreath of white flowers that had a picture of K.C smiling in the center of it.

As they reached the doors to the family room K.C's sister suddenly glanced over in the direction of the casket and started to scream hysterically. My sister said that she continued to hold and support her to keep her from falling down the small hall which led to the room where the rest of her family had gathered.

The atmosphere of the funeral home along with seeing her best friend so upset become too much for her. She felt herself sweating and her hands had started to shake. She wanted to run away but knew that she couldn't leave her best friend because she needed her now more than ever.

She was going to have to find a way to be strong for her so she stepped of the room and into the small hallway to try to regain her own composure. As she wiped her face with her handkerchief suddenly there came the sound of a shotgun blast. It had come from the direction of the viewing room.

At first she thought that it had come from outside of the funeral home. She ran from the hall where she had been standing to lock the outer door in case whoever was shooting wouldn't be able to try to take cover inside. The same time that she opened the doors from where she had been standing, K.C.'S casket slammed to the floor. As it fell on its side the lid popped open allowing the upper part of K.C.'S body to come halfway out of the coffin. Showing the results of what the gunshots had did to his body. K.C.'s sister heard the shots and came running to see where the shooting was coming from but stopped dead in her tracts alongside of my sister. Now both stood looking at a figure wearing a long black coat that was stood aiming a shotgun directly at them. K.C's sister turned her head quickly towards where the casket had been. Seeing it on the floor and how K.C's body lay with the top half out and the rest still held down due to the hinge that held the bottom of the casket closed, was more than she could handle. She started to scream but stopped she fainted and fell like a ragdoll to the floor. My sister never moved from the spot where she was standing. She stood frozen looking at the person who now stood looking back at her holding a gun. By looking at it she could tell immediately that it was a double barreled shotgun. Mostly everyone was familiar with guns from having seen them or having someone they knew who had one. K.C'S sister had promised her to secrecy after having shown her K.C.'s gun once before. Her blood ran cold as she recognized him it was Oswald. She had told me that they had stared at each other for what seemed like forever, although it probably was for only a second or two. She had told me that Oswald had had a crush on her at one time. She knew by the way that he looked at her and would sometimes smile at her when he would walk by. One time he had even winked at her as he walked by. When he did she said that he had said hi. It had been so soft that although she had heard it sometimes she pretended that she hadn't.

She said that she never liked him because there was something in his eyes that when she looked at him it made the hairs on her neck stand up and gave her the creeps. He gave her one last hard glance before turning the shotgun away from her, firing again into the casket which had held K.C.'s body. She said that the sound of the blast was even louder now that she was in the same room with the gun that had been firing, and even though she had closed her eyes and covered her ears, they had started to ring inside.

Afterwards she heard a small popping sound inside of them and was unable to hear anything. She told me that she never understood why K.C.'s family never came out of the grieving room to see what all of the noise was about or even what was going on. She thought that maybe the emotions and pain that came with losing their son was why they couldn't think of anything else.

The only thing that they could do was to be together and hold on by being lost in their own thoughts. She could not imagine how bad the feeling was to lose their son and how badly it felt to have their hearts broken because she had never had lost anyone to death. Oswald was really angry. As a gang member himself he knew that Tommy's gang would never think of being caught in a place like the funeral home.

A setup would have been too easy. He even knew that gangs never attended viewings, only funerals to avoid ambush but that didn't stop him from doubting himself he had lost a member who had been like a brother and the only rational thought was the same as Tommy's, that he would make them pay.

At a funeral, in the cemetery a gang could take cover either behind the people there or they could shield themselves behind the trees, bushes or even the headstones. Everyone knew how close K.C and Tommy were and Oswald thought that because they were blood brothers, Tommy would try to sneak in to get one last look. In his own anger he had forgotten a lot of important things. In doing what he did, had been the wrong one.

My sister said that as the popping in her ears stopped she heard voices coming from the outside. People who had gotten there early to get a good spot in line were standing outside talking loudly. The viewing of people who had lived in the projects and had died usually went on for a whole day because of the number of people wanting to attend. As the shots rang out she could hear people screaming and telling others to run for cover. She heard people in line, not believing what was happening, question in disbelief why there would be shooting <u>inside</u> the funeral home.

Tommy and his gang didn't go inside the funeral home but they weren't far from it either. They heard the shots and came running towards the funeral home just as Oswald kicked open the doors, shooting while he screamed out the affiliation of his gang. He kicked the bar on the door so hard that the door itself almost came off of its hinges. He must have checked the doors before he entered the funeral home to know which door was locked and which was open.

Tommy wanted nothing more than to find out who had killed his best friend. Mark had never told Tommy what I had seen. But now Tommy, his gang, and everyone else especially people who lived in the building all knew who it had been. **It was *Oswald*.** The person that they had least expected. But Mark and I had known something wasn't right with Oswald for a long time and would have known long ago if Mark had told them what had happened when they had left the building after Tommy's fight with Shannon.

Because the gang hadn't paid any attention to him when they returned they continued to allow him to come and go without having second thoughts about it. It had been the one time that Tommy had allowed himself to become complacent probably because Oswald lived right in the building where everyone lived. He had been right under their noses the whole time and Tommy's complacency had cost him the life of his best friend.

Tommy and his gang crouched down behind cars lined up on the street. They started to shoot at Oswald. As Tommy reloaded his gun he probably remembered the promise that he had made when he had held K.C.'s body that fatal night. Now everyone from the building knew who had killed K.C. Everyone

including Oswald knew that if he ever got out alive
would never be able to come near the red brick
projects again.

My sister told me that the funeral director who
ran and hid had now returned from the safety of his
hiding place to see what damage had been done to his
place of business. She mentioned that K.C.'s sister
struggled to get up from the floor. She seemed lost
and confused so my sister helped her get back to the
grieving room. Another of my sister's friends told her
what had happened as soon as Oswald stepped outside
the doors of the funeral home.

Tommy, his boys and Oswald started to exchange
gunfire. People who had started to cross the street to
attend the services quickly turned away, running for
their lives. Everyone ducked, dived or ran to keep
from getting hit by any stray bullets. Oswald, now
walking backwards used the shotgun once more before
dropping it to the ground. He pulled a gun from the
pocket on each side of his coat as he continued to
fire. Ducking into every doorway that he could to
shield himself. He had counted on the cover of those
doorways as part of his plan. He needed two things if
he was going to live to make that happen. The doorways
were his only cover and Tommy and his gang were
starting to get closer. If they boxed him in it would
be over. He needed to get to the alley as soon as
possible. He reached onto the pockets of his coat,
pulled out the two hand guns and used them as he
continued to fire. He stood as close within the
doorways as possible to shield himself and to return
gunfire from Tommy and his gang.

He knew as he poked his head out that he would
soon run out of doorways and he was almost out of
bullets. But he had to make it to the alley. At the
last doorway he had nothing else to shield himself. He
came out shooting both guns at the same time, trying
to point them in the directions that he heard the
gunfire. Tommy and his gang continued to shoot
nonstop. My sister said that while she was inside of
the funeral home it had started to sound like the
building was in the middle of a battle field. And
throughout it all, none of K.C's family came out of
the grieving room to see what was causing the barrage
of gunfire. Oswald was still shooting when he got to
the alley. He had taken a bullet to the arm and
another one in his knee. He had made it to the alley

but Tommy and his gangs were almost on him. He knew he would be killed execution style if they caught him. He had run out of cover and had nowhere to go. As he stepped out in the clear, still willing to die for the alliance to his gang an old dark blue Chevy screeched up right behind him, as it stopped his gang members helped him inside while others covered him by firing back in all directions. Before Tommy or his gang could do anything the old Chevy revved its engine, the car lurched forward while making a sharp turn onto the street its tires burned rubber as it completed the turn and in an instant it was gone.

As it sped away Tommy stood in front of his gang and watched it go further and further down the street until it could no longer be seen. Tommy slowly dropped his gun arm down to his side. To his gang he looked as though he would fall apart any minute. It was Emmett who reached down and slowly took the gun out of his hand. Tommy let go of it without any resistance. My sister told me that she was still standing in the viewing room as Tommy came in followed by Emmett and the rest of his gang. T-Bone was the last member to enter and as he turned to close the door to lock it a hand grabbed the inside of the door to keep it from closing. It happened so fast and with so much strength behind it that instead of trying to keep the person attached to it out, decided to grab whoever it was that was trying to force their way in. The hand belonged to Shannon. The damage was done and the danger was now gone. My sister told me the gang members never attempted to make any eye contact with her what so ever.

My sister just stood by the door not speaking not moving and almost too scared to breathe. T-bone pushed the door and at the same time Shannon yanked the door again with such force that T-Bone almost came flying out. She walked into the funeral home followed by her mother, Tommy's mother and Deidra. They had arrived for the viewing, but only saw the aftermath. The four of them just stood in their place with a look of disbelief at the condition of the funeral home. Tommy, T-BONE, and Emmett were in the process of picking up the casket stand as the other gang members were trying to put the wreath of flowers, or what was left of them back on its stand.

The bullets had disintegrated the picture of K.C so they wouldn't be able to use it. Tommy and the others hadn't paid any attention and didn't know that both mothers, Deidra and Shannon had all entered the funeral home. Both mothers looked at the damage that had been done to K.C.'S body along with what had been done to his casket and the stand and both of them immediately started screaming and crying at the same time. Shannon tried to hold her mother but she broke free and ran over to where K.C's body lay and kneeled on the floor as she put her arm across his body screamed, "my baby! No, Lord, not my baby!" Tommy ran over to help Shannon's mother off of her knees.

As he helped her up she just put her face into his chest, still shaking her head. Tommy held her and rubbed her back, trying to do everything that he knew how to try to console her, knowing inside of himself that there would be nothing that he or anyone else could do. He couldn't even hold back his own tears anymore. He Said, *"Momma I would gladly trade places wif K.C. if I could, I wud give anything, my soul if it wud bring um back and yu no it. But I cain't, ain't nothing I can do. But don worry WE WILL GIT -EM, MY HAN ONA STACK A BIBLES WE GONE GIT HIM, I PROMISE YU DAT.* My sister said it was so heartbreaking to watch. Tommy's own mother didn't know K.C. as well as K.C.'s mother knew Tommy but by the look on her face anyone could tell that she was hurting inside just as much. What mother wouldn't feel the same pain? Mark, Cisco, and Roy walked the mothers, Shannon, and Deidra to the grieving room to join K.C.'s parents. She said Shannon came out of the grieving room quickly wiping away the tears from her eyes. As she walked past my sister, she said excuse me but really didn't act like she knew her at all. She excused herself and walked over to where Tommy and the others were trying to make things as presentable for the viewing as they could. Looking around to see what she could do to help, she saw the cartridges on the carpet and got on her knees and started to pick them up. The gang watched her but she never looked up. Cisco walked over to where she was kneeling and handed her his bandana to put the cartridges in. It was his prized possession. In a soft voice she said thanks. Their eyes met for only a moment before he turned around and walked away. It didn't have to be said, everything was on hold, No apologies, or words of appreciation were necessary. No anger, no hatred, and no animosity. Nothing.

The tension between Shannon and Tommy was also

on hold. Everything could be resumed later if
necessary. The only thing that was in the room was the
love, pain and sadness that was felt by all. Once the
casket was placed back on the stand my sister said
that Tommy and the others repositioned K.C.'s body as
neatly as they could into the casket. The mortician
had done his best under the circumstances but there
was no way that he could do anything when it came to
what should have been K.C.'s face. There just wasn't
anything to salvage. Before closing it, each gang
member bent over and placed their face on what was
left of K.C's chest. The embalming fluid had made it
firm and after it had been completely closed for the
viewing. No one was meant to see the damage that had
been done to the body. Only the gang, my sister and
the family would know that there was nothing at the
top but something that looked like a mannequin there.
Everyone there would never forget him. They would
never forget how the bullets made what was once a
person so ugly, that they would carry the site of how
his damaged body in their minds for the rest of their
lives. Before closing it, each gang member bent over
again and told K.C. that they loved him; each one
closed their eyes for a moment to say their personal
goodbyes. Also out of respect each gave him the gang
sign as they walked away. It would be the last time
that anyone would call out for K.C. He would never
answer back

     Tommy, Emmett, and Roy all walked slowly back
towards the grieving room to get K.C's family. They
reopened the casket for one last time. K.C.'s sister
and Shannon's mother fainted. My sister said that she
and Shannon waved their hands across their faces to
try to make a breeze and gently patted their faces to
revive them. K.C's mother didn't react at all after
viewing her son's body, neither did his father. They
just stood at the casket and stared. Tommy, Mark and
T-Bone gently helped them to the closest pew to sit
down.

     The police had been called by the funeral
director but by the time they arrived there was really
nothing that they could do. They took the cartridges
from Shannon who was still holding them in the bandana
and placed them into plastic bags. My sister edged
slowly into the back room so that they wouldn't ask
her any questions.

     She told me that one of her friends who lived in

the apartment above and next to the funeral home had a front row seat and had watched everything from her window. She later told my sister what had happened from the time that Oswald had backed out of the funeral home to the time the car pulled up and his boys in the car had pulled him in.

After it was said and done, even though she never went up to the casket to view K.C.'s body, what happened at the funeral home would haunt her for the rest of her life. I knew that it had scared her half to death. So much so it had gotten to a point that she started to have nightmares that would have her waking up screaming in the middle of the night. My mom would come to the door and she would see me holding and rocking her as I told her that she was going to be alright. She had no idea of the event that had happened that day. My sister would hold me and tell me that in her dreams Oswald did not let her go, but had pulled the trigger and had killed her. I would sit on the bed with her and hold her. At other times I would crawl into bed with her just to be there if she needed me. The nightmares caused her to have such paralyzing fear in her dream that she would wake up, reduced into a trembling mass, of uncontrollable screams.

Only after being held and in spite of my reassurances becoming completely exhausted, the screams gave way to her helpless sobbing and tears, and finally sleep. My mother wanted to take her to the doctor to see what was causing it. My stepdad knew why she was having the nightmares and convinced my mom that if she took my sister to them they would start giving her pills that would have her like a zombie. So my mother dropped the issue. I promised my sister that I would be there. Noone knows what goes on inside the mind of someone that has seen too much too soon, and had even been the one having stared into the receiving end of the barrel of a loaded gun.

I thought about my sister. She was lucky enough to escape unharmed physically, but would she or anyone else in that same situation ever escape the memory mentally? For some, the image of a traumatic moment has such an impact, that sometimes the person tries to remember it to face their fears.

Others cannot and then use anything that they could get their hands on to forget like Snookie had. He was drinking heavily all of the time. And then there are the last ones, who can forget but for

whatever reason of their own, won't. I never asked my
sister what went through her mind when she stood there
that day looking into the barrel of the shotgun as
Oswald had pointed it directly at her. After that
entire episode, I really didn't need, or want to know.
At least not the details. But I do remember thinking
about what she had shared with me, and as I looked out
of my bedroom window at night for a long time
afterwards my only wish was that she would be okay.

Chapter Forty-Three: Mark

After K.C. was laid to rest it rained for a whole week. It rained at different times and in intervals. Sometimes it came down in sheets that seemed that it was never going to let up. Mark and I would get together as often as we could. We would sit on the damp porch at night and he would put his arm around me as we talked about how things between us would be when everything was over. I would always tell him how worried I was and although it would soon be time for him to go back home I would tell him how much I would miss him.

He would tell me how much he was going to miss me too and try to reassure me that he was always going to come back to me. But in my heart, I knew that there could always be a chance that he wouldn't. Especially now, after saying how obsessed Tommy had become in wanting to catch Oswald and the others for killing K.C. without having shown him any mercy on.

Mark always kept me informed of what was happening within the gang. At the risk of getting caught by anyone finding out that he had been telling me. He said if I knew I would be safer. Usually it was the other way around, the less you knew the better, but in the projects Marks way kept me knowing so that if I needed to I could stay one step ahead of the Dragon. I knew that he trusted me and really cared for me. We had even started saying I love you to each other when we parted.

Chapter Forty- Four: Tommy Goes Rouge

Everyday that passed after K.C's death, Tommy's anger grew. He became more and more impatient and for reasons that no one in his gang understood he wanted all of them around him or readily available at all times. The anger that was inside of him soon started to give way to rage. He would constantly come up with new ideas to what they would do if they caught Oswald and how they would make him suffer before killing him then, he would say how he would make him tell who was really behind K.C.'s hit. Shortly after K.C.'S death he verbally gave every gang member a lecture for not keeping an eye on each other at the party. And used K.C.'S death as an example of why it was important. After dismissing the gang, Emmett, Mark and Roy reminded him that it had been his idea for all of them to go to the party. They left the laundry room with Tommy still inside to think. He needed to take responsibility for this as much as they.

But Tommy knew deep inside that he was just as responsible and had acted as irresponsibly as they all had. But the revenge on his mind would never let up until he would have the chance to release the anger inside of him by taking it out on those that had caused the death of his best friend. Slowly the gang noticed that Tommy became almost like a different person. His temper was meaner; He would get impatient and showed no tolerance for even the smallest of things. He seldom spoke unless he absolutely had to or if he had called a meeting. One night during a meeting two of his gangmembers, Cisco and Roy were rough housing with each other and Cisco accidently pushed against Tommy who, ordinarily would have joined in or completely ignored them.

That night he just lost it and almost beat both of them to a pulp. He shouted at them, "When I call a meeting yu heah to lisen to me only. Yu ain't pose to be doin nut-in else. Anybody got som-um to say bout it? I ain't think so. So stay in yo place when a'm talkin." He wanted everyone that he had contact with to get involved, even the older ones. First, he would have to have to find out which ones were available, because a lot of them were in prison. He also knew that as a rule a total retaliation meant all gangs from the youngest to the oldest needed to join in to find Oswald. His request for help would mean that everyone had to be voted on by the older gang leaders. They would determine if what they would be fighting for would be worth their time to get involved in. A leader, younger or not, Tommy felt K.C'S death was important and reason enough. To his dismay, those that he counted on most had been caught and were now in prison. Others that were doing well would not interrupt their jobs of dealing drugs, which was easy money to risk their life on member that wasn't even 18 yet. Others were actively protesting the way that Blacks were being treated through the NAACP and weren't available. A few from the 20 year old age gangs did come to the meeting but made it clear that it better not have been a waste of their time

Tommy felt his leadership skills were strong. If the older members were at least willing to listen to his cause. After all, a gang member was also a brother. All any gang had been each other and to be separated and divided would cause a breakdown that no gang could afford. But the elders still turned him down.

Chapter Forty-Five:
Predators in the Rain

The weather was bad on the first night that Tommy planned to go on the Westside to hunt down every gang member that he and his gang could catch to get his revenge. The gang members who were to join them had not arrived. Tommy was mad at the elders' decision but knew that there was nothing that he could do. He decided not to wait any longer after the meeting time had passed. He would go with or without their help. He and his gang were going to go that night, raining or not. T-Bone had borrowed his father's old work truck and they all piled in and left for the Westside.

Tommy thought the rain would let up for at least a little while he was wrong in fact it came down in sheets so thick that because of it they could hardly see through the windshield. Finally they reached the Westside and parked the old truck across the street from the park. Mark said that they sat and waited hoping to see any of their rivals. But it was still raining hard and no one was out. Then Tommy spotted a rival. He knew he was one by the colors that he was wearing. He was running down the street trying to get out of the rain. Tommy whistled, the gang member looked across the street and took off running with Tommy and his gang on his heels. It only took a minute before they had caught him. Tommy already had a plan. This was not a member that he wanted to use his plan on but as far as he was concerned he would do. He now knew the gang that Oswald was loyal to. He had seen the gang's colors before they drove off. He knew that the rival they had in the circle; now on his knees, was a small fish from the gang. None the less, he would make this rival talk.

He was trembling and crying already showing a sign of his weakness. He was a follower and if they hurt him enough he would squeal on his own to save his own throat. He was young, he didn't have a strong alliance with his gang; otherwise he wouldn't have been on his knees begging. What this young rival didn't know was that he was going to die anyway; Tommy was just waiting to see how much he would be willing to tell him first.

After giving him a thorough beating it was obvious to Tommy that he didn't know anything, he was nothing more than a lookout. Lookouts weren't told very much until they had moved up within the ranks. Begging for his life had started to bore Tommy and after looking over at Emmett they both lifted up their guns and fired at the same time. The shots killed him instantly. They walked back over to the old truck leaving the body where it fell.

As they rode in the old truck Tommy was angrier with himself than he had been before. He had taken a chance that turned out to get him nothing. His only saving grace was that the other gang members wouldn't find out through gang members that had been loaned to him because none had shown up and the only ones that really knew of his screw up again, were his own. As they drove back home in the rain, Andrew pulled out liquor to share with everyone to try to lighten up the mood. As they emptied their bottles, they threw them out of the window, laughing as the bottles broke against the concrete. Roy told Tommy that he needed to take a wiz so T-Bone stopped the truck. They were at the corner of forty-seventh and state. Directly across from the white buildings were.

Had it been a night were it wasn't raining the lookouts would have been everywhere on the street outside of the building selling weed and watching for strangers coming and going from the buildings. If the night had been clear, Tommy and his boys would have been dodging a hail of bullets that would have been raining down on them because they were intruders and everyone would know that their truck had not been seen around the area. But that didn't happen. The rain had slowed down everything for everyone. After waiting without seeing anyone they decided to leave. Tommy's anger and disappointment
became fueled and everyone started to open their bottles of alcohol and drink. By the time the truck pulled up to the light at 47th and state everyone inside was completely drunk. A pregnant girl walked across the street in front of the truck towards the white buildings

As she walked Roy hollered out of the window, "Hey bitch can I get dem digits? The girl turned around and put both hands with the middle fingers up and said "Fuck yu an yo momma! Tommy was already pissed off not being able to find Oswald. As the girl turned and started to walk away. Tommy pointed his gun through the window and shot her, she turned around and looked at the truck in disbelief for only a second before falling to her knees and the completely down with her eyes wide open. Tommy said, "Bitch shudda kept her mouth closed, she woudda lived longer. He took another drink then looked back over to where the pregnant girl lay. He told Roy and T-Bone to stop acting like slobs and go and put the girl's body up on the sidewalk instead of leaving it halfway in the street. Roy waved his hand as he playfully said, "foget yu man." Then he remembered that Tommy was already in a foul mood. This was not the time to kid around with him. A woman who had seen the whole encounter came running across the street. A woman came running down the median. She was screaming at them saying, "How could you do that? Just kill people like that! dat girl was pregnant!

    "I'm gonna call the police!" She turned around and started to run away. Tommy wasn't fazed. Andrew rolled down the back window and shouted, "Tell this Bitch!" then he put his gun out the window and shot her. Tommy pulled out another bottle from the floor under his seat and took a long drink. Tommy told Roy and T-Bone to put the pregnant girl's body onto the side walk. Andrew asked Tommy if he wanted Roy and T-Bone to pick the other woman's body off of the median too. Roy yelled, "Hell naw, I'm done being a undataken carrier Fa da night. Anyway, I ain't got no bag fa ha anyways. Ain't nobody paying me to load no bodies, leave dat shit fo the police or the ambulance drivers." Everybody in the truck started laughing. Suddenly a car sped through the red light. As it passed Tommy and his gang guns came out shooting a hail of bullets at Tommy and his gang. Tommy shouted to them, "Take cova!

    Tommy's gang ran in the opposite direction and crouched down to take cover in the door way of a building called, "THE FIRMAN'S HOUSE." It was a small white brick building that offered activities, where kids could go on field trips, to parks, or to watch programs and other things to give them something to do. A place attended by adults. Anyone could come as long as they had a note from their parents to attend.

    The attacking car's wheels screeched as the driver sped up, and jumped the curb causing the car to end up on the grass in front of the building. The driver was driving the car as fast as he could causing the wheels to make deep tire tracks in the grass as the wheels struggled to gain traction to keep the car

184

moving fast at high speed. As the car came closer
Tommy jumped out waiting for the car as it sped
towards him with his gun pointing directly at the
driver. Bullets were flying in all directions. Tommy's
boys opened fire from their hiding places in the
doorway to cover Tommy. The others had started firing
from the other side of the truck too. Mark said that
it seemed like Tommy had a death wish. K.C. was gone
and he didn't seem to care if he came out of the gun
battle alive or dead. Tommy continued to pull the
trigger on his guns, emptying their clips. As he fired
the last shot from his gun the car slid on the grass
and stopped as if it had parked itself in a parallel
position. The windshield was completely shattered but
remained in place. Every bullet that he had shot was
reflected in it.

He dropped the gun on the grass as he called out to
see if everyone in the gang was still alive. They all
answered as they came out from their hiding places. T-
Bone walked over to the driver's side and opened the
door. When he opened it, the upper part of it fell
half way out. There was a clean bullet hole in the
center of the driver's forehead. Roy and Andrew opened
the back doors. The bodies sitting in the back seat
were still sitting up and riddled with bullets. It was
the same for the bodies that sat on the other side.

But the best gift for Tommy was yet to come.
When Cisco opened the passenger door the body that
fell out onto the grass made Tommy smile. With bullets
to his throat and all through his body there was no
question that Oswald was dead. He had died with his
eyes open. Tommy went around to where his body lay and
slowly took the gun from Emmett's hand. He stood
looking at Oswald for a minute. He kneeled down and
gently cleaned the blood off of his face with the
bottom of his shirt. While kneeling down he put the
gun directly in the middle of Oswald's forehead and
fired. Even as the rain poured down he smiled. He felt
good, so good that he lifted up his arms and screamed,
"HELL YEAH."

The gang raised their fist high to show their
alliance. Tommy turned around to face his gang, the
smile on his face showed victory. He had kept the
promise he had made to K.C. He announced that what had
happened that night was good, but it wasn't over.
There was still someone that they had to deal with...
Oswald's leader. As Tommy and the rest of the gang

walked over to T-Bone's truck they were laughing, and told T-Bone that they would make it right by his uncle by get the truck fixed. Everyone was happy, except one.

Tommy had become a predator that night, one of the worst kind, He had killed Oswald but he wasn't satisfied. He felt that he still had a bigger fish to fry. His killing had gone from revenging K.C.'s death to just hunting and killing people. He had killed six people, seven if you counted the unborn baby that night. He had broken the cardinal rule not once, but twice and worst of all he had killed a pregnant girl without having any reason at all. The older gang members ran their operations even when they were in jail, they were swift in punishment when it came to keeping and enforcing the rules. There was some honor among thieves but tonight Tommy had crossed the line. Women were the heads of the house. They were the ones who raised them, taught them right from wrong even when their sons and daughters had chosen the wrong path. The mothers had done the best that they could. They were both mother and father. Women were never to be killed ever.

If the leaders had ever found out what Tommy had done, even while they were in jail a quick death would be easier on him than being given a slow one to remind him of the law. Tommy was in the debt of his gang members now and he was scared because now they all held a secret over his head. But he wouldn't let them know it. Because they would be held responsible for the deaths as much as he was.
Tonight Tommy was only second to which was considered the lowest of the low. It was even lower than that of a pedophile. Tonight Tommy had become a killer of women. He killed a mother that was going to have a child. He had become a predator, a predator in the rain.

Chapter Forty-Six: The Gate Keeper Am I?

The night after the massacre, Mark came down to talk to me. He looked bad as he told me in detail everything that had happened the night before, even the way he thought Tommy felt. He told me that as soon as he got home he went to the bathroom and threw up. What had happened had made him sick to his stomach. The worst part was that he had participated in the shootings as well. While looking down at the porch he slowly put his head down. I'm disgusted at what I've been a part of. I don't know how I'm gonna be able to live with himself after I get home. He looked at me with tears in his eyes and said, "I'm not a gangbanger. I never should have gotten involved in the first place. I thought it was only gonna be smoking a little weed and some drinking, If I had known this coulda happened I would have taken my chance in trying to get out with a beat down."

"I might not have lived through it and that's what scared me. "Instead I caved in, I never even dreamed of anything happening like that. I'm alive, and I killed somebody and I'll have to live with that every day of my life." He sat next to me and as I looked at him I could see tears running down from his cheeks to his chin. I could only put my arm around him and hold him. I couldn't tell him that it would be alright because like he said, he would have to live with what he did for the rest of his life.

The only thing that I could do was hold him. Nothing was going to undo what had been done. I could sense his pain, but I couldn't feel it because I had never been in a situation where I had killed anyone.

Nor would I ever feel the guilt or know what it would be like for him. We were teens, nowhere even near being adults. I couldn't even summon up what the length of a life time was. Everybody had seen old folks and I guess if he lived with his guilt that long it would probably feel like he was going to be feeling guilty for a very long time. It was sad because he had a conscious and was truly sorry for what he had done. But none the less he had participated in it. There was nothing that I could say. Nothing would ever change that. To tell him that it would be alright would be telling him a lie so I just held him. We must have sat there huddled together on the porch for over an hour. I had started shaking but I didn't want him to leave feeling the way that he did. He felt my shivering and slowly stood up. I've put enough on you tonight. As I stood up he grabbed me and just held me, resting his head on my shoulder where it was faced away from me.

I felt so bad for what he was going through the tears had started falling from my eyes. The first thought that came to my mind was how much I hated Tommy for what he let happen to Deidra, And now for what he had put on Mark. For Tommy and his gang it wouldn't be a second thought for what they had done, they had no conscious but Mark had. I wished that he was dead for what he had done, he and all of his gang. He had lied to me when he had told me about how cold Shannon could be. He knew he was lying when he said it. I guess to him it was no big deal. But when it came down to it the truth was, that Tommy was just like, if not worse than Shannon. If there were anything that was colder than ice it was him. He had no heart and without a shadow of a doubt he was worse. I didn't know about Shannon but now I did know about him. I remembered how when he spoke of Shannon the night that we sat in the laundry room, how he had told me that she would shoot a person dead without any second thoughts. But he left out the important part, *so would he.* I had been stupid to think that he could have been anything other than what he had shown me. He hadn't changed, it was my blindness in wanted to think that he could. He had been himself all along. It had all been a lie, and a cheap one at that. He was who he was. He wanted what he needed. He needed me to teach him to read but his reason was not to be able to leave the gang, get a job, or to do something good. His reason was to keep his rank as the gang's leader, because anyone could take his place if it had gotten out that he couldn't read that He was illiterate. He also wanted to impress Renee. He was arrogant, he was cunning, but above all, he was very, very smart. He knew what to do to keep his gang members in line; he knew what to do to make them happy. By giving them things, but he really didn't give them anything. He allowed them to rob the railroad trains and he allowed them to give the families shopping from the stores using the small welfare checks that would have taken months to fill the books with the S&H green stamps the blenders, irons, coffee makers and other things to make himself look good, To make people think that he really cared.

He helped his gang members carry the heavy groceries for their own families as well as the other families that lived in the building. And the families knew that he and his gang were the enforcers who kept them safe. So to everyone he looked like the hero that they needed when it came time for them to be protected since they could never count on the police. But Tommy didn't do anything that if caught, would have got him sent to jail. He only stood by and watched as his gang did the actual stealing. I never saw him climb on the train or carry any of the goods. Again it was his gang. It was his gang that took care of the WA WHO BA MAN and had provided the protection for the little kids that usually played unsupervised around the building.

But he was still the one who the gang looked up to. Tommy was for Tommy. He was who the families looked up to. By everyone's standards everything he did was justified even when it wasn't. The people that knew what he did wasn't right and didn't want their sons involved in the gangs moved away. And the other families that lived there and knew what was going on kept their mouths closed. Tommy was smart; there was really nothing that he could be tied to directly. It would always be someone else. I had tried to do what they had done, to stay on his good side or like others before me ended up meeting--THE DRAGON--. But I really believed in him, and all the reasons for everything that he said, I helped to justify everything all of his reasons and excuses even when It made no sense. When I saw Tommy and his gang give the working men respect when they walked by, It gave me a reason to believe in him. But the real reason was the men that had steady jobs had problems enough.

I know mine had, and they weren't going to take any crap from Tommy or his gang. They had no fear of the gang and the gang knew it. They had a family to help feed. Because in being there their wives and girlfriends didn't get public aid stamps. Trying to make it on the small checks was problem enough. Those men were like papa bears to their young; and they would kill or go down trying if they needed to. Gangs in the projects could be large. Gangs like Tommy were still considered as shorties by the older gang members who dealt with more serious issues like drugs, being enforcers and doing the killings of important people.

When gangs were caught their crimes would always be aired on the news. And so would the lengths of time that they would serve in prison. To reassure those who worked that they would be safer on the streets now that the real threats were finally off of the streets. So the men who worked were left to come and go alone. But what most knew was that for everyone caught, there were three more to take that one's place. The unspoken law still applied for everyone when it came to the interference of a fight but that was where the line was drawn.

When the Men came home in the evening if Tommy and his boys were out in the back of the building, or even if they were in the front, they would speak to them. The men would speak back to them, but would say nothing more. When they spoke, they would always maintain eye contact with the gangs. To not do so was a sign of weakness. Maintaining eye contact let the gang know that they were not intimidated. Men minded their own business and the gang did the same.

I never saw a working man walk past the gang and look back over his shoulder. That too was considered a sign of weakness. Working men that had been raised by a male role model taught their sons about eye contact, about the responsibilities that came in getting a girl pregnant and that a girl would like him more for the way he treated her than the gifts that he could or could not afford. This is the way Mark told me that it was how he was raised. I knew because I would hear my step-dad when he had talks with my brothers. Afterwards I would think to myself, that's the type of man that I want, one that was good to us like my step-dad. One who was like Mark.

The majority if not all of the members in Tommy's gang had no father. So they didn't have a role model. And I guess since the girl's mothers hadn't been treated in a good way, they couldn't tell them what to look for in a good man. So to a lot of girls any man/boy was good. No matter what he did, as long as she was theirs.

Chapter Forty-Seven:
Inside the Devil's Hopscotch

The next night, Tommy sent for me as he had when
we would have our reading class together. As I entered
the laundry room, he sat the book that I had brought
to read gently to the side. He said that he wanted to
talk to me. He had no idea that Mark had told me
everything. And acted as though nothing had ever
happened. And as I sat next to him I kept my head down
to keep from looking into his face because everything
about him disgusted me. What he had done out of
revenge for K.C., in a way if that had been all that
he had done maybe I could have tried to understand
although there was really no excuse for him to kill.
But that's what gangs did, for the killing of K.C. it
would have been considered by all to be justified. I
knew what K.C. had meant to him. That part I would
have expected to happen. I knew it wasn't right, but I
knew it would have had to come. But the rest, the rest
was just sickening.

I sat listening to Tommy as he told me
everything that he and his gang had done. Everything.
The killing of the one rival gang members, then the
four others, which included Oswald, he even told me of
the killing of the pregnant girl and the other woman.
Tommy tried to justify the killing of both women.
That he killed them because they could identify him.
As he continued to talk I started to feel sick and had
to think of other things to prevent myself from
throwing up. I turned my head away and told him that I
didn't want to hear anymore. "What reason did he have
for keeping me around, to continue to teach him to
read? No. I was a sounding board for his conscious.
The thought made me shiver. Now, instead of reading he
was telling me everything down to the last detail of
what he and the gang had done. He told me he had shot
the second woman because she could identify him. He
said it so matter of fact that it made me shiver. He
lit a cigarette and did his usual blowing of the smoke
rings into the air. "I dunno yella girl, I just feel
betta after you read and listen to me. I guess its
cause I ain't got shit to lose." He looked at me,
reaching for my face, he put his hand under my chin
and lifted it and said, "But chu do. Yu gat som-um to

lose Yella Girl, yu got plenty. Besides, I ain't gonna
go to no jail. Eva." Na les fo-git about dat stuff
and yu can jes read ta-nite. For Tommy, not only was I
his teacher but I had become the gate keeper for him
to tell all of his wrong doings. I couldn't sleep that
night. I kept thinking about Tommy repeated what Mark
had already told me about the pregnant girl being shot
dead, lying alone with a baby inside of her belly like
some animal that had been dumped on the sidewalk in
the rain after they had shot her.

And the other woman, whose only mistake was
saying what she, had seen and was going to do. Tommy
had killed her without even hesitating and had showed
no remorse for it afterwards.

He had sat there and literally told me that I
had something to loose and threatened me, wearing a
smile as he said so. He would go back on his word if
it became convenient for him. When he told me that I
had a lot to lose, it had all been lies. The promises
that he made to me were meant to be kept for only as
long as he wanted them to be. And he told me all of
the things that he did to clear his own conscious
because there wasn't anyone that I could go back and
tell, and neither could he.

The next day I walked across the street, sat on
the stoop and pulled out a package of cigarettes from
my pocket. As I lit one I inhaled it deeply. I could
feel the smoke against the back of my throat. I didn't
even cough; in fact I didn't even get dizzy. Under
different circumstances I would have been angry at
myself for smoking. I closed my eyes as I exhaled the
smoke and let it out first out of my nose; I opened my
eyes as I copied the way that Tommy exhaled and blew
little smoke rings up into the air.

I was preoccupied with so much of what he had
told me about the killings; now with everything
circling around inside of my head the cigarette had no
effect on me. Instead it soothed me; it calmed the
shaking that I was feeling inside. I even found myself
liking it. Last night was the real Tommy that I had
been reading to. He had killed and had liked it, and I
was really afraid, because now I knew that he could
look me in the eye and blow my head off without even
thinking twice about it. Then, I too would meet the
Dragon.

He knew that none of his boys would ever tell
anyone that he had broken the gang law and killed

those two women. The backlash for their part in the killings would have been worse than Tommy's, because they would have been considered a snitch and every gang hated a snitch. It was felt that if the snitch would squeal on someone else, he would do the same to his gang. Snitches had no loyalty to anyone. There were very few snitches that anyone had talked about. The few that had been snitches that I had heard about had happened a long time ago, they had not been just beaten; they had been fed to THE DRAGON.

When I looked down I saw that I had smoked ten of the cigarettes from the new pack that I had just bought. Would the snitch have been missed? Probably, would people know that he hadn't been seen? Yes, did everyone know what happened to snitches? Yes.

Would anyone tell? Tell what? End of story. I made sure to keep my mouth closed about Mark. He made sure that if there was going to be trouble, especially in the building he would tell me to stay inside. But all in all to the gangs, if they had found out that he was telling me anything he would have been considered a snitch even though most knew that we were dating. But girls were not allowed to know anything about gang business. I was no different. But as far as the killing or the gang was concerned, no one ever knew.

When Mark and I were seen together we always made sure that they saw him trying to pull me close to him to try to kiss me or see him putting his arm around me. Yesterday we had let them see us kissing while we sat on the monkey bars. They were all saying, "Way to go Marky Mark! Hit that ass!" Afterwards Mark didn't look suspicious when they saw him with me. When Tommy saw us he would give a short smirk and go on with what he was doing. I held on to that thought knowing that Mark was not going to be looking out of place with me. Roy came over to the monkey bars, "Man why u won't yella girl?" Mark's eye brows furrowed.

"Why not? Why don't you have someone?"

The look that Mark gave Roy sent him on his way. As I sat there thinking about everything I dropped the cigarette butt to the ground and as I put it out, I had smoked two more cigarettes. I felt like I had been there for only a few minutes. It had actually been over an hour. A nauseous feeling came over me; it made me so sick that I could only walk a few steps to get to the corner before everything that I had on my stomach came up and out of my mouth like a volcano.

It was what Bright's mother had said when she had listened to us and had said as we had talked about the first killings that Tommy had done. As I wiped off my mouth, her words came as a whisper in my ear. *"Neva make a deal wif the Devil he'll cheat ya eva time."*

The conversation that I had had with Bright had taken place well over three weeks ago. As I stood there by the stoop I thought to myself, "What had made her say that when she had looked in my direction that day?" How could she have known then, what I had just found out? I felt goose bumps as they moved the hair on my arms. I thought, "No, it's just my mind playing tricks on me, I've just been involved in too much stuff. Mark told me of about Tommy and what he had done, Then Tommy literally hitting me in the face with what he had said to me the other night, I was just tired that's all." I was tired but not that tired. She was an old woman, and people used to say that those types of old women could tell about things that would happen in the future. Soothsayers they were called. I never believed in that sort of thing, but I had never been out in the world where I could have experienced someone who was supposed to have the ability or know anyone that did. I didn't know at that moment what to believe. But I do know that she had called it before I found out what Tommy really was. She said the Devil. Could she have been talking about Tommy? And what was I supposed to do now? Now I was with him at night reading and being his sounding board. I sat there thinking about what Bright's mother had said and the situation that I was now in. I put my head down and slowly shook it in disgust.

My mind kept going back to her. Some people had to see things to believe it. I had been no different. Her words had been in my head ever since. Now I was like the others, she had been right and now I was in too deep. I didn't know what to do and there was no one who I could go to. I was just like Mark. I had been fooled. I was in the same situation that he was in. He had one saving grace, he would be leaving to go back home soon, and he had the option of never having to come back. I loved him and he had said that he loved me. But everyone knows that self-preservation was the first law of nature. And that's what it would come down to. In my heart I knew that he would not risk his life after what had happened that night to come back to a place where he had killed someone. Not to a place that would forever give him nightmares. I didn't want to believe that he wouldn't come back to see me the next summer. But I thought to myself, "Who do you think you're kidding?" If it were me it wouldn't have been a question. I already knew the answer. He wasn't coming back. And I didn't want to look into his face to ask him and make him lie.

Chapter Forty-Eight: Goodbye Mark

Mark left a week after we talked to go back to his home in LA. It had been so hard for us to say goodbye. We had held each other tight that night because we both knew that this would be our last time together. I cried into his shirt so hard that by the time I finally took my head away from his shirt it was completely wet. I remembered the trembling in his voice that night, when he told me that he didn't want to leave me. He told me that he couldn't imagine me holding someone else, that just the thought of it was tearing his heart to pieces. We knew that it was the best thing for both of us. It didn't make the hurting stop but I didn't want him to go through anything else. He was already going back with much more than he came with. What hurt so much was that I knew that I would never see him again.

I finally let go of holding on to him. He said how this was so wrong and that he would never forget me and that for the first time he had spent the summer up here, he had finally found a reason to look forward to coming back. With tears in his eyes, he put his finger under my chin so that I would look at his face. He looked at me and said, "Then I met you." He walked slowly towards the hallway door. He looked back at me once more. He said, "Bye babe. I'll be thinking about you always." I couldn't let the word goodbye come out of my mouth, it hurt too much. It hurt even more to watch him walk away. I closed the door behind me as I went inside. I walked into my room and sat on the bed as I thought about him and what he had said to me as we stood together. It was so wrong. I lay down and cried all night. The more I thought about not ever seeing him again the harder I cried. As I looked out of the window up at the moon, I felt the tears roll down my face and fall onto my arm. I took a deep breath as said softly, "I guess that's the way it is." Or at least the best way that it could be done. And it was all because of Tommy.

Later that night Tommy sent one of his gang members for me. When I got there he was sitting against the mattress with the book that we had been reading next to him. I walked in trying to sound normal, as though nothing was wrong but I didn't hide it well and he saw it in my face immediately.

"What's wrong wif you?"

"Nothing."

"Yu lying, what got yu lookin like dat?"

"I guess I just miss Mark."

"Yella Girl, he sho got yo nose open wide, you look like you been cryin all day. Don't worry he be back be-fo yu know it and yo kin be all happy agin." Then he crossed his hands and put them under his chin, batting his eyes mocking the girls did when they were in love and had been hurt. He started laughing at the top of his lungs at how I looked Then he said, " Or, you can do what I do wif Deidra, just find sum-body else to take his place till he gits back. That'll make da time go faster."

"I don't feel like reading tonight Okay? I'm feeling too bad, missing him too much you know?"

"Naw I ain't got no feeling like that fo no bitch. Yall get all teary and shit and I own wanna see yo eyes all swoll and yu breakin down an cri-in by me. Jus go on till yu get him out yo system. We kin git back together den. "Damn, yu got it bad girl, yu got it real bad."

I turned around and reached for the door knob. I walked out the door and turned my head sideways as I looked at him.

"Yeah I guess I do." Before I closed the door, I heard him call Emmett inside and then I heard the two of them laughing. I didn't care, Tommy didn't care who he hurt in fact, he was still seeing Renee *and* Deidra at the same time. Although he preferred Renee, when he couldn't see her he used Deidra instead. I thought to myself, "What a piece of shit! He's playing Deidra and doesn't care how she feels. How low could he go?" I didn't care that he and Emmett were in the laundry room laughing at me because I missed Mark.

What I knew, that Tommy didn't know was that Mark wouldn't be coming back. Tommy didn't feel anything; he didn't have any regrets at all after having killed anyone that night but Mark had. And because of the regret that he felt, He wasn't coming back. I wouldn't see him anymore and by Tommy telling me how to keep my mind off of him only made it worse. He figured that by tomorrow I would be okay. But I wasn't. The more I thought about it, it seemed to me that Tommy was wrong in more things than he was right.

Chapter Forty Nine: Used and Alone

The next evening I just wanted to be alone. Mark had left that morning, I saw from my window when the car pulled up and he got in. He had looked up at me and waved, and then he was gone. Everything that I had tried to put in the back of my mind wasn't staying there anymore. It was getting harder and harder not to think about it. After the car pulled off I wanted to smoke badly that my hands were trembling and my nerves were a mess. Leaving the house would be the only way that I could do it. I went down stairs across the street by the high school and sat on the stoop looking up at the building and thinking of all of the things that had happened not realizing that I had already lit a cigarette. I was smoking more and more. I found myself lighting up one cigarette with the flame from the last one. With each one I would Inhale deeply, letting the smoke leave my nose and mouth as slowly as I could.

I wasn't even eighteen and I had lost one boyfriend and Rafael, a friend back to back. I had initially liked Rafael. I think that Rafael liked me as a friend as he did all of the other girls. Mark and told me that he loved me and I had said the same to him. Mark had always been there for me he was a boyfriend and a friend, he told me things to keep me out of harm's way at the risk of getting himself caught doing it.

In the summers before I had seen Mark come and go. Sometimes he was with Tommy sometimes he spent time with his relatives but I didn't think that he had it in him to start talking to me. We started out slowly just as friends but it led to something more and before I knew it I fell in love with him. He later told me that he had felt the same way about me. He would tell me so when we kissed. He would hold me and we would talk about the things that we would do when he came back the next summer. Plans that now would never come true. All of our plans were gone and it was all because of Tommy. Sitting alone, the only thing I could do was cry. I cried for everything, for all of the old crap that I had been holding inside for so long the physical and mental. Now for the new crap that had been added, I felt bad for the senseless deaths of those that I didn't know and for the ones that I did. Before any of this happened, I thought that it had been better to hold it inside than to let it come out. Now, I was sitting here thinking that I wanted to run in front of a bus or even jump out of our window because I couldn't think of a way out of the mess that I was in.

My thoughts kept going back to my family and what could happen to them, especially to my brothers. My mother used to let us go to church from time to time. The pastor would ramble on about fire and brimstone, to repent before it was too late. Sometimes I would look around to see if anyone was sleeping because he seemed to preach forever. I used to snicker because half of the members would nod off and wake back up saying, "Praise the LORD. " One Sunday at our church I had dozed off and had only heard the last part of the sermon, something about having thrown the lamb to the lions. If I killed myself that's exactly what I would have done to my family, thrown them to the lions. My brothers would have a choice but to join Tommy's gang.

I didn't have a clue what would happen to my two sister's maybe they would have been watched and then caught up in the girl gangs. So I couldn't even think of dying. My responsibilities were to my family and here I was feeling trapped like a rat with my back against the wall again. The only thing that I could do was come up with a good reason to stay away from Tommy for a while, to clear my head. I was going to have to come up with it fast because he was expecting me to come to the laundry room to read at night after I had gotten over Mark. The very thought of him, just the thought of being near him, knowing what he had done, made me want to kill him. For me though, it wasn't even an option.

The week before school started I told Tommy that I wouldn't be able to come to the laundry room at night for a while. I had to get things ready for myself and for my brothers and sisters for school. I told him that I had gotten busted coming in past my curfew from having been outside with him that last time. He asked me how long my (OG) old girl mother had grounded me. I lied and told him that I didn't know but it would be a while before she cooled off. Now she thought that I had been sneaking out to meet someone to get laid. At first he just looked at me. Then he started laughing.

He told Emmett why I was grounded. Emmett laughed too; both understood and believed that I

199

wasn't lying. Almost every girl in the projects had at one time or another been grounded by their mothers for the same reason that I had. Tommy laughed as he told me that he had been surprised that I had gotten away with sneaking out to meet him as long as I had. He said," jus let me know when yu git otta jail so we can get started readin again."

"Okay, I will." I came out of the laundry room and as usual he had one of his gang, Andrew this time, to follow me as he usually did to make sure that I made it home. I walked in the house as usual and went straight to the bathroom. It was the only place in the house where I would be able to have any real privacy. Once inside, I closed the door and put my elbow up with my hand clinched and silently shouted! "Yeeeessssss!" I had done it! I had gotten a reprieve! I didn't have to be near him. Although I didn't know how long it would last, but even if it was only a short time that would give me a chance to not have to look at him or listen to him. Thank you Lord! Just for that saving grace.

It was late after I took a bath; I started to fall into a much needed sleep. As I drifted off, the thought came into my mind that there was always tomorrow. For now, tomorrow was another day that seemed to be a few hours away.

The next day, I went back across the street to sit on the stoop by the school. It had become my thinking place. I didn't worry about what was happening with anything, there or anywhere else. As I sat there by myself, I took a cigarette out of my pocket and lit it. I was not really paying attention to how easily it had become to just pull one out whenever I was frustrated, which seemed to be happening all of the time.

As I smoked the cigarette I thought about everything that had happened to me that summer. As I looked down at the cigarette it dawned on me that my cigarette smoking was starting to become a habit. My free time was going by much too fast and with all that had gone on I hadn't had one day to enjoy it without something happening. I didn't have enough time to digest everything that had happened to me. Having been beaten up by the girl gang, Rafeal's death, Deidra's beating and rape, the argument between Deidra and me. Then there was Tommy's payback for having done what he did and Mark having to take the punishment that

Shannon and her gang had given him even though he had not raped Deidra.

He had been cut just for being there, which made him a part of it. Then there was K.C's death, having to deal with my sister and the nightmares that she had that after what had happened to her at the Funeral home. Later there were the killings of the woman and especially, the pregnant girl. There was Mark leaving with no intentions of ever coming back, And last but not least, my having to go back to school. Without a doubt I knew that sooner or later I would have to face the girl gang all over again. As I sat there I kept thinking how wrong I had been in thinking that the past had been bad but nothing compared to what I had gone through in the last few months. But living here, in the projects, was all that I knew.

Although I did have cousins who lived in the projects not far from mine, they cared for my family very much but were barely able to make ends meet themselves. And I didn't want them to get involved. There were too many things, bad things to risk getting them involved in some crap involving a gang, although I think that If I had asked them they would have helped but I didn't. I would have gone to live with them but there would have been no room for me and someone was bound to see me staying in another building to avoid Tommy and his gang. There was nowhere for me to run and nowhere for me to hide. I didn't know how much more my mind could hold. My brain was like a sponge and it had absorbed as much as it could. The problems started to leak out like water coming from it. I had no idea of what the sponge could hold.

I wondered if the way that I was feeling was how people that were considered crazy had gotten that way, where things seemed to happen, never letting up until it made them just let go so they wouldn't have to deal with it anymore. Noone ever paid any attention to people that acted crazy like the winos. Or the people who walked down the street talking to themselves. They were treated as if they didn't exist when they started stumbling and falling on the sidewalk. From where I stood at that moment it didn't seem to me that winos weren't in such a bad place after all.

The fact was I was afraid to go back to school, although I wanted to I just didn't think I would be able to live through another beat down. My mind kept going back and forth stay away and be safe, go back and probably get killed. I wanted to do both although I knew that that would be impossible. Very soon I was going to have to choose.

I had seen Death, or maybe I thought that I had seen him, I had seen The Dragon, well the name that I had given to the incinerator and I had met The Devil who was beginning to seem to be Tommy more and more. The question that I hadn't thought about until then, as I sat by myself was when was I going to meet GOD? "Maybe you didn't get a chance to see him till you died, after it's all over. Or maybe he just didn't bother to listen to the prayers of poor people, especially those of us who lived in the projects.

Chapter Fifty: The Misinformation of Candy

It was only three more weeks until school started, which meant that Candy knew that she wasn't going to have that much longer to make the extra money that she had been making when she was having them every weekend. As we sat across the street on the school steps she had told Brenda and I that she was going to have only two more. People were going to be busy getting things for school and everybody's money would go towards helping out their families for school clothes and supplies. For a while now, Brenda and I had noticed that Candy had been acting differently. She seemed to always be tired and she ate much more candy than before. Her change wasn't in a bad way there was a change but neither of us could put a finger on it. She had stopped being her playful and sarcastic self. This was very different than the way she had always been.

Even when it wasn't hot outside, she would start sweating and was sometimes too weak to walk up to 47th street with us anymore to get apples or to see what was playing at the movies. So we sat mostly by the school and talked about what she would have at the last of her parties. Sometimes she would start shaking badly; we would take her upstairs so that she could lie down until she felt better. Two days later I found out that something bad had happened to Candy. She had been rushed to the hospital and had been kept. She returned four days later and seemed to be in a good mood. She told us that she was feeling better. While she was in the hospital she told us that her mother had told the doctors all of the things that she had noticed about Candy in the previous weeks. She told them about Candy's night sweats, about her shakiness and her blurred vision. She even told him that Candy had been sleeping much more than usual. That's when Candy showed us the medicine bottles, all were labeled Insulin. She even showed us the large bag of syringes that they had given her. Candy laughed as she mocked the doctors. Now we don't want others to have access to these so don't pass them out to your friends.

She showed us the professionally typed note that gave her permission to legally carry an insulin bottle and one syringe. Both were placed in a case and the doctor told her to keep the note inside the case just to be able to prove that she was a diabetic if she were ever stopped by the police. Brenda didn't think that his remark was funny at all. Did all people that lived outside of the projects think that everybody that did live there was shooting drugs? Brenda asked Candy if the doctor had checked her arms for track marks as he made that statement. I looked over at her and said, "Now don't get mad because Candy has more syringes then you." Brenda had an angry look on her face. She looked over at me but her anger went away and we both started laughing. We asked Candy if she had told the doctor that she smoked cigarettes, drank wine, and ate candy like it was going out of style. Candy looked at us and started laughing and said, "Of course I did and afterwards he asked me if he could have a cigarette and one of my twizzlers." We all laughed until we had tears running from our eyes because we knew that she hadn't mentioned a thing. She told us that while she was in the hospital they taught her how to give herself insulin by giving her an orange to practice with. They never told her to change her diet or what would happen to her if she didn't take her insulin. She said, "The doctors didn't ask me if I drank alcohol so I didn't tell them that I did." She said it didn't seem to be a big deal anyway. All they were concerned with was that she took the insulin. Two days later, as Brenda I was at her house, Candy begged her mom to let her go and sit across the street by the school. She promised not to move from that spot. She told mother that she couldn't stand being in the house in bed another day. Her mom finally agreed and after eating half a sandwich and gulping down a glass of Kool-Aid we were off. Kool-Aid was almost as important as water. It was Kool-Aid with lunch, Kool-Aid with dinner and Kool-Aid with snacks, and Kool-Aid by itself. We talked about her upcoming party and the kind of records that would be played. What she didn't know was that we were planning a surprise party for her the next weekend because it was her birthday, not just a quarter party. A few hours after we had been sitting on the ground leaning against the wall Candy started shaking and sweating. She kept saying, "I'm all right I'll be okay. Just let me sit here a little longer."

We continued to sit there for a few more minutes but she didn't seem to look any better. We started walking across the street she seemed to become more

unbalanced and her shaking increased. Once we got her
into of her house she told us that she just needed to
lie down for a while to take a nap. Before we left
Brenda told her that she would give her a call to see
if she felt any better and if so, would all get back
together the next day after school.

We took the elevator down one flight, where I
lived. I went to my house and Brenda rode the elevator
down to hers.

The following day after I had finished my homework
and made sure that my chores were done I went down to
Brenda's house and knocked on her door. Her brother
told me that she and her mother were up at Candy's
house. I didn't think anything of it so I left a
message with him, telling him to let her know that I
had stopped by and that when she and Candy were ready
I would be on my porch waiting for them. I stayed on
my porch just hanging out until my mother called me
in. I thought it was odd that neither one had come to
get me so I took my bath, ate dinner and watched
television knowing that Brenda would call sooner or
later to let me know why they hadn't come by.

The next day after school and not having seen or
heard from Brenda I decided to go to Candy's house
first figuring we would then go down together and get
Brenda to finish talking about the party. When I
knocked on Candy's door Brenda's mother answered. I
looked at her and could see that she had been crying.
It bothered me a little to see her just standing in
the door dabbing her eyes with a tissue. I asked her
if I could speak to Candy she started crying louder,
the door open wider and Brenda stepped out closing it
behind her. Her eyes were just as swollen if not more
from crying than her mother's. So I asked her, "What's
going on? Why are you and your mother crying? "She
quickly wiped her eyes and just stood and looked at
me. I barely heard her as she whispered, "Candy's
gone." She told me that Candy had died the other night
in her sleep after she had left her. And that's why
she never made it to my house. I looked at her as I
felt the tears well up in my eyes. We both started to
cry. I asked her, "Died how? From what?" Brenda was
looking down at the ground shaking her head she said
that Candy went to sleep and just never woke up. Her
mother had said that all she knew was that Candy's
mother had told her that earlier she had tried to get
Candy to eat dinner but Candy kept telling her that

205

she was too tired and that she was going to sleep awhile and get up later and eat. Her mother let her sleep and didn't think anything else about it. So she and the kids ate then went to bed.

Candy's mother had told Brenda's mother that when she went to wake her up that morning she couldn't get her to move. That's when she took a good look at her and saw that her lips were blue and when she had touched her, her skin was as cold as ice. She had probably died sometime that night. Now we were crying hard, hugging each other and rocking back-and-forth. We just sat and held each other until Brenda's mother opened the door and asked her to come back inside. I hugged her one last time before walking toward the stairwell. Brenda was still standing in the door when I looked back. She was taking it so hard and I could definitely understand why. She was Candy's best friend and she, her mother, and Candy's mother were going to have to make the plans for her funeral. It was really going to rest on Brenda and her mother because Candy's mother had started to drink until she passed out. She wasn't going to be in any shape to do anything. Candy was gone a few days before her birthday. She would give no more parties, no long walks for apples no sitting around talking girl talk. In the blink of an eye she was gone. I had only four friends to start out with. Featherhead was dead, Mark was gone, and Now Candy was gone. Now I only had one. As I sat my bedroom looking out of the window I thought to myself, "Crap doesn't Death have something else to do or somewhere else to be? Couldn't he have given her more time?" Out of all the people he could've touched, he had to go and touch two out of the only four friends that I had. Out of all the buildings that were around, he seemed to stay in mine.

Everyone knew that Candy's family didn't have any money so I decided to do what I thought would be the best way that I could. Brenda and her mother had their work already cut out for them. I thought that by taking up a collection for her funeral would help. Everyone knew her, so I decided to go to as many people as I could to get a donation.

I started in our building first; I went to every apartment on every floor. The word had already gotten out about Candy so I didn't have to explain why I was taking up a collection. Mostly everyone that I collected from knew her and cried as they put money in the jar. No one wanted to believe that she was gone. Tommy and his gang gave a large contribution and Tommy told me if there was anything he or his gang could do to help would be to just let them know. Word had spread faster than I could have ever expected about Candy's death. People dropped money into the jar freely and asked if there was anything that they could do. I didn't know so I gave them Brenda's telephone number and told them to call her; she would be able to tell them better than I would. After the jar was filled I went home emptied the money in a bag and put it under my bed. Then started off to the other three buildings to do the same. The jar that I was carrying was a large pickle jar and so many people were donating that before I could make it to the middle of the second building I had to stop because the jar had become so heavy. Again, I would go home and repeat the process over and over until I had finished them all. I had never seen that much money in my life! After receiving a collection from one house, I thought about how good it was that people cared enough to give in order to help her family out. When I came to the next apartment, I knocked on the door and one of the boys who came to her parties regularly answered but I couldn't say anything. I just broke down then and there right where I was. I sat the pickle jar to the side and sat next to it and cried. I brought my knees up; I put my head down and wrapped my arms around them. I couldn't hide the pain of why I was doing this anymore. Every door that I knocked on made me remember Candy's face and how she laughed. Now here I was taking up collections because she was gone.

   In the background I heard the door open again. The boy that had come to Candy's parties came out and walked over to where I was sitting. I looked at him as he helped me up from the porch and without saying a word, held me. He was tall and muscular just like Tommy. With his arm around my back and the other around my shoulder I started crying harder. He held me and kept saying, "It's gonna be alright she's in a better place now she's gonna be alright." For a moment it didn't matter that I was Yella Girl, I was someone who was trying to help out someone else who everyone had cared for. He said, "Hold on a minute he closed the door but came back quickly handing me some toilet tissue, gave me one last hug and took the jar that I had been holding. He looked at me and smiled. He said,

207

"Cain't be going all over the place with my house shoes on. Now we're ready."

He took the jar from me and as I went from door to door he carried the pickle jar for me. After the jar was filled he walked from his building to mine and came up to my floor and after handing me the jar he said, "It's gone be alright, God's got her now." Then he turned and walked away. He didn't even know me or ask my name and I didn't know his but he took the time to help me. Which I thought was a good thing. It showed just how many people cared about Candy. She would've been happy to know how many people cared about her. Tommy had seen me with the boy from the other building as he helped me with the jar. After the boy left he walked up to me and said, "Didn't I say if yu needed sum help to let me no?" T-Bone and Andrew were with him. He motioned to T-Bone, who came forward promptly and told him to carry the pickle jar to the rest of the buildings.

When I got home I had to get another bag because the third one that I had, had become so full that the money was coming out of it onto the floor under my bed. So I went into our pantry and found our laundry sack and poured the money into it. I knew that when it came time for me to give the bags to Brenda I was going to have to split them up and get One of Tommy's boys to help me with them to make the carrying them easier. T-Bone and I covered the last two buildings, making frequent stops back to my house to empty the jar. By the time we had finished it was late and I could barely walk. That's just how hard it was. But I knew that I had done something and I knew it would help. I could almost imagine her laughing and crying at the same time knowing that so many people thought so much of her and cared, and were more than willing to help. It was right then as I carried that jar that I knew what I wanted to be. I wanted to be someone who could help people who were sick. I wanted tobe able to help and to make sure that they knew the type of illness that they had on their level not just some fancy hospital talk that they wouldn't understand.

How important it was to do and not do what they had been told by their doctor. I would have them to repeat back to me what had been taught to them so they understood what the consequences would be if they did or did not follow those directions. In Candy's case they had diagnosed her with diabetes, but they didn't say how serious it was. They just told her to take her insulin, how and where to give it, and what symptoms would let her know that she was in trouble and needed to come back to the hospital.

I often thought about candy and the symptoms that had continued to make her much sicker. They had told her to take her insulin; they didn't tell her she needed to eat when she took it. I knew she would have eaten less junk if she knew that it would have killed her. And because they didn't I had lost a friend and was now going around the buildings taking collections for her funeral. She just went to sleep and never woke up.

# # #

Seven years after high school graduation. We had long since moved, I enrolled in nursing school, after graduating I started working with diabetics doing patient teaching. I always thought of Candy and how she might still have been alive if she had known more, been taught more, If the doctors had placed more emphasis in what was to forever be her disease and hers alone and how very hard it would be to adjust to it all. But no one knew, if anything about her disease, what it was doing to her body, or if Candy just chose to ignore that information. It was the lack of information and the misinformation that killed her. After all, she was just another one of those people from the projects. Anyone from the projects that went to the doctor knew how they would be treated so most of the older ones chose not to go at all.

# # #

After I had collected all of the money from the three buildings I waited until Brenda came home and gave it to her. As I handed to her I was thinking, "Hopefully it would help her mother with the money that would be needed for Candy's funeral. Brenda and her mother hugged me and her mother even cried because she said that she didn't know where she was going to be able to come up with the money that would have been needed for even a basic funeral. Brenda put her arms around my neck after her mother had walked away and just held on to me. We held on to each other. We both missed Candy more than words could say. She looked at me and said, "You know you came through right on time I don't know what to say."

I looked at her and said, "I guess I did a good thing because this is the first time that I've ever known you to be speechless." She tried to smile, but it was a tired one. "Everybody in the projects will know what you did for Candy when this is all over."

"I think they already do."

Candy's mother was in no condition to do anything afterwards Let alone take the responsibility in planning any of her daughter's services, the funeral or even the care of the rest of her kids. Brenda's mother had gotten in touch with Candy's aunt because when Candy's mother wasn't crying and screaming, she was drinking and cursing at the kids and it scared them. They didn't know what had happened to their sister or if they had caused it. She was taking it out on them. Their relatives came and got them and I didn't see them again until the funeral. Candy's mother continued to cry and drink to the point of getting falling down drunk to numb her pain. Sometimes when she was drunk she would lie on the floor and call for Candy, telling her to come back home and stop playing games with her because she and the kids needed her. Brenda told me that her mother would get so mad at her that she would help her to bed then give her orders not to get out of it unless she had to go to the bathroom. She did as she was told. Brenda's mother was going to have to step up to the plate and plan the services and the funeral. With the money I had collected her mother was able to buy a nice casket, flowers, money for the viewing services and the funeral. The services for Candy's viewing were held at a larger funeral home than K.C.'s. There was more space for people to move about and twice as many pews for them to sit in. In the back, on a podium, was a large cross with Jesus crucified on it. It was the first thing that caught my eye when I walked into the room. The Bible lay on a beautifully shined pedestal and behind it was an area that was large enough for a choir. Further back from that section was a large stage where sitting to the left side was a baby grand piano. The way all of the flowers had been placed made the room look beautiful. There were flowers everywhere. Even though the room was larger it was still not large enough to hold all the people who wanted to attend. Some of the people stood by the entrance of the parlor where the service was held. Further back from the door on a beautiful wooden stand was the guest book to sign.

There were so many signatures that the people

who greeted guests at the door had to get a second book for others to sign. The pastor said the eulogy and a man played the Piano and the lady with a beautiful voice were a duet, performing two songs from the hymnal. Tommy and his gang were there. They went into the funeral home two by two. They went ahead of other people because everyone knew that after what had happened at K.C.'s service Tommy's gang was not only there to pay their respects but also, to protect each other.

People that had been standing at the back near the entrance of the room were allowed to come in first. Everything was done in an orderly fashion. As Candy lay in the casket she looked just like herself, as if she was just sleeping. Row after row of people walked up to the casket to say their goodbyes, kissing her forehead as they walked away.

Lots of people broke down sobbing and had to be escorted outside. The services went on for almost three hours because that's how long it took until the last person had had their chance to say goodbye. Brenda and I went last. Brenda looked at Candy, kissed her and told her, "Don't worry girlfriend you're in a much better place than this living hell that we still have to live in. GOD is going to take good care of you. And I'm telling you now there ain't gonna be no drinking up there so don't even ask." With that she looked over at me and gave a little smile. Then it was my turn. I looked down at her, as I stroked her forehead I whispered so that no one on my side could hear me, "I didn't get as much time as I wanted to get to know you better but in the short time that I did, you were a really cool person to be around. Everybody's going to miss your parties but the main thing that they'll miss is the same thing that I'll miss, *YOU*. Don't worry we'll see each again." I sat down next to Brenda, her mother, and Brenda's brother. The funeral was so sad. As I stood looking at Candy's casket in its final resting place, I thought to myself that it would be a very long time before I would attend another one. There were so many people there that you could see heads all the way back to where the cars were parked.

Candy's mother and her siblings, with the exception of the baby, were holding hands. Brenda's mother, brother and I stood next to the pastor, as he read from the bible I looked up briefly. As far as I

211

could see every head was bowed with respect for Candy. From a distance I could hear girls screaming and crying for the loss of their friend. I had not known that she had so many friends but it was a good thing to see that so many people cared. All of a sudden Candy's mother just lost it and tried to leap onto the casket as it was being lowered into the ground. It took several men to hold on to her as she kicked and fought them with all of her might to go with her daughter. She had been drinking and now completely out of control. A I looked over at Brenda, she had turned her head away. It was already sad but her mother made it worse by acting out because she had been so drunk. It was almost too hard for anyone to bear.

When the blessing by the pastor was finished and the people started to walk away, there was not a sound to be heard. The sad look on everyone's face said it all. Candy had really been loved. She would be missed and most of all, she would never be forgotten. Brenda and I tossed two red roses on the casket. As we both walked away, neither of us looked back.

Chapter Fifty-One: School

I made up my mind to go back to school, knowing what was eventually going to happen. After I went back I was glad that I had. I loved my biology class most. We dissected frogs, made volcanoes and best of all; our class went on field trips. When we did our school teacher told us that we would be going to areas that were dedicated to the protection of the animals and that we would have to collect specimens to look at under the microscopes once we got back to class. On the field trips the buses took us to places that we never knew existed. We went past homes that were so beautiful that they didn't look real, where grass had beautiful flowers and all types of birds were just flying around. As we talked in the evenings I told Brenda that as our class rode the bus and passed different places I remembered thinking, "So this is what the rest of the world looks like?" I wanted to become a part of it.

There were things that I saw that I knew that the two of us had never seen up close. The bus rides were very long but it was worth it to have the time to see how beautiful everything was. I didn't know this world and I felt very sure that they didn't know about ours. Those few bus rides took me to another place, a more peaceful place. The longer the ride took to get there, the easier it was for me to forget about where I had to go back to. As I looked out of the windows as the bus went past the well-kept houses I was willing to bet that when those people had disagreements they didn't take it into the streets like they did in our world. Brenda shook her head agreeing with me.

She said, "I know. Sounds like it was a pretty nice place, I wish I could have been there to see it." I told her about having seen raccoons, deer, chipmunks and other animals that wouldn't ever be seen by anyone living in the projects. We brought our own lunches and when it was lunch time we sat in the grass to eat. Listening to all of the different sounds that the birds and other animals made, Learning the names of different plants and flowers were all so different for us. When you took a deep breath even the air smelled fresher out there.

When it was time to leave I hated it, sometimes I felt like I wanted to cry. I asked Brenda. "Why couldn't we live out there?" Why did I have to come back here to where we live?" It was dirty, people always cursed, or fought. Someone was always getting killed, we were living in buildings that looked like prisons with cages that made us look like animals.

At home there were no birds or animals like those that we had seen while we were out in the prairies that we were visiting. There were garbage cans that read, Please be responsible, put litter in its place. And that's what had been done with it. There was no garbage or empty bottles anywhere. As the bus left to take us back to school I looked out of the window at the places I thought that I might never get a chance to see again. Others on the bus may or may not have missed being there but I knew I did.

We had one history class but we studied American history and Black history. Both were requirements in order to graduate from high school. The classes were to be taught to study both cultures. I learned that the way the whites had treated the blacks or Negros as we were referred to at that time wasn't the only race of people who were mistreated and sold as slaves as well. Chinese and other immigrants were as well. The whites would take what they wanted by force. The Indians had been treated just as bad if not worse. They had had their land taken away from them, they endured harsh winters and their bodies lacked the immunity that the colonist had grown a resistance to from being in the outside world. It severely weakened them and nearly wiped out their tribes by the thousands. They were forced to become Christians and read from the bible which forced them to forsake their native beliefs In fact both races had to endure the wrath that was inflicted on them. They were beaten, starved, the women were raped. The colonist did marry some of the women from the different tribes. We never heard about them marrying any African Americans or any of the Chinese women when they made them slaves but they used the African slaves for their sexual gratifications and their wives knew that they were doing it. Some slaves became pregnant by their owners and their children could pass for white. The slaves who the owner had sexual favors with were usually given jobs inside of the house although the work was hard it could in no way be compared to that of the other slaves who worked in the cotton and sugar cane fields. We learned that some were sat free by their owners, others escaped like Harriet Tubman, but many

214

did not and they were hug from trees as a reminder of what would happen to them if they tried.

We learned about Christopher Columbus the names of his ships; The Nina, Pinta and Santa Maria which would probably be ingrained in our brains forever and that he was the man who discovered America. We also studied about Thomas Edison, The Civil War, The Constitution and other well-known documented writings that were in every history book. We were told about Amelia Earhart, who was admired and known for becoming the first white female to fly across the Atlantic in 1928. But when it came to Blacks in history we were taught very little. Of course they had to tell us about Jean Baptist Point DuSable because he was who the school. They spoke of Fredrick Douglas, and George Washington Carver.

When it came to the African-Americans and their contributions and to an extinct how they even gave their lived for our country. The things that they did could be mentioned in one paragraph. American history took up most of our time. The African American History class took twenty minutes. We had a Black teacher who told us things about African Americans that were not mentioned in the American history class. Sometimes when he was teaching, we would see him glance towards the back door. When we turned back to see what he was looking at, we saw a white teacher walk by the classroom, and briefly peer inside before walking on. When they left he would talk to us quickly and quietly and go into detail of what our African American people had accomplished for our country but were rarely mentioned. He told us about Sojourner Truth and how she and her daughter escaped to freedom in 1826. He went into depth about a young man named Emmett Till and what happened to him and supposedly why. He did go into depth about Robert Taylor what he did and why the projects were named after him. Even with that short period of time, each time we had class he made sure that he covered a lot more than we would have ever known. He talked about segregation between blacks and whites especially in the south. Where the signs hung everywhere to let the colored people know where they were and were not allowed. Bathrooms, stores, schools, even the water fountains had signs "For whites only."

Gym and Health were actually two classes in one which lasted for an hour. In the summer the girls and boys had gym class outside at the same time. Gym class was good most of the time. Sometimes In the summer if the girls and boys coaches decided, they would make an exception and allow the girls to play against the boys. Sometimes they would monitor us to make sure that the games were played fair, other times they became so engrossed in their own conversations that the hardly noticed that we were even there. The boys would play fair because they were cocky, felt they had the advantage and that they were better than the girls. The two teachers leaned against the wall by the school and talked and laughed with each other usually getting closer and closer at times as they spoke. They wouldn't notice when we stopped playing ball to watch them. As they spoke, the girl's gym teacher would twirl her head and touch the coach on his arm.

We would laugh and make jokes about what the teachers were going to do when the school day was over. When they finally stopped and saw that we were all watching them they would stop, come over and monitor the game. By the time they did come the bell would ring and the softball game would either be a draw or sometimes because the boys would steal bases and cheat, they would say that they had won.

We would argue but it would never amount to anything because the two teachers had not been paying any attention so they couldn't say if the game had been played fairly or not. At other times we would come out and play softball by ourselves and the boys would go to the other side and play touch football. They couldn't tackle each other because all of the ground from the DuSable Upper Grade Center to the high school was all gravel. And the school didn't want to take any responsibility if someone got hurt from falling on it. Then when it became too cold outside both the boys and the girls had sex education classes. What a piece of crap. The teacher would turn on the movie projector and show a picture of what was called, "A uterus and fallopian tubes. It was made like a vase and the tubes were made to look like wilted flowers. They would show the sperm which was made to look like a tadpole with a smile on it swimming towards into the flower. The teacher would stop the projector and finish up by telling us that's how babies were made. And that was it nothing about abstinence or birth control, just not to have sex because everyone else was doing it. Then she would move on and talk about our periods. She very seldom used the word menstruation and how it would come every month and the cramps, and how to ease the pain.

She would show us a box of sanitary pads and the belt that would hold it in place and tell us to read the instructions from the movie projector. A lot of the girls in the class were having conversations about other things amongst themselves because a lot of them were not only having sex, but were either already pregnant or had had babies already. The class was a crock but everyone came because we needed that class to pass to get the credits needed to pass to the next grade. When the bell rang, we would all come out of class at the same time. The boys would walk up to one of the girls and say, "open your flower so my little tadpole came swim up there, other boys would come out laughing pointing to their crotch and say, "Hey! Want to see a big tadpole?" everyone in the hallway would breakup in laugher. Then they would chase us down the hall screaming, "My little tadpole is going to turn into a big one and it's gonna get your flower tonight!" Then they would give each other the high five. While everyone was laughing and walking to our next class we could hear the teachers screaming from their class rooms to stop using that language, and to stop laughing! The more they said it, the funnier it became. There were other times in gym class that we had swimming class. Again our time to use the pool was either before or after the boys had used it. The teacher would show us how to use our arms and how to paddle our legs. They gave us demonstrations on how to float or to do a backstroke. They would tell us that until they had checked us off of the list we would be limited to the shallow end of the pool. We would then gradually get a chance to swim in the deep water. Afterwards when it was time to take a shower and put our clothes. We would laugh and tease each other about who had the largest or smallest breast but no one that I knew of ever took it to heart and no one was ever hurt by the teasing that we did too each other.

As usual after getting dressed we would leave to go to our next class. While in school I was able to do my schoolwork, have fun in gym class and for the most part forget about what went on after school let out for the day. On what I considered a perfect day consisted of being able to go to school and get home without having any problems from the outside. From inside the safety of my bedroom I could concentrate on the homework from whatever class I had received it.

But the end of one day always lead to the beginning of another and every time I walked out from the safety of my house I expected to see the girl gang waiting for me and found myself always looking over my shoulder. One day school let out and I saw some of the girls from the gang. It reminded me that they hadn't forgotten about me. Sometimes when they saw me they would say things to each other and then start laughing among themselves. It was only a matter of time before the real action would start. Sometimes they hung around the school, sometimes they didn't. I guess it depended on what, if anything they had going on that day.

When the bell rang to signal the end of the school day I would be walking on eggshells wondering if they were going to jump out from behind the side of the school building or just be standing at the doors waiting. When I came out and they weren't there I felt better when I got home. The headaches were so bad that they made me take aspirin because my head felt as though it would fly apart into a thousand little pieces if I didn't.

The gang left me alone. But something in my gut told me that it wasn't over yet. I continued to help Tommy from time to time but not nearly as much as I had before. When I did meet with him, he showed me some books that he had started to try to read on his own. I always kept the thought in the back of my mind, If or when, he would want more of the time than I was able to give him. Even when he would show me the books, it was mainly to show me that he had them because he was still seeing Renee I knew that he hadn't put as much interest into them as He thought I would believe. He hadn't sent for me for over a month. I was still on reprieve from the girl gang. How long it would last I didn't know. The only thing that I could do was take it a day at a time. One day after school, Brenda met me and had a big grin on her face. She told me that she had found out that the girls in the gang had had a party of their own in an empty apartment they knew of and had invited their boyfriends over. She laughed as she said, "It had to be one hell of a party because later they found out that they had all gotten pregnant! I bet they won't be so tough now with a baby on their hips!" I started laughing with her. Imagine that! I was going to be able to breathe! They had their pregnancies to deal with and then and having newborn babies to tend to afterwards. I figured that that would keep them busy for a while. I'm sure that they were mad and pissed. For them it meant no more parties, and no more running the streets for a while. It had been said they most of the boys who had gotten them pregnant had broken up with them leaving them, Leaving them to raise their babies without a father and having to get help from their mothers and public aid. They had not become an exception to the rule, they just been added to it. More statistics for the census takers to add and for the board members of the Robert Taylor Homes to pay for under the heading of Female, black, unwed, on public aid with a child and no education to speak of. Another generation to add to the rest of the generations that were already living there. Another addition added to an apartment. Every now and then I would see some of them come out of their building because most of The Robert Taylor buildings faced each other.

I was walking through the breezeway of the buildings that faced mine and ran into one of the girl gang members. As soon as she saw me she turned her head in the other direction to ignore me. But the look that she gave me said just wait!

She was holding her baby tightly as her mother carried the diaper bag. I thought to myself that she was probably on her way to the clinic for her baby. Her mother had a look of anger and disappointment on her face. I was still friends with her sister, who was not in the gang who told me that her mother was very upset with her sister because she had had high hopes for her sister to graduate and get a job so that both of them would be able to get out of the system. But because her sister was ignorant and careless trying to act like she was grown by ignoring her mother, she had just become another girl who had gotten pregnant. Her care free life as well as the others in Bay-Bay's gang who had babies had been caught up in the updraft of an airplane going into the sky, stopped, did a nosedive that them back to earth and poverty-causing a crash and burn for their futures. Most of the girls in the gang could have come back to school after having had their babies. They had dropped out long before that and hadn't wanted to come back because after having

219

left school so early, there were so far behind there was no way that they would be able could catch up. From the very beginning they had said that they thought school was boring. That's why they had dropped out in the first place. Now with babies, they would be stuck in the same hell hole as every other girl that had not continued or tried to go back to school and nothing to look forward to. There were a lot of girls who got pregnant and after having their babies had returned back to school and even graduated.

It hadn't happened to me, Brenda or even Candy and certainly not for a lot of the girls who lived in our building as well as many girls who lived in different buildings but it did happen to many. In school I had heard lots of girls were very interested in going to college. They had the grades to go there if given the right direction. A lot of them talked about going to colleges that were in other states where they felt that they would have a better chance at getting accepted. Most spoke of moving there and living with a relative so that the college or university wouldn't know that they had lived in the projects. Just that name put a foul taste in anyone's mouth, the chances of them getting accepted would be narrowed greatly if it were known where they had lived and the High school that they had attended. Everyone looked down on the people in the projects, Chicago the place with all of the ghettos. But to me DuSable High was still the place to be. A lot of good kids went there. I probably only knew half but even if someone didn't know you they still spoke. One of my favorites was watching the ROTC when they did their drills on the stage. The school had held talent shows, everyone on stage was good. There was one girl that sang a song and when she finished, everyone gave her a standing ovation.

We even had James Earl Jones and Ruby Dee to come to the school. And in case I didn't mentioned it our mascot was the Mighty Black Panthers, who we were proud of it. The football, basketball and softball team were all good. The cheer leaders were very good too and always had their dances together when they came out before the boys that played football.

Chapter Fifty-Two: - I Told It All

Brenda was now the only person after school that I associated with and sooner or later, if I didn't tell her at least some of what I was going through, she was going to put it together. The more things happened and I and tried to keep it to myself the worse that it got. It had gotten to the point where I felt that I wasn't going to be able to hold it together much longer. I wanted to tell her but I had to be sure, I didn't want to say anything too soon because she knew people in and around the buildings that I didn't. I hadn't told her what had happened to me until we were sitting by the school one day. I started with the argument between me Deidra but I had a feeling that she knew because it had happened downstairs. I tried to hold back but the pressure inside of me made me feel like I wasn't going to be able to take it anymore. I needed to tell someone. That evening I took a deep breath, knowing I was taking a chance and told her everything.

It all came pouring out all at once: I told her about my fight with Tommy's gang for my brothers; why I was teaching him to read; why he had let his gang rape Deidra, which was why Shannon beat him half to death and was why he went missing; I told her about the killings of the rival gang; how I knew about their being killed from Mark, and how even after it was clear that Oswald was dead after the shooting; what Tommy did to him afterwards. I told her that Mark was never come back because of what Tommy had made him do. I even told her how Mark had told me the night that it happened, how Tommy and his gang had killed a pregnant girl and a woman who was coming to her rescue.

I even told her that Mark had felt so bad for what had happened, that he had always came to visit, get with Tommy on a friendly level like Rafael but wound up in the gang. I told her that he had told me that he had fell in love with me and all of the plans that we had made were gone, that he told me that he would miss me but he was never coming back. I started crying. By the time that I had gotten to the part about his not coming back and sooner or later the girls in the gang were still going to come after me to

even the score, I was shaking and rocking as I cried-
so hard that I made myself sick. We sat on the ground
not saying anything until I could get myself together.

Finally she said, "Why didn't you tell me any of
this?"

"I didn't feel I had anyone that I could trust but
I was tired of holding it in and if Tommy had found
out from anyone about the things that I knew about and
spoke of I was just as good as dead."

"You've been holding in all of that? along with
Candy's death too? I'm surprised that you haven't gone
crazy! That's too much for anyone to hold inside.
Don't worry I won't tell. As far as those bitches are
concerned, I've got your back. I hate them with a
passion. I always wondered why they never said
anything to me I guess they know that I don't play.
We'll do whatever needs to be done together now, my
lips are sealed. After school I'll wait for you and if
you get out of class before me, you do the same."

I finally felt good knowing that I wasn't all alone
anymore. I was glad that I had told her everything it
was better than the school trips that I had taken.
Well not that good, but almost as good. We did that
for the whole year and I was surprised that I hadn't
had any trouble at all and almost forgot about that
that I did have before. I still hadn't forgotten about
what I was going to have to face and that gave me a
bad feeling inside. One evening after dinner I went
down to Brenda's house to study. When she came to the
door she had a wad of Kleenex up to her nose. Her eyes
were watery and puffy and as soon as she spoke I could
tell that she wasn't feeling well.

"What's wrong? You gotta cold?"

"Naw it's these damn allergies I got. I'm not
gonna come to school tomorrow I'm just gonna lie
around and take this nasty medicine that I have for
it. It usually makes me drowsy and I don't want to
fall asleep in class. I'll be alright by tomorrow
though; it's just on the first day that it really hits
me hard."

"OK I'll see you tomorrow. Hope you feel
better." I turned and walked back to the stairwell to
go upstairs to my house. When I opened the door and
walked inside mom was standing at the stove cooking
dinner. She looked over at me and asked what had
happened. I told her that Brenda had allergies; they
were acting up so we were going to try to get together

tomorrow to do our homework. I walked to my room to get started on my own. The teacher told us before class was over that we were going to have an open book test the next day and I wanted to be ready for it.

Early the next morning Brenda called me but didn't sound any better than she had the other evening and had called to let me know that she wouldn't be coming to class after all. I told her not to worry, that I would pick up her homework and bring it down to her when I got out of school. I hurried my brothers and sisters off to school. I crossed the street to go to class; I made it to my class a minute before the tardy bell rang. School went by fast and before I knew it the bell had rung letting us know that we were dismissed for the day. After having collected Brenda's homework, I headed out of the door. As soon as I opened them I saw that my nightmare was standing in front of me and no one was wearing a grin. I don't know why I thought that had forgotten about me. After a year, they had delivered their babies and had reassembled. They had gotten back together and had come to the school ground for me. By the looks on their faces they looked meaner and more hell bent on killing me than ever. The only thing that I could see was the rage and revenge that they wanted in their faces. In the past year Brenda and I had become very close. We had done everything together, I had met some of her relatives when they came to visit her family, and we did our homework together and just hung out. Now as I stood looking at them standing only a short distance from the doors The only thing that I could think of was Brenda, boy; I sure do need you now.

Chapter Fifty-Three: My Nightmare

They had come to get me and even though Brenda
wasn't there I was glad. I had been walking on
eggshells and praying too long for this day to come
and go, no matter what the outcome would be. The bell
was on its second ring signaling for everyone to be
out of the building. They usually didn't need to ring
it twice. When it rang the first time everyone was
already rushing out of the doors. Then the kids
stopped rushing and had started to linger around. Most
of them knew that if Bay-Bay and her girls were around
the school after the bell rang that they were waiting
for someone and that there was going to be a beat
down. Bay-Bay and her girls were as well known
throughout the buildings, almost as Tommy and his gang
were except Tommy's reputation expanded to places I
had never been. But I was tired of ducking and dodging
people, tired of the name calling, the threats and
just tired of being tired. I was ready.

They made sure that there would be plenty of
space so that they wouldn't get too close. Bay-Bay had
stepped in front; next to her were Sweet, Corkey,
Jean, and two more who ran with her. I thought to
myself; *This was it*. Fear was no longer welcome. They
had greased their faces and removed their earrings.

I let my books drop, as they slid down the
stairs the pages flipped open and all of Brenda's and
my homework fell out and had started blowing across
the gravel. The books ended up facing upward as they
hit the ground. As I stood there a moment, there was
something going on inside of me that felt different.
It wasn't the fear that I had felt in the past. It
wasn't even the same feeling that I had had before I
had had the fight for my brothers. This feeling was
mean and vicious. It was a type of anger that was
strong and had been waiting to come out for a long
time. For a split second there was no adrenalin rush,
and no thought of getting hurt. I didn't even want to
run away. I could feel the anticipation inside. At
first this fight was what I had dreaded and now here I
stood, wanting it more than ever. The anger inside of
me was so strong that it was tunneling upward inside

of my body like a volcano waiting to erupt. What they
didn't know was that I was not going to be fighting by
flailing my arms like a windmill or trying to scratch
any of their faces. I had learned a new way to fight.
I had been taught by one of the best in our building,
and now I was ready to show them what I had learned. I
walked slowly down the stairs as Bay-Bay started
taunting me. "What? I didn't hear you; you say you
don't want to fight?"

"Bitch I've waited a long time for yo ass and
this time you gonna get" Before she could get the
words out I suckered punched her. We were only a few
feet from the wall; and then it started. I grabbed her
and hit her in her face so hard that she started to
stagger. I stepped up to her and grabbed her by her
neck. I held her head back and said, "You know what?
You talk too damn much." I held her head up straight
and took my fist and hit her in her throat. She
started coughing up blood, tightly holding onto her
throat.

She held her head down coughing and while she
was bent over on her knees I looked at her just a
second before kicking her in the face. Sweet stepped
up "You hurt my girl bitch" and before she could
finish I brought one fist up and used the other and
connected into her face as I heard her nose break. I
hit her with my fist over and over. She landed on the
gravel; straddling her I took a handful of the gravel
and started stuffing it into her mouth. There was
something inside that didn't feel like me. I had hurt
two of them then and I liked it. In fact, I was
looking forward to the next two. I was breathing hard
but wasn't out of breath. Corkey stepped up and
brought her fists into boxing motion. And Jean came
making a windmill motion with her arms. As soon as I
saw it I felt a smirk as it came across my lips. I
even felt a spark in my eyes.

I didn't have to think about what Tommy had
taught me. He had told me to watch out for when
someone started to do a windmill and how to avoid
getting hit. I had remembered it and used what he
taught me to beat sweet. Everything came naturally as
Corkey, who was the thinnest of them all started
moving towards me. I could see out of the corner of my
eyes the others were coming towards me, they were
going to box me in. I took a deep breath and as I let
it out slowly I said, "So you want to box?" Tommy and

his gang had moved up. Tommy especially wanted to see what I had learned from his coaching me; he wanted to see if I could handle myself. I did just like he had shown me. Without thinking about it I brought both of my hands up to my face as my guard.

The next girl took a wild punch; I sidestepped her and took a shot that connected perfectly to its mark. Her head went back and I moved in, one punch to the left the other to the right and the last was an uppercut that took her down. One had hit me and blindsided me, I went down to the ground on one knee then I felt her kick to my stomach I saw the blood as it dripped from my nose onto the gravel. As she went to stomp me I rolled over and got up behind her. I took my elbow to her back and brought her to her knees, I did it again and she flattened to the gravel. Other from the side grabbed my hair and had my head down. I was feeling the pain now, all through my body, the rush was slowing down. I brought my fist up and hit her one more time and she went down like a broken doll. I had my back to the school wall; I was not looking at Tommy, who was on the fence. I turned my face away from the wall to listen to the sounds of the shoes running, coming closer and closer.

Tommy had taught me in a situation like this you had to be able to turn around at just the right time to deliver the knockout punch, miss it and you lose they will get the chance to finish you off. My body was shaking badly I was running on gas fumes and now I couldn't focus. But all I could do was try, so I waited for it. But I waited too long. I felt the fist as they caught me on both sides of my back, but for some reason I didn't really feel the pain. As I turned around I found myself looking at a new member. After she had hit me with both fist she stepped back, waiting for me to fall. She just froze as I turned around and stumbled up to her. I drew back and hit her hard in the mouth. One of her teeth popped out. I said, "I don't know who you are, but thanks for the prize." No one else was coming towards me; no one was paying any attention to me at all. I was finished; my body was too, I had nothing left. If there had been just one more or if they had all gotten up and started coming for me I wouldn't have been able to do anything. I was spent.

Tommy and his gang started clapping and whistling. Bay-Bay and the others were trying to crawl

to each other to help them up. I only looked over at
them once before I stumbled back over to the stairs to
pick up my books. After picking them up I just half
limped away. If I hadn't held in everything for so
long they would have eaten me alive in the first
round. The element of surprise is something. I had
fought for my life. Had I won? Yes. Was I extremely
lucky to be able to walk away? Without a doubt. Was it
over? I hoped to GOD so. As I walked/limped away the
anger and fear disappeared because I had changed. I
had become just like them, liking the fact that I was
able to do what Tommy had taught me. It had made him
proud. They were whistling, clapping, and passing
money back and forth. Those bastards had taken bets on
the fight. I was too spent to get mad; I just walked
towards my building, using the bottom of my shirt to
wipe my nose. Cisco caught up with me, took the
bandana off of his head and threw it towards me, He
never said a word, I caught it, and neither did I. I
didn't want to be what Tommy wanted me to be. I didn't
want to be like Bay-bay's gang and I didn't want to **be
in it**.

I just wanted to prove a point and I wanted to
be clear about it. *I wasn't running anymore from any
of them again ever.* I wasn't going to duck or try to
dodge myself to keep from being seen, or worry about
being caught by them. I think that as I walked away
they knew. Tommy and his gang walked a short distance
behind me laughing and slapping each other's hands
still giving high fives. I heard Tommy say, "Fuck you,
shudda bet on huh yo broke dumass" I heard Tommy tell
Emmett I knew she could do it! I knew she'd do like I
showed huh and kick dey ass! Damn, she fights betta
than yall asses!" I didn't want to feel good after
beating someone the way that I had beaten them but I
did. At least for me, it was over. They wouldn't come
back for me. We were even. No more walking on
eggshells anymore. When I walked into my house my
mother was getting something out of the refrigerator
and didn't notice the scratches or bruises on my face,
arms or legs. Then she glanced over at me.

"What's wrong? Are you alright? "

"Yep, I'm okay; in fact, I'm feeling pretty good
Mom."

"Okay go get washed up for dinner." She stood
looking at me with a worried look on her face. I
walked to our bedroom and looked out of the window.

227

Then I heard the sound of her house shoes and knew that something was coming. She came to the bed and handed me a damp wash cloth.

"Did you get them off of you?"

"Yes, mam, I did."

She turned around to walk out of the room, without looking back she said, "Good."

That night as I looked out of my window up at the sky there was no moon showing, only clouds. But I asked quietly anyway for God to take away the anger and the happy feeling that had through me during the fight. The person I had become at the fight, the person that I was slowly beginning to turn into. Because I was wrong and what I did that afternoon was wrong. Fighting and acting as cocky as I had could have backfired on me and I could have gotten killed. And I didn't know how much more my ribs, back, knees and face would continue to take. That attitude and fight could have easily been taken as an invitation to everyone who thought they could, or who was better in fighting want a piece of me. And whenever I came out of my front door I would have to look over my shoulder every time. I didn't want to have to do that either. Doing it all of that time with the girl gang had been more than enough for me. The odds of getting killed would have no end. I just wanted to go back to being Yella Girl. But for some reason, I didn't know if I could.

Chapter Fifty-Four: Brenda and the Parties

Brenda took Candy's place in giving the parties. She didn't have them nearly as often as Candy did because her mother was usually home. Even then, everyone was glad. There had been no other ones since Candy's death. Being invited to a few parties in our building made it better for everyone because then we felt safer in our own area than having to go over another building that we didn't feel as comfortable in. It also took off some of the tension. When Brenda wanted to have a party she would first have to get permission from her mother. After getting it her mother would get Brenda's brother who was older than her by five years to come over to make sure that things didn't get out of hand. She felt more comfortable and would leave for the weekend. Her brother usually got high and drank with everyone who came to the parties but he didn't allow anyone to go into any of the bedrooms in their house the way Candy had done. Most of the same people who had attended Candy's parties were at Brenda's parties. There were people sitting in every place that was available because The back of the house was off limits because Candy let people go everywhere in her house except the room where her brothers and sisters slept. So the party poured outside, onto the porch. People sat in chairs on the porch. And those without chairs sat on the porch or if their boyfriends had a chair they would sit on their laps. Everyone was drinking, playing cards, smoking and having fun. What happened next surprised me.

I was leaning against the wall in Brenda's front room near the record player holding what was supposed to be a glass of rum and coke, but it was actually *all* coke. The alcohol just wasn't my thing. People were really having a good time. Brenda walked over to where I was standing and turned the record player off. Everyone inside and out stopped talking, wondering what was wrong. There was no screeching sound so everyone knew that the record wasn't scratched. There were a few people who had continued to talk but soon there was absolute silence. Brenda stood in the middle of her living room and said, "Quiet down everybody I want to say something. I want to thank everybody here, relatives, friends and everyone who gave donations for

Candy. We all loved her without the money her family and mine wouldn't have been able to make her services and funeral as nice as it was. But the person who really made it possible is standing next to me, this Brenda." Some of the people looked at each other and started snickering and laughing because most of them didn't really know what my real name was. Brenda put her arm around my shoulder and looked at me, then back to the crowd and said, "Most of you call her Yella Girl. She was the one who, I'm sure you already know, was the one who went building to building, floor by floor and door to door. She did more than any of us. She really made it happen so we could pull it off, and as you all know it came off beautifully. So we're going to do two toasts. Everybody hold up your cup for Brenda. Yes, yall didn't even know that we had the same name but we do now, you know. Okay now that we got that out of the way, She laughed and looked at me saying, "She'll still answer to either one but don't fuck up and call her something else cause then she'll kick yo asses." She was laughing so hard that she spilled some of her drink, everybody held up their cans, cups, bottles and whatever else they were drinking from.

"Here's to you Yella Girl," then she held her cup up again and said, "Now, raise your drinks again." Everyone did. "Now "Here's to you Candy. We all miss you but we know you are in a much better place. While you're there keep a watch over all of us." Again that everyone held up their drinks and said, "Right On!" I was still blushing after the toast to Candy was said and done. I poked Brenda on the shoulder.

"Why did you do that?"

"What? I don't know what you're talking about!"

"You know, telling everyone about what I did and having them to make a toast to me!"

"You deserved it. You never get your props and it's time that they know what you did."

"I'll get you back for that!"

"Sure you will, Sure you will." Then we started hugging and laughing. Brenda turned the record player on and the party continued. For once I was glad that my mother had given me permission to go to Brenda's party. This time, although nothing had changed, I had been recognized. The boys patted me on the shoulder and smiled. One offered me a beer but I held up the cup that I had been drinking from and told him that I was good, but thanks. And I was okay with that. Even though I had been the center of attention, what I did was not a big deal. It had all been for Candy, to show her how much I cared. In my mind I hoped she would have done the same thing for me. The party continued I tried to blend into the walls as everyone continued to laugh and talk. I missed Rafael and thought of him and Candy. For a moment I wanted to think that Rafael was gonna come walking through the door and ask me to dance. Of course I knew it would never happen but it was a wishing thought. After the partying was over and I lay in my bed, my thoughts went from Rafael back to Mark and I realized just how much I missed him. Monday meant going back to school I didn't want to dwell on what was or what wasn't to be so I pulled up the covers, closed my eyes, unplugged my memory, and went to sleep.

Chapter Fifty-Five: Tommy's Homework

Tommy and I had started to get back together but not as much as we used to I tried hard to keep our meetings to a minimum. Making the readings last half as long as before but it didn't seem to bother him as much as I thought it would. He knew that I had to go to school myself. The laundry room had no heat and got cold very quickly. Now I noticed that he had really gotten better with it. He wasn't hesitating as much as he had before, his handwriting was better and his sentences had fewer mistakes in them. He didn't have one temper tantrum even when he made a mistake while reading. He was more patient and had stopped smoking when he read. His math was to a point that he would take his practice paper out and do addition, subtraction, multiplication and division. I would put math problems on the paper and he sailed through them. I had done as he asked and taught him what he had asked, I had kept my promise. I still hated him for the person that he was because I no longer knew if he was ever going to keep his promise or not. He had written down all of the books that he had read and like a child, proudly showed his list. He had worked his way up to reading books that kids in grammar school were reading. I looked at the list then back at him and said, "You didn't really read all of these books did you?" His smile was gone and his eyebrows were now furrowed. He was mad because he thought that I didn't believe him and in an off the cuff way had said that he was lying.

"Look yella girl, I said I red-um I ain't gotta lie bout shit. If I say I red it, din I red it! An next time I-mo bring one wif me an yu can pik a page an I'll read it fo you. Now I'm otta heah got things to do, I'll sen somebody to git yu when I'm ready agin." He opened the laundry room door and told Andrew to walk me home. I thought to myself now I've done it, but I didn't think he would have taken it so seriously. For our next meeting, I would know better. And if I did or didn't believe him I would keep it to myself.

Chapter Fifty-Six: Deidra Forgets

The next day after coming from the store I walked to the building and made my way towards the breezeway I saw Deidra. This time she had the same angry look on her face that she had before Tommy had raped her. Her girls were with her just like before. The first thing out of her mouth was, "Yu meeting back with my man again? I heard yu was in na laundry room wif him *again last night!* People gone tell me when yu innare yu shud no dat by now." She was standing in my face ranting and raving about Tommy going on and on and on. Now I was really getting tired of Deidra, she and her crap were getting old.

Deidra this is going to stop, <u>TODAY</u>! "The last time you got in my face you asked me if I heard you last time and I told you that I understood." "Now I'm going to give you some, and you can take it any way you want. I'll hurt you Deidra; I'll beat you like you stole something from me. And your girls? I won't have a problem with them either. I'll snap their necks like chickens. And you know what? I want you to go get Shannon; she'll kick your ass. Let me think, who was it that got help for your sorry ass after her own man had let his whole gang pull a train on her, and who was it that when and got help for the same stupid sorry person whose ass was ripped from one part to the other? **IT WAS ME DEIDRA! Tell me that Tommy hasn't knocked all of the sense out of you!** Now you're telling me that people are telling you things about us? Deidra I don't give a fuck, should you! Want to take me on now and see? Or do you want to take **my advice** this time and just walk away?"

This time I was in her face, the same way that she had been in mine the last time. I meant what I said to her and I think she knew it did too. Her girls had turned lit their cigarettes and were walking away. I watched as she dropped her head without saying a word and turned, walking slowly to catch up with them. I watched as she walked away and then I called her back. When she came back I could see that she was crying.

I said, "First of all Deidra, I'm not trying to take Tommy from you I don't even like him like that."

"Then why yu keep messing wif him and go-in in da laundry room wif him?"

"Why don't you ask him yourself Deidra and see what

233

he says."

"I luv him, an yu and everybody else knows it. It's like yu just doin things to try to git him to foget bout me dats all."

"Deidra, let me let you in on a little something. If Tommy let all of his boys gang rape you while he just stood there not saying anything, just standing back laughing, If that's showing you how much he loves you then I'd hate to see how much worse it could be if he decided that he hated you. He breaks your arms and your ribs, he gives you black eyes and that's what makes you think that he loves you? If you kicked my ass in front of the whole building *which you won't*, do you know who they would be laughing at? *You!* Are you acting blind and crazy? Or are you really just that *stupid?* The whole building, including *your friends* knows that he's messing around with T-Bone's cousin. He's with her all of the time right out in the open where everybody can see him when he tries to kiss her. Now tell me that you don't know that. Your friends don't tell you because they know that you already know, and just don't want to accept it. So you use me because you know and there's nothing that you can say to him without him beating you." "What I want to know is why do you keep taking him back?"

"Yu ont even no what yu takin bout Yella Girl, yu need to mine yo own biz-ness."

"Your wanting to fight me over some shit that ain't really about me *is my business!* They might call me Yella Girl, but they aren't laughing and talking about me and calling me stupid, which is what they're calling you! You really are stupid!" I looked at her and just shook my head not believing what I was hearing. "You know what? If the girl that he's seeing now is pretty, smart and won't let him beat the shit out of her, then that's who he's gonna be with but he'll still beat the shit out of you because he can." And the bad part is there's not gonna be a damn thing that you will be able to do about it. I helped you. Do you remember how he left you? All that you seem to worry about is why I'm in the laundry room! Is that the only place that he takes you? Why don't you ever come to school; or to any of the parties? Does he ever take you anywhere else besides the laundry room, Deidra?"

She put her head down and I knew the answer about the laundry room but she wouldn't answer why she never came to school. "Can I ask you something? After all of these years of being with Tommy how is it that you never got pregnant?"

"Doctors told me I can't have no babies cause som-ums wrong wif my female parts I don't really remember dose big medical words he told me, cause every time I did get pregnant I would have a miscarriage." I thought to myself, thank God for small miracles. He knew that she needed some. "Me and Tommy go way back. He'll always be my man and he'll always come back".

I had only gotten as far as the third stair. When I heard her say that, I came back out of the hallway. "Deidra, I don't know what you're gonna do and I really don't care but maybe you should talk to your sister about you and Tommy. Cause you need to wake up or one day you *won't*." I started walking up the stairs again to go home. I walked up the stairs thinking about Deidra. Even after what had happened between us I had lied. I felt bad for her. She was caught up in something that for her, I didn't think would ever change because it seemed to be all that she knew. Being treated the way that she was, was to her a sign of love.

In a way I was glad that no one around the building thought about me in that sort of way. For the first time ever being Yella Girl was the best things that could have happened to me as far as relationships go. Except Mark, and he was gone so that didn't count. I wouldn't have to worry about going through the crap that Deidra was.

I was glad that no one in Tommy's gang had been interested in me. A smirk came across my lips as I reached the tenth floor because the first time they would have hit me I would have hit back. In my mind my thoughts would have been right. I most certainly would have ended up dead.

I thought about Tommy and Deidre. At different times I had seen him going to different floors where his gang members lived to see Renee. Deidra knew when Renee was in the building because her friends would tell her or there would be the whispers that spread quickly but she would just stay in her house. Renee knew about Deidra too and made sure that she was seen by everyone when she came into the building with Tommy. She seemed to be hoping that Deidra would see them together and Tommy certainly didn't care, it

235

wasn't the first time that he had cheated on Deidra
but this had been the longest. One day when I was
coming through the breezeway to get to the stairs
Tommy and Renee were on their way out of the building.
Tommy smiled when he saw me and spoke, "Hey Yella
Girl".

"Hey Tommy."

I wanted to see where they were going so I
slowly walked behind a group of other people who were
also on their way out of the building too I stopped
short of coming out. In the parking lot Tommy and T-
Bone were standing next to his uncle's truck. I saw T-
Bone drop the keys into Tommy's hand. As soon as Tommy
had them he walked around to the other side of the
truck and opened the door to let Renee in.

Once she got in he closed the door for her then ran
back around to the driver's side of the truck jumped
inside and after giving T-Bone a high five he sped
off. I'm sure Deidra was looking out of her back
window, watching her man drive off with another girl
instead of her. Slowly Deidra's friends stopped coming
around as often because they felt sorry for her.
Deidra never went to school and there was no obvious
reason because her mother was always home to take care
of her brothers and sisters. she should have been
able to go if she wanted to. But then I thought, maybe
she did want to go to school But Tommy had something
to do with that. I wondered but never asked anyone if
Tommy had something to do with it. I was the only one
who knew that he hadn't been able to read or write. I
didn't know if she could or couldn't either.

Tommy really liked her, he had gone all out to
keep her from finding out that he hadn't been to
school, or had even graduated. Two nights later when I
met with Tommy in the laundry room I didn't say
anything about Deidra. He would really hurt her to
find out that she had disrespected his orders. I
didn't want her to end up with broken ribs that she
had received many times before when Tommy had gotten
mad at her. Now with Renee in the picture he would
really hurt her. I had my head bent down, reading
along with Tommy But my mind was somewhere else. It
was a while before I noticed that Tommy was watching
me.

"What's wrong wif you? Yu lookin like yu got a
lot on yo mine."

"Nothing, just stuff going on at home," I lied.

236

He sucked big time. I was glad that Renee was taking up so much of his time when he stayed on the Westside. When he came back and when I could, I continued to meet with him to practice on his reading. I often wondered to myself how long it would be before Deidra blew up, not being able to take it anymore. Or if she knew her place and would just let Tommy do as he pleased until he got bored and came back. That's what she had said to me when we had had spoken. That he always came back and she always took him back. One day, when I saw them together I smiled and thought to myself of what he had said to me when Mark had left.

Except this time it was the other way around. This time it was him. Renee sure has his nose opened wide and he loved it. I also remembered that he had Deidra to fall back on if he got tired of Renee or however it would go if they broke up. When Mark had left Chicago, I didn't have anyone.

Chapter Fifty-Seven: Déjà vu

It was Wednesday Brenda and I met after school to do our homework. She was grinning from ear to ear as she told me how much she had made from the party; she said it would help her mother from struggling during the middle of the month. She knew her mother wouldn't do her like Candy's mom had done to her, and had told her so. Brenda had already decided to help her and then she would keep the rest for things that her mom couldn't give her. In fact her mom was going to let her have another one this weekend. We decided that we would go to the store the next day to get an early start.

The next day, we were going to walk to 47th street to go to the grocery store to get stuff for the party just to have something to do. We had just crossed State Street and were at 46th street when out of nowhere, walking towards us were Bay-Bay, Corky, Sweet and the rest of her gang. As Brenda and I continued walking towards them I took a deep breath, shrugged my shoulders and said to her, "Might as well get this over with. You go on across the street and keep walking." As we continued walking, without looking at me she said, "I'm not gonna leave you I hate those bitches. If we go down then we go down together. Within a few steps we were standing face to face with them. Some of Bay-Bay's girls had slowly started to circle us. At first, I could see a blank look on Bay Bay's face.

She and her gang had never seen Brenda or anyone else for that matter with me before and now I was standing in front of them with someone who instead of walking away from me was standing by my side. As more of her gang continued to move slowly around us, Brenda turned slowly in their direction until we ended up standing back to back. Bay-Bay looked in the direction of the girls who had surrounded us and a smile came to her face but still hadn't said a word. It was though she was sizing us up. I knew Brenda could fight. When her older brother was over to her house I had seen her spiral and play boxing with him. He was good and the more Brenda had practiced with him the better she had become. She had gotten so good at it that more often than not she won. As we stood back to back, the realization of us being outnumbered and what could happen to us became very real.

My thoughts returned from the last fight. "Take the one who comes for you first. If Brenda could get ahold of Sweet we might have a chance." I moved sideways, took my stance and put my fist up to guard my face. The swelling from my fingers was still there callouses has started to form on some, and my left pinkie finger had been broken. I had only bandaged it, and it was taking forever to heal. It had started to look deformed as it was growing crooked away from the rest of my other fingers. The pain from trying to make a fist almost made tears come from my eyes. At the same time I said, "Bay- Bay call off your girls, remember what you said when I was at your get together."

Bay-Bay kept looking at me as Sweet said, "Fuck that we were wasted." Bay-Bay turned her head to the side, and Sweet stopped talking. The girls behind us were quiet, looking for a signal or for Bay-Bay to speak. Bay-Bay surprised them started laughing. Her girls followed her lead and did the same. She looked at me and said, "Hey it's cool we ain't come here to scrap." Sweet chimed in, "You down by us." Bay-Bay and her gang gave each other the high five.

I didn't trust them. I went into my pocket to get a cigarette. Bay-Bay beat me to it and offered one to Brenda and me. Brenda never bothered to look up as she took her own from her pocket and lit it, afterwards blowing the smoke in the direction of Bay-Bay and her girls. I did the same I still didn't trust them as far as I could throw them.

Inhaling the smoke then releasing it through my nose like I had been smoking for years. Corkey at looked Bay-Bay and then at me, "Check huh out! She's been doing shit behind our backs! She's smokin like a pro! You definitely no you and yo girl are one of us now!"

In my mind I thought, "No I'm not, not now, not ever."

As we all stood smoking, out of the corner of my eye I saw Bay-Bay give Sweet a quick look. Smiling, she said, "Hey I'm given a little get together Friday night, Wanna come? Without smiling Is I had my head down lighting another cigarette I said, "Yeah I guess so, I'm not busy. Bren's party is on Saturday night, what time is your get together?"

Bay-Bay said, "It's gonna start at 9:00 sharp."

"Okay, but I gotta leave by 11:30 my curfews at 12:00 midnight sharp. Corkey put her hand over her mouth to squash a giggle but it came out anyway. "Girl, you still got a curfew?" Bay-Bay and the others started laughing.

I said, "Yeah, my momma wants to know where I am because she cares about me, What about yours?" Corkey's smile faded fast. She was really pissed. Everyone including me knew that she had no mother and lived with her father. So my remark brought her joke back to her and bit her in the ass. She tried to lunge forward to get me for my remark but was held back by the others. Bay-Bay cleared her throat as a signal for her to stay where she was. Bay-Bay said, "Okay we'll be looking for you at 9:00 sharp."

Looking past her at her girls I said, "I'll be there."

When Bay-Bay and her girls needed quick cash they usually went up on forty-Seventh Street near Kings Drive to steal some of the Johns away from the prostitutes without getting caught by them or their pimps. Sometimes when Candy had been alive, we had all gone to see what was playing at the movies and would see girls from Bay-Bays gang in the alley's kneeling down with a man who either had his fly opened or had his pants down around his knees. Once some other girls who lived in our building had seen them on 47th street, they usually gave oral sex because it was quick and had even invited them to join them if they wanted to make some quick money. They had told the girls and they gave (head jobs) because the men were too dirty to do anything else with. The talk about them doing johns didn't bother them at all mostly because it had been true. They were much younger than the women who walked the streets, and they were always preferred by the Johns. When a car would cruse by and lower the window once inside, the car would drive a short distance around the block. For Bay-Bay and her girls it was easy money. It gave them money to buy their alcohol, smokes, weed and even have some money left over.

Brenda and I changed our minds and decided to go to the A&P store which was closer to our building. We stood where we were and finished our cigarette as they walked away. I looked back just to make sure that they were still going in the opposite direction that we were. When I looked back I was walking alone. Brenda had stepped up her pace leaving me to do a quick run to catch up to her.

As I caught up I could see the anger on her face. "What's wrong with you? What did I do?"

She was screaming at me. "Have you just lost your damn mind? You didn't see that coming? Do you just want to get yo ass killed? Why do you think they want you at *their* get together when it wasn't even a week ago that you kicked their asses by the school?" "Do you think they gonna just let you get away with that? You just set yourself up, I just can't believe you!" They're gonna get you in that house and beat the life out of you and you told them you would be there! Damn, sometimes I think that you really want to die." You said that you never went to look for trouble that it always seemed to find you, well what about now? Did it find you or did you go looking for it?" She was looking down at the ground shaking her head like I was already dead. I kept walking, not bothering to look over at her because she was right. She was crying now, "I'm sorry for saying that but why are you doing this? You don't have anything else to prove to anybody. Just tell me why? Why did you accept that invite?" the tears were running down her face. "I'm your friend, I meant that. Did you see me walk away when they were all around us? I stayed by your side and they could have beat us to death! Then they baited you and practically invited you to a beat down and you take it like it's an invite and accepted." "Are you that crazy? I just don't get it! Why you're doing this to yourself?"

"I don't know, I guess maybe it's that I've got to finish playing the hand I've been dealt so I'm gonna play it to the end." I gotta let them see that I meant what I said. If I go by myself they will know that I don't need a crowd to be there. They won't think that you'll show, you know that, I lit a cigarette and said, "Yeah, I know."

"Fuck that! What TV westerns have you been watching? This isn't a western and this definitely isn't a bid wiz card playing game; this isn't where you play rise and fly! When they get through kicking your ass that's gonna be the rise and you gone be flying right into the incinerator."

"You finished?"

"Yeah, I'm finished. I'm gonna get some of the girls that I know and we gonna go up there with you."

"No you're not. If it makes you feel better you can come down to my house at twelve-thirty and knock on the window. If you don't see my hand waving through the window then come and start looking for me. You know what floor it's gonna be on?"

"I know more about them and that building then you'll ever know. You know that I'm gonna be pacing the floor all night." Man! This just fucked up the rest of everything that I had planned." This is just plain ol fucked up. Period!

"Don't let it," I put my arm around her shoulder as we started walking towards the building. "It's gonna be alright." But neither one of us was really sure about that. Inside of my mind, I think that I was just hoping that it would.

Neither of us said another word to each other for the rest of the walk home. As we entered her house I sat down at the kitchen table. She went to get something out of her kitchen cabinet to eat after getting it when she turned around she kept her eyes on the sandwich that she was fixing, trying hard not to look at me. I thought that she didn't want to talk to me anymore. I got up from the chair and started to walk to the door and shouted, "Why'd you have to wait until we got so close before you decided to make up your mind to go and get yourself killed?" I just turned and walked out closing the door softly behind me.

Chapter Fifty-Eight: I Promise

This was going to be another miserable Friday; this would make it two in a row. School was a bust; I didn't hear or learn a thing that day. The only thing that I could concentrate on was what would be in store for me that night At Bay-Bay's get together. After my family and I had eaten dinner, I heard a knock at the door. It was Brenda. She asked my mom if I could come down to her house for a while to help her with her geometry. My mom said yes without hesitating. The one thing that my mother was big on was our education. I asked her if it was alright if I stayed with her until my curfew. She looked at Brenda first, then me and then she did hesitate but only for a moment, before saying that I could. The weekend was here so if I was going to do some studying first, for her that was ok. After we were out of the door, I asked Brenda, "What's up? You know you don't have any homework to work on."

"I need you to come down to my house for a while before you go tonight. I want to get you ready first so at least you'll have a chance if things start to go wrong."

We went down to her house and when we went into her room she had it set up like a beauty shop. Her dresser top had combs, picks, brushes, hair oil and something that I hadn't seen before, razorblades. I turned and looked at her,

"What are the razor blades for?"

"You'll see. Like I said earlier I'm not going to send you down there with no protection at all. With what I'm going to do at least you'll be able to give um a run for their money." Now sit down." First, she combed out my hair then took a thin section of my hair and threaded it through the middle of the razor blade and very gently pushed it down then she braided the rest of the braid to the end. She did this in different places all over my head. When she was finished all of the razor blades were gone, hidden into my hair. She left the back bushy and placed a rubber band on it. She carefully separated the ponytail and put a razorblade in the middle and put a rubber band at the end of it. As she sprayed afro sheen on it she told me, "Make sure that you don't touch your head or you'll come away with a fist full of nubs."

I couldn't believe how well she had hidden the blades in my hair! I couldn't even feel where they were. Then she went into her top drawer and brought out a pair of brass knuckles, pulled up my pants leg and put the knuckles down inside of my slouch socks. "Don't forget which side it's on and don't let it slip out." I went to touch my hair because it looked so nice and shiny and I thought that I looked good with my new hair style since I hadn't ever worn my hair that way. Just as I put my hand up she slapped it away.

"Don't touch, don't scratch! Don't forget I'll be up to your house at 12:30 sharp. Then we're coming to get you."

It was 8:15pm and time for me to go, to be able to take my time to walk and get to their building. As I opened the door Brenda ran up to me and said, "One more thing," she took the earrings I had on out of my ears. Now you're ready. She gave me a long hug before turning to walk away. She didn't look back at me. She just walked back to her room and closed the door. I got to Bay-Bay's house on time; I took a deep breath and knocked once on the door which opened after the first knock. Corkey was sporting a big smile. "Come on in girl! We thought yu wudn't coming!" By the sound of Sweets loud mouth in the background I could tell she had already been drinking. When I first walked into the house, I thought one of Bay-Bay's girls was going to jump from behind the door but no one did. The lights were low but I could still see everyone who was sitting there on the couch I counted seven crammed there and sweet was sitting on the arm of the couch. The girl that I didn't know was coming out of the bathroom. I heard the toilet when it flushed. She just looked at me as she went over and got a beer off of the table and started to drink. I still felt that something wasn't right. I had had that feeling all day long. Since school they had moved up in the liquor department. Everyone was laid back on the couch I saw one jug of Boone's Farm and a pint of White Port off to the side. After a moment I was able to focus my eyes better and could see everything on the table. The rest was hard alcohol. There were Pints of Beefeaters Gin, Gordon's Vodka, Grey Goose and Bacardi Rum. The majority of it was expensive by everyone's standards, but I knew that by them going up on Forty-Seventh Street they were able to get the money to buy it.

I knew about the Beefeaters Gin because my stepdad drank it from time to time. Sweet picked up the Beefeaters bottle put it in her mouth and took a large gulp. She slammed the bottle on the table, shaking her head and making a nasty face to signal that it was strong. Bay-Bay and Corkey glanced at her, them at each other but I saw the glance too. Sweet passed the bottle over to me. And said, "Your turn." I took the bottle, put it to my lips and put my head back. As it went down my throat it tasted like rubbing alcohol and hit my stomach like a burning flame. I thought I was going to choke, "Oh shit!" As I started to gag everyone at the table was laughing so hard that they started falling all over each other.

Next she passed the bottle to Corkey, "Come own bitch go for it! Do dat shit!" Then Sweet stood up, half wasted and staggered from the couch holding up her fist in the air, She started shouting, "Hell yeah! We bad we da badis bitches in the 'jects!" The others followed her lead, all except Bay-Bay. Who had sat on the couch quietly sipping on her Rum and coke I could see that she was watching me. Sweet was stumbling as she made her way back to the couch. She Corkey and the others continued to drink what was on the table. After drinking the Vodka I was through. I had my own fight to deal with as I tried my best to keep that God awful crap down but I could feel it moving like a wave in my stomach and feeling like lightening. Corkey took out a joint and everyone including me took a drag off of it. If their plan was to get me messed up then fight me, it had worked.

I couldn't have fought if I tried. But I had gone there half expecting it. As I lay back on the couch, completely out of it in my mind I HAD to keep it together, even if it was for show. Another of Bay-Bay's girls who usually kept a low profile named, Cricket asked me, "Where'd you learn to fight like that?" My head was swirling as I said, "Some from when you all kicked my ass and the other along the way." Then I lit a cigarette, not bothering to look back at her.

Now it was Bay-Bay's turn. "Yu know yu never did tell us who taught yu how to smoke a cigarette and be able to let it come from yo nose and mouth at the same tam?"

"It doesn't matter who, the main reason I learned it was from always being stressed and pissed

245

off; I guess I learned two things for the price of one you can have the credit for that."

"You no yu kicked our ass and made us look bad in front of ever- body." I felt the same smirk that came across my face when I had last fought them.

"Yeah, I know. And if I have to I'll try my best to do it again. I looked over at Bay-Bay, It got personal. You almost killed me the first time that you got hold of my ass, I swore to myself that you wouldn't ever do what you did to me again." And if you try to get me again, I'll kill you. One by one even if it takes me a lifetime, you can take that to the bank." This time I picked up a can of beer, popped the lid and took a drink, looking into my can, "I'm fucked up now and everyone here knows it. If you gonna do something to me now's the time to do it." "Otherwise as far as I'm concerned, it's over." I was drunk but I knew a grilling when I heard one. Then I looked over at Bay-Bay and flashed a wide smile. Bay-Bay looked like she wanted to eat me alive; instead she smiled back and said, "Our beef wif yu is ova." That's why yu was invited so I could tell yu myself. "I looked at the clock on the wall and blurry as it was I could tell that I had missed my curfew.

"Oh shit! I missed my curfew. Damn! I gotta go my mom's not gonna let me out again till hell freezes over!"

Everyone started laughing but it wasn't funny at all to me. I had really messed up and to make it worse not only had I been drinking, I could smell the alcohol and the cigarettes smoke all over my clothes and in my hair. I was supposed to have been in the house and here I was almost a block from my own building! I had peppermints in my pocket and I sucked on two at a time. After spitting those pieces out I was still able to smell the liquor. So I popped two pieces of gum into my mouth. When the sweetness went away I popped in two more. I did that until I reached the building and then my floor. Hoping and praying that the gum would save me by hiding the smell. The alcohol was starting to move up and it wasn't going to be long until it was going to come up and out just like a volcano.

I put my key into the lock, took two steps inside and standing in the middle of a fully lit apartment in the middle of the floor was my mother with her arms folded. For some reason she looked so tall that her head seemed to touch the ceiling. She looked at me for an instant before she screamed, "You're Grounded!" I was so drunk that my mind was telling my mouth to ask, "If that meant until she forgot about it, or until hell froze over" But I was no condition to try to duck or forget to duck and end up getting hit in the face with a shoe thrown from an angry woman with an arm that reached so far back, that that shoe would have traveled from Mississippi. And if, or when it did hit me I would have been wearing that shoe print on my face for a month or in my case, until I was old and gray. Instead she turned and walked back to her room and slammed the door. My mind was saying, Thank you Lord that she didn't feel like giving me a lecture before grounding me and that GOD had kept his hand over my big mouth.

I was starting to lose the battle with the alcohol. It was ready to erupt so I staggered as quickly as I could to the bathroom. I lifted up the toilet seat, fell to my knees and dropped my head into the toilet bowl. The alcohol came out of my mouth without forgiveness. The force was so strong that it went pass the toilet and onto the wall. I must have filled up and flushed the toilet three times. Finally it stopped. While on my knees with my hands holding on to the sides of the toilet, my head down in the toilet bowl, I promised God that if He let me get past that moment he would never ever have to worry about me doing that much drinking again. After kneeling for what seemed like forever, I was able to drag myself to the front room to lie down on the couch. Just as I was turning on my side to try to get comfortable, I heard a soft knocking at the front window. I parted the curtains, it was Brenda. I raised my hand to give a short wave to let her know I had made it back safely. I dropped my arm to my side. It felt like it weighed a hundred pounds. I fell asleep as soon as I closed my eyes but it was not for long. I felt a couple of gentle taps on my shoulder. As I half opened my eyes, I could see my stepdad standing over me holding a rag in his hand. He bent over and whispered in my ear, "You better take this rag and go into that bathroom and clean that mess you made up before your mother gets up and goes in there and sees it." I took the rag out of his hand and staggered to the bathroom.

I could hear my dad behind me laughing softly. He said, "Bet you won't do that again." He walked past me to the back of the hall where the bedroom was and closed the door. I went into the bathroom and kneeled down; I could barely see the wall let alone the mess that I had made. I did my best, probably not *the best* but it was passable, now I could get some sleep.   It happened so fast but I felt like I had just lain down and now it was time to get up to go get everyone ready for school. NOOOOOOOOOOOOO! I had been through everything that I thought I could go through in the past but the hang over that I had made everything in the past was pale in comparison. The price that I paid for feeling like a piece of crap that day was far from worth it. I met Brenda on the first floor. She was grinning as she said, "What brick wall did you run into? You look like,"

        "Yeah I know, just don't talk so loud okay?"

        "That must have been some night! You still wreak, Pew! What the hell did you drink or better yet what didn't you drink?"

        "Just give me a break okay? We can talk about it later." As we walked to school every sound that I heard was amplified. My head hurt, my ears were ringing, my stomach felt like I had been kicked, even my eyebrows and eye lashes hurt. The whole school day was a total loss mostly because everything was a blur. The school bell rang and classes were over for the day. Finally my torturous day was almost over all I had to do now was get my brothers and sisters home, do my chores and try to stay awake just long enough until my mom made it home. Dinner was out of the question all I wanted to do was lay down and slip into a coma. As Brenda and I walked home every time she looked at me she would crack up laughing. The only thing that I could do was give her a dirty look. It didn't bother her at all. It was the first time that I ever wanted to slap her, she knew that her laugh was making angry but she didn't care, she thought it was funny. Once I got home and looked at myself in the mirror I could see why, I looked like a zombie. I even had to smile, I tried to laugh at myself but I couldn't. Just trying to, made even my eyelashes hurt.

Chapter Fifty-Nine: Seasons and Holidays

There were very few things that changed in the projects except the seasons. In summer those who passed to the next grade looked forward to what they would do with the time they had earned out of school. That's when everything came to life. Once again that's when you could look forward to going to the parties again or stay outside, and go to the movies. Most of us would do this. It was also the time that you would hear the gunfire and remembered to duck when the sounds came too close. That's when Tommy and his gang were most active.

The winter weather brought with it the same cold wind that had slapped you in the face and froze you to the bone as a child and still had the same strength years later, continuing its same methodical cycle year after year. People either went from one person's house to another to watch TV or find other things to do. There were very few parties held so everything became dreary and boring.

Winter brought holidays and family gatherings. There was Thanksgiving, Christmas, New Year's Eve and New Year's Day. Everyone in all of the buildings looked forward to Christmas. Although Thanksgiving was more about food and church, it was good for my family, we ate and all of us kids went to church. For some families it was bad especially when the day ended on a bad note. When relatives got drunk and argued with each other, cursing and screaming to the tops of their lungs, wanting to fight or threatening to kill and saying as they left they would never speak to the family that they were visiting again. Only to be seen with those same family members again at the next holiday gathering.

At Christmas some families had white flocked trees. If any of the dust from the branches got onto your skin it would itch and you would end up scratching yourself like crazy. Our tree was silver. Everyone in the house would help to put popcorn on strings that would reach around the whole tree, along with our decorations and ornaments. After the tree had been decorated my mom would place a rotating light with colors of red, blue, green, and a regular bulb to make it look white. Then my mom and dad would place Christmas bulbs around the windows.

Once the lights in the living room were turned

off the windows and the tree with its decorations made the living room look completely beautiful. We even had stockings on the tree limbs. There weren't always a lot of boxes under the trees but even with the ones that we got not counting the boxes that usually had clothes in them, we would shout and jump up and down with joy at having gotten the very thing that we had hoped for Christmas. Everyone in the projects knew that none of the social workers were going to come around, The Holiday meant not having to deal with families in the projects, but having a chance to be off enjoying the company of their own families. That's when the men could come around without having to sneak in or out to spend a few days not have to worry about any unexpected knocks at the door. Fathers and boyfriends could all be together with their families. It was a time that everyone everywhere could be happy.

New Year's Eve was strictly for the adults. We would giggle when we saw my mom and our step-dad kiss under the mistletoe. she would catch us peeping and shout with a smile on her face, "Go to bed! Can't a mom and dad give each other a little peck without five pairs of eyes watching?" We would snicker and bat our eyes at them like the ladies do and go back to our rooms to play with our gifts. After they had gone to bed we all went into one room and from the darkness of the night looked at the fireworks from the windows. When the clock struck at midnight everyone outside the building would run for cover. To bring in the New Year, everyone that had a gun or access to one would start shooting and the sounds of the shots being fired made you think that you were in the middle of a war. Not just in our building, shots seemed to come from every building around. Some of the shots sounded like fire crackers, others sounded like cannons. There were even some that sounded like machine guns. For some reason my mom seemed to know what we were doing and would come back and made us get away from the window. Then she turned off the lights in the house and sent my brothers to their rooms and made us go to bed. For us New Year's Eve was over. On New Year's Day the women would cook for the family, which meant that their men could come or been seen and really make it a real holiday. Some families would go to other family members who had invited them over and they would eat and drink while the men made bets on who would win as they watched the football game. My step dad did the same thing. He would invite some of the men that he worked with over to our house and my mother would serve them dinner and they would do the same, eat drink and make bets on the football game.

The next holiday was Easter; on our way to church we would see some families wearing the best clothes doing the same. We were all hustled into the family car and driven to church. Everyone wore their best. The women at church strutted around like peacocks wearing their large hats and matching suits. The men paraded around like rosters in their silk like suits with ties and shoes to match. Lots of women brought food and would always show off to the members in the church. After church services were over families including ours returned to the building. Everyone cooked ham and potato salad along with other foods that were made on Easter. The ham was the main course on every table. My mom made potato salad too and other side dishes that I can no longer remember. The one thing that I never forgot was how our mom made a cake into the shape of a lamb and brought and placed in the middle of the table for dessert. We would all stand at the edge of the table with our mouth's watering watching the lamb cake as though it was going to jump off of the table and run away.

We all had the same thought, when was she going to cut it? When was she going to hurry up and cut the cake? My mom would smile, she knew by taking her time that it was torturing us. Afterwards we would see the kids in the building with Easter baskets. We all had one too. Although I only ate the candy out of mine, I gave the gifts to my sisters. My mother knew that I was too old but she always bought one for me. Some of the baskets kids had smaller ones that were filled with toys and different colored eggs hidden in the play grass. Some had chocolate bunnies and others had chicks in them. The kids didn't seem to mind and that's what made everyone happy.

The next holiday was Memorial Day. That's when everybody that had one and even those that didn't, went down in the playground, to the parking lot in the back of the building, or over to the lake front to bar-b-que ribs, hamburgers, hotdogs and everything in between. There would always be a lot of drinking going on. People would bring down chairs and sit four to a table and play bid wiz. Usually my family would go over by the lake to meet with our cousins, aunts and

253

uncles to grill meat and do the same. Except at our get reunions none of the men drank alcohol where any of the women and kids could see. They usually found a place under a tree where they would lay out an old blanket, open the cooler and pull out bottles of beer and laugh and talk together.

Some of my older cousins and I would walk to the shore and put our feet into the water and run from the waves. It was some of the fun things that I remembered that we used to do. We took the ones that were a little older to the shallow part to let them play too. The last was Halloween. Mainly for the kids but teenagers got into the act as well.

Every kid in costume would go door to door and say, "trick or treat!" then hold open their bags for candy and Goodys to be dropped in. Sometimes the older one in the family would take the little ones to the other buildings to get candy. Sometimes there would be trouble where another older kid would snatch a younger kid's bag but it didn't happen often. But it was the perfect time for Tommy and his gang to go and start trouble because they could wear ski-mask and go into the white buildings and not be noticed or get caught. They always came back laughing about who they had caught and beat up without that person being able to tell who it was that did it.

The fourth of July was as fun day too. The men and boys set off cherry bombs, lit firecrackers which made loud noises, there were twizzles and flares and always every kid had the snakes that when lit curled and made a hissing sound until it had burned up and was completely ashes. Tommy and his gang had the rockets which were too loud for some of the younger ones. It usually scared them so Tommy and others who wanted to set off the rockets went behind the buildings to set them off one after another most of the night.

For weeks afterwards people were still setting off firecrackers which were scary. Sometimes you wouldn't know if the sound was from a firecracker or a gun. And the sounds could be heard echoing off of the buildings everywhere. Other people would watch the firecrackers that were lit from their floors, others even bar-b-qued on their porches. The little kids laughed in delight when the fireworks started. They would clap their hands and point as the rockets went high into the air. The excitement was shown in their smiles and somehow their innocence always seemed to peek through.

Chapter Sixty: The Hippy Lady

The last school holiday had given us a two weeks off, some of the other girls and the building had gone to play softball. We played on the one side of the playground that had grass which was close to the street. The batter had hit a home run and as I ran and turned backwards to catch it, I heard a voice behind me that cheerfully said, "Hi." I turned around and was so shocked that I completely forgot about the ball and it came down on top of my head almost knocking me down onto the grass. There standing on the side walk was a young white woman who looked like she was a college student. One of the girls who had seen me get hit by the ball ran over to make sure that I was alright, but after seeing the white lady seemed to forget what she had ran over for. She just stood next to me with her mouth open but no words were coming out. She just stood there staring at her. The lady smiled at me and asked, "Are you okay?" Then the others soft ball players ran over to see what everyone was looking at. You could hear the excited whispers that were being repeated as they came closer. A white lady! It wasn't like we had never seen one; the majority of them were the teachers at school, but we weren't in school and she didn't look like a teacher! She had put her long blond hair into two braids which lay on her shoulders, that made her look like an Indian squaw. Her headband and blouse were psychedelic colored and her blue jeans were wide leg at the bottoms. She had sandals that were open at the heel and toes. She also had on a brown suede jacket with fringes along the arms and across the back of it. The Jacket, braids and headband changed her squaw look into The Lone Ranger's sidekick, Tonto.

As more people started gathering around us to get a better look at her, she held up her fingers making a peace sign. A lot of the girls giggled while the others put their fingers up to return the peace sign back to her, laughing as they did. Out of puzzlement and fear for her, my heart had started beating like it was going to jump out of my body.

The Projects were a place where if you were white and caught *in* or *around* them the outlook for their survival at best was bleak. Brenda said, "Lady, are you lost? Do you know where you are?" I kept looking behind the crowd to see if I could see Tommy or any of his gang coming over. I was thinking maybe she was from out of town or something and had no idea of the danger that she was already in. Just by standing there, she was attracting more and more attention. One of the girls named Deborah, who had been playing ball with us was looking back behind the crowd at the same time that I was and as I looked at her our thoughts collided.

Maybe we could do something to take the attention off of her so that she could get away. Maybe we could flag down a cab! Now what the hell was I thinking? Cabs never came to get a fare in the projects because they always got robbed. Our building had a bus stop sign on forty-ninth and state, at the corner that was right next to our building but the busses seldom stopped there. They would go a half block further when going south where the strip mall was and then let passengers off leaving them to walk the half block back to their destination. They would do the same when going north.

We didn't know what to think. Standing here in front of us was this white Lady smiling and handing out leaflets to each of us and while doing so, was telling us that "God loves you." Each leaflet had a scripture quotation from the bible written on it. Deborah and I took her by the hands hoping that we could get her to the mall quickly where she could stay in one of the stores until someone could come to get her. All of a sudden the expression on her face changed leaving an almost questionable and uncomfortable look on her face. Just by looking at her, Deborah, Brenda and I knew we were too late. Just by the look on her face we knew who she was looking at. At least I thought I knew. I thought it was Tommy and his gang but it wasn't. It was worse; when I looked back I saw who she was looking at.

Now I really thought her time had run out. From out of nowhere walking towards us was Bobby. Bobby was one of those people that everyone considered crazy. He even acted crazy, talking and laughing to himself, cursing out people who weren't there, even doing cartwheel flips in the streets. People said he had a hair trigger temper, he didn't care who he hurt or killed and he would sell his own mother if it would turn him a quick buck. Bobby didn't like Tommy or his gang. And it was said the feeling was mutual. Both would speak when they ran into each other but nothing

more. The older gang didn't want Bobby around because
when he was, somehow the police had always been one
step ahead of what they were planning to do and
someone would always end up getting caught and sent to
prison. It was known that everyone in the older gangs
were true to their alliance, they would even die for
it but on rare occasions there would be a question in
a gang-members commitment for life. Sometimes there
would even be someone who thought they could run the
game better. Usually that gang member would be taken
care of. Somehow word on the street would get back to
the building that a gang member had disappeared and we
knew what that meant. The older gang members hadn't
had any real proof that Bobby was the snitch. What
Bobby didn't know was their not having any real proof
was the one thing that had kept him alive. Once he had
questioned an older leader's decisions he was kicked
out with a warning that he better keep his mouth shut.
They told him that he wasn't worth killing because he
acted like he was crazy. One of the soldiers in the
gang was said to have told him that he wasn't even
worth wasting a bullet on, but it didn't mean that he
wouldn't come up missing if they ever found out that
he had snitched on them. Everything about Bobby was
old news in the building. Bobby didn't like Tommy; he
definitely didn't like the older gang. I don't think
that Bobby even liked himself or the world, but what
everyone did know was *that Bobby hated white people!*

Unfortunately, what Bobby had in common with
most of the people from the projects was the mutual
hate they all shared for white people. It was Bobby
who put everything in motion. He walked up to her and
started looking her up and down. Then he snatched the
leaflets from her hand and threw them on the ground.
The wind did its job scattering them across the
streets along with the litter that was already on the
ground. Two of the girls from the team jumped in front
of the lady to protect her. They told him that the
lady was only giving out scriptures from The Bible to
everyone. They weren't afraid of him because both had
come from a large family with mostly brothers who, if
they had been called because their sisters were in
trouble, Bobby and everyone else knew that if their
brothers caught him messing with their sisters there
would be hell to pay. Bobby's face contorted, his
mouth curled up at the corners and his eyebrows almost
came together making him look like he was going to

tear them apart as he told the one girl to get the hell out of his way. She stepped aside then started running back toward the building. She looked back and screamed, "We'll see how bad yu are when my brothers git yo ass.

He screamed back, "Tell em to be packin when-nay come." I felt really sorry for her but there was nothing that I could do. If everyone could have jumped him, she may have had a chance, but with just us trying to fight him would have been a death wish coming true. When I didn't think that it could get any worse, we turned in the direction of the laughter and saw Tommy and his gang walking towards us. GOD, I hated this place! Somewhere along the line Tommy had picked up some new recruits. I didn't recognize any of the new ones. As Tommy got closer, he looked at me. Then he looked through me as though I wasn't there. I don't know why I thought that by him seeing me that it would change. When I looked into his eyes I could see that same evil look, the one he had when he let his gang rape Deidra, but he was going to participate in this one and the grin on his face showed that he was going to enjoy every minute of it. Tommy didn't bother to speak, he told Bobby to go about his business before they made *him* their business. Bobby started to mumble but did as he was told and turned around and walked away.

Tommy looked directly at me and yelled, "Erbody get the fuck out of here!" Everyone who had been standing there started running away; I just stood there looking at him. He put his face so close to mine that I could smell the alcohol on his breath.

"Dat goes fo yu too yella girl, don't even think that yu can stop dis. I ain't hit yu yet but dat don't mean I won't so I'm tell in yu fo the lass time, go!"

As I backed up I saw that one of Tommy's gang had pushed the lady hard against her chest. By the time I had gotten to the playground I heard a scream. As I looked back they were dragging her across the grass by her hair. They had already taken off her coat. All of us who had been playing ball slowly came together. Some had their hands over their mouths others were crying as the lady started screaming for someone to help her. Most of the girls put their heads down and covered their ears. I didn't do either, covering my ears wasn't going to drown out her cries, it wasn't going to stop the creepiness and disgust because we all knew what was going to happen. I had grown numb to it, the screams, the begging sounds of the other girls when their boyfriends had beaten them, I put all of her cries in a bag and in my mind I put that bag behind a door and quickly closed it so that I could silence it, and keep my imagination from running away with it. Even in doing this, I couldn't stop the tears from welling up in my eyes. We all watched as they dragged her into the stairway and that was it. Brenda, Deborah and I sat on the ground by the outside of the playground for hours before we saw them drag her out. We stayed where we could see what was going to happen next. Even at a distance we could see that she was a mess. There didn't seem to be a place on her body that wasn't bloodied and she didn't seem to be moving. From what we could see as they dragged her from the stairwell, was that they had cut off her braids, her glasses were gone and although none of us wanted to say anything out loud about it we were sure that each and every one of them had raped her. They dragged her to the curb and tied her with a clothes line to the light pole. Then they left her there, laughing and pointing at her as they walked back to the building. Cisco hollered out, "That's what we do to honkey women!" and again the gang started laughing. They had tied her where she was facing the street.

We all watched but stayed hidden for what seemed like forever wondering if they had tied her to the pole using her as bait to rob anyone who tried to stop to help her. Cars went by; some even slowed down but wouldn't stop. We didn't know why no one tried; maybe they knew the game or just didn't want to get involved. Maybe the driver wasn't paying attention and had missed seeing her tied to the pole. There were so many reasons there could have been for the reason that no one had stopped. The ropes were the only thing holding her body up. She just held her head down. A bus went by; as we watch I kept thinking to myself why didn't any of the passengers say anything to make the bus driver stop?

If the bus driver had stopped the bus, it would allow Tommy and his gang to get on, rob and possibly kill all of the white people have be long gone before the police would have been able to get there. Even if they got there, once the gang ran in the building there would be nothing that they could do. The six of us who decided to take the dare and go and untie her.

Slowly we walked over to the pole where she had been tied; some of the girls watched to be able to warn us just in case Tommy his gang or Bobby decided to return, they never did.

One of the girls named Andrea took off her outer shirt and wrapped it around her; the rest of us did the same because she had been left with only her bra on. Jackie ran back and told us she had called the police. Shortly afterwards she came running back and shaking her head as she told us what had happened when she called. She had her hands resting on her knees, trying to catch her breath from having run so hard. She told us that after she told the police what had happened the police said, "Yeah, sure," and hung up on her.

Brenda said, "You know they weren't going to believe you. You should have said that the gangs were holding up a bus and robbing everyone or that the bus had been pulled over and you heard gun shots." "You know they weren't going to believe that there was a white woman tied to a pole near the projects. Everyone knew not to come around here, but we'll get them here somehow." Andrea said, "And I know just how we gonna do it!" Once she told us what her plan was we all looked at her and said, "Have you lost your damn mind?" Sheila repeated what Andrea had suggested. "You want us stand in front of a moving bus with a white bus driver driving it. " Shit this ain't no peace rally for Dr. Martin Luther King! He'll try to run all of our asses over just for the hell of it!" Andrea looked really angry as she said, "Look yall, she came all the way over here giving us leaflets about God. Tommy and the rest of um tried to kill her. The Least we can do, or try to do is show people that we ain't all animals." As dangerous as it sounded Andrea's point struck home in all of us. She said, "If you don't believe in someone telling us about GOD then you ain't nothing no way.

She must have believed that not all of us were dat bad or she wood-na came. She had to been told what kind of area dis was. She had to, but she believed she could do it and we wud take it an read it. Just cause Tommy did what he did don't mean dat we don't believe an are like dat. Why do we go- ta church den?" I think GOD gonna help us." It wasn't the believing in God that I had a problem with, we all believed in Him. Question was, was I willing to die for someone like he did for us. For the first time, I wasn't that secure in my faith but if the others were willing to do it, then so was I. I had been talking about dying and wanting to die for a long time now. So now was the time for me to see if God had really been there when I needed him. If not, well... I'd be eating my breakfast with him the next morning.

We untied the hippy lady and laid her on the ground while Saundra stood in the street looking for a bus to come our way. Her face was a bloody mess where they had hit her so many times in her eyes they were swollen shut, her lips were swollen and bleeding, they had wacked off her hair which was uneven almost down to her ear. And she was bleeding a lot between her legs; there was no guessing why on that. Finally Saundra said, "I see one! Ones commin! Okay now everybody get ready, One, Two Three! As the bus came close to our stop, we all ran out into the street and waved our hands to get the bus to stop. For a moment, I really thought that God was going to grant my wish to die and it was going to come true soon because the bus didn't look like it was slowing down. Just as the bus got to where we could see the driver's face through the windshield, I thought to myself, "This is it" and closed my eyes and waited. At least it would be quick at the rate that the bus was coming. The bus tires screeched, the bus did a short rocking motion before coming to a full stop. The bus driver opened the doors and stepped out screaming at us, "What kind of game are you niggers playing? You almost got me, my passengers and yourselves killed!" As he continued to scream Andrea, Jackie, Brenda and I carried the hippy lady's body up on the bus.
The bus driver took one look at her and said, "Good Lord." He immediately went to his seat and phoned the police for help. The passengers who were sitting on the long seat that was up in front got up quickly, leaving the whole seat empty so that we had room to lay her down on. One white woman that was sitting behind us in the next seat shouted, "Look at what they did! They're nothing but animals. They need to stay locked up in those cages."

Suddenly from the back of the bus a voice rang out and a black man seated next to three others screamed, "Did you fo git that we on this motha fucka? If day had done nat to-a day damn sho wouldn't have risked they life tri-in to flag dis bus down. If it

waddunt fo that honkey, he would of ran all of day
asses ova, so be glad dat dey did what dey did." Now
yu betta shut up fo We really git mad back hea and
tare dis motha fucka up!" The bus went completely
silent. Thank God for those brothers! One of the other
men in the back shouted to us, "Yall did a good job
God gone bless shall." Five minutes later there were
police cars and an ambulance surrounding the bus.
Another police car had driven north to the next block
to stop the traffic from coming towards us. He
redirected traffic in the other direction. As we got
off the bus the police didn't say anything to us. It
was Jackie who spoke up. "It wouldn't of took so long
if yall had listened to me when I first called yall, I
told yall that it was a white woman over here and she
was hurt and needed help but what did yall do? Yall
hung up the phone in my face so don't act like we
didn't try. And if we are animals we would-na tried to
git huh some help."

Then Jackie just walked away. One policeman
stopped and looked at Jackie and just stared at her as
she walked away. Could he have thought for just one
minute that she was right? We would never know because
he turned his attention back to the ambulance drivers.
As they were putting the hippy lady into the ambulance
we stood by the door. All of us had tears in our eyes.
As the ambulance driver started to push the stretcher
into the ambulance the hippy lady put her arm out to
stop him, she put out her hand and we all walked over
to hold it, we held her hand and arm together. She
whispered again to us, "God loves you and so do I."
The ambulance drivers pushed her inside both giving us
dirty looks as one went to the driver's seat and the
other got into the back with her. The driver turned
the siren on sped away. After the ambulance was gone
and the bus driver had finished talking to the police,
he gave us one last hateful look as he closed the
doors and sped away. Their world and ours when they
met and collide it was always in an ugly fashion.
You'd think that the bus driver would have thanked us
but he never did. In their world, the white world,
that's how it we were seen, as animals. And that act
of violence against a lost white woman made the
headline for the next day's news. It was spoken about
all day on the television and was on the radios too.
The newsmen had a field day with it reinforcing how
inhumane, even the poorest and poverty stricken blacks

could be even when they were unprovoked. They let some whites voice their opinion as far as what had happened. Everyone that was interviewed voiced how outraged they were. People who spoke kept saying that Blacks and Whites would never be able to mix. Nothing was going to stop the hatred between the two because we, the Blacks weren't willing to try. The hippy lady's incident was used in every example. There was no follow up to the hippy lady's status or the extent of her injuries. As the six of us sat talking about it some days later we all wanted to tell her how sorry we were and that everyone was not like that, we had tried our best to help her and we all hoped that she would be okay. For us that thought would probably be of little consequence. As our world collided, theirs with discrimination, for the hippy lady, ours was with determination to get her help, we saved her. We reached across the gap, held her hand... and touched.

Chapter Sixty-One-Senior Year

From the beginning of my freshman year up to and including my senior year, I had experienced prejudice up close by the people who lived around me. In school as freshmen everyone was teased and picked on just for being freshmen-not just me. There were teachers who made little jokes about how the majority of poor Black people were unwilling to learn because they could use the excuse that they had been trying to get a job and couldn't afford to look for work and come to school at the same time. After having been turned down once or twice they gave up knowing that the government would take care of them. Which we all knew was not true. They would say Black people would use this example for every situation, and would take their anger out on the whites who tried to help them as well as outside of it. Citing the cases of the good humor man and the hippy lady to try and prove that their case true. But nothing about those same poor blacks who tried to save her. What they did was relied on what was said by the media, their friends and anyone else who had those same opinions about us and because of it they had carried their own prejudices and the stereotypes back to their friends, neighbors and others that they knew to add fuel to the fire. They were just as bad if not worse. No one in class would ever say anything, especially about what happened to the good humor man and why it happened because we had come so far to get where we were in school. The last thing any of us wanted to do was to get into a debate with a teacher who could determine if you would pass their class, one which would be needed to graduate? That was the ugly part.

Disagreeing with a teacher could now be considered inappropriate behavior and that was enough to get you thrown out of the class and when that happened that was it. There would be no walking across the stage. That student would get the opportunity to go to summer school and then get their diploma. But it wasn't the same. As a teen when you graduated and walked across the stage you wanted your family, friends, and anyone else to take pictures and clap because you had made it. You had proven them wrong. Even with their discrimination and what they said, putting all of the blacks in one box, those who were good as well as those who were bad But there was no deterring those who were smart and capable of passing and meeting those standards that put before us. With that same determination We made it.

It seemed like only a few would get straight A's or B's no matter how hard we tried. I'm sure that there were other students in the school who did get those A's and B's in school. There may have been other students who were treated completely different by teachers and counselors. Those teachers and counselors might have even shown them compassion. But a few were better than none. But for the record There were **Many**.

As you are reading this please understand I am only referring to what *I experienced.* As school went on everyone noticed that things started changing. The regular teacher for a certain class became absent more often and was replaced with a substitute teacher who was Black. It happened slowly at first. Then it seemed that in the months that followed I started to notice more Black teachers than Whites for the junior and senior classes.

After being in school for what seemed like forever, it came time for the seniors to go to the counselor's office so that he could evaluate their grades to try to give ideas and how to inspire us in ways that would help to help us to reach our goals. In the hall by the counselor's office, sat six to eight chairs for students who were there waiting to see him. The counselors were still white. When my name was called I got up and slowly walked into his office. Without looking at me he told me to sit down. Not to have a seat, but that was okay with me. He was looking at a sheet that had my grades printed on it. I was worried, because I wasn't an A student but I did have a good portion of A's and B's I had one C but no D's or F's. The counselor looked through his books and kept saying, "umm" as he did so. He picked up a book whose title I glimpsed was called, "College Careers". He looked at it for a few seconds before closing it back and putting it at the other end of his desk. He crossed his arms and laid them on his desk before proceeding to commend me for the effort that I had put forth to achieve my grades. Then he said, "Well I have some good news and some bad news." Hearing him say how well that I had done had made me flash a big smile and I felt butterflies inside of my stomach. Then he said,

"Now comes the bad news. I don't see any college that would match your grade point average <u>BUT</u>! There are positions where you would be phenomenal, like a supervisor for the cafeteria or even the head of a maintenance department; just maybe you could be a teacher's aide. They're their own bosses now days and they make good money too." Then he winked his eye at me saying, "I'll see what I can do." He put my papers down onto a pile that was also at the same end of his desk as the college books were. He started to shuffle some papers excusing me and without looking, he asked me to call in the next student. When he looked up he realized that although I had stood up I was still standing in front of him. I remembered using my arms to lean on his desk to put myself closer to him.

My tears dropped on some papers that he had on his desk and made the ink smear. He dared not try to move because; he didn't know what would come next. He wasn't smiling anymore. No he had a very, very angry animal leaning over him as he sat at his desk and he didn't know what to do. He didn't know what I was going to do and for a split second neither did I. We locked eyes I never shifted my gaze. I was so mad and full of rage that I really couldn't see him anymore. I screamed, "I wanted to become a Doctor! A Nurse! A Teacher or maybe even have *YOUR* job! My grandmother is a maid she's a good one, better then you could *EVER BE!* And you know what? *SHE NEVER EVEN WENT TO SCHOOL!* For a moment he looked surprised as though he couldn't understand why I was acting so ungrateful!

Then he slowly stood up and eased towards the door. I was only trying to help you, you people are so ungrateful! As he got to the door and had it open, he turned and glanced quickly at me over his glasses and said, "My job? I don't think so." After he was in the safety of the hall he told the other students that he would reschedule them for another day. Everyone was already talking about the conversation inside. The window to the door was so thin that you could hear a pin drop inside anyway.

I came out of his office and I slammed the door with as much force as I could, hoping the glass on top of the door would go crashing to the floor. I walked down the hall and tried not to blink so my tears wouldn't fall, so no one would know that I had been crying. I walked as fast as I could to get my books out of my locker for my next class, but not before making a quick stop to the girl's bathroom to put some cold water on my face. After drying my face I went to my next class. While I was in the bathroom a lot of girls were already inside, laughing, doing their hair and using the bathroom. As I came in they all gathered around me handing me Kleenex. A lot of them put their arms around me and kept asking me what was wrong. That's what was good about being at Dusable, people would always try to help you, especially if you were crying or sick they didn't even know me but it seemed that everyone in there was offering me what they could. After wiping my face as I tried to run up they shouted if They could do anything, each shouted their name and told me what class they were going to be in and to come and they would help me. If I had told them what the counselor had said to me they probably would have gotten together, cornered him somewhere and beat him to death. There were so many spaces there in the building they could have gotten him and no one would have known. He had no idea how lucky he really was. I never told anyone what the counselor had said to me, not how he had humiliated me, but how he had also insulted me. I had worked my butt off to get those grades good ones considering what my life was like at home. After school, at home, I lay across my bed and cried so much that I almost made myself sick. I never forgot what he had said to me and I never forgot what I had said to him, in fact I never ever forgot him.

\#   \#   \#

Fast Forward: Twenty Years

After I became an adult and received a degree, I still remembered what he had said to me. How I wished that I could have placed Nurses Aid certificate, my License practical Nursing, my Associate degree, my Bachelor's degree, and finally my Master degree I wished that I could have put them all on his desk to show him what I had thought of his suggestion to become a housekeeping supervisor. But I'm sure he had retired or had died long ago. But I had stood up to his challenge and had won. Instead of making me weaker it gave me something to work harder for. For myself and because of him.

\#   \#   \#

A couple of weeks later my grandmother asked my mother if I could come over and spend the weekend with her since She lived alone I wanted to go to keep her company. With my mother's permission I would make the long walk over to her house. When I would visit she would always cook enough food to it feed an army. My favorite was her macaroni and cheese, fried chicken, chicken salad. For dessert she would make a lemon meringue pie which she made from scratch. I ate so much that when I finished the only thing I could do afterwards was lie on my back and groan. She would lean on the door with her arms folded and with a big smile say, "I told you not to eat so much, you little pig!" I would roll on my side and say, "Granny, please don't make me laugh again it hurts my stomach too much." Then she would look at me and we would both break up with laughter.

One weekend when I was over visiting my grandmother, my older cousin who was from Memphis, Tennessee was there. To all of my family and relatives in our eyes we saw her as being very privileged. She wore clothes that looked like they had been made just for her and it made her look just that much classier. She was attending college at the time to become a teacher. When she came into town she would sometimes stay with my grandmother. She went out that night but came back earlier than I had expected. I asked her if I could talk to her about some things that had happened to me at school. She said, "Sure just let me change my clothes and then we can discuss it". I waited anxiously for her, spreading my papers for her to look at on the bed in an orderly fashion. Finally, she came into the room wearing her robe and sat down next to me. I showed her my report card then I told her what the counselor's suggestion were regarding what my job outlook should be after my graduation. She shook her head as she told me that things were not that different from what I was going through at the college that she was attending. She suggested that I take my papers to the principal and inform him of what was said by him. I nodded my head while she spoke but my mind had already left the conversation. That conversation was never going to take place but I told her that I would think about it first, and then make an appointment with him to tell what had happened. She kissed my head like she always had since I had been a

269

little girl pulled up the covers on me and turned out the lights. Well, that went well.

I lay on my side quietly thinking *Yeah, Right* go to the principal. This wasn't Memphis; this was Chicago and she lived in a house, not in the projects. I think that in her heart she thought that the principal would do something. It would have been a total waste of time. I had asked her for her opinion and she had given it to me so I couldn't be angry with her. Although useless she had given me an answer, but she told me something that I would always remember. This was to never give up. No matter what the situation was. *NEVER GIVE UP.* I had heard it only once and the explanation of what it meant. After hearing it I never thought much about it. Or that it would ever apply to me. Now I knew what low self-esteem was. I hated that word. I knew what it meant and how it made me feel. It was happening to me. It hurt deep down in my gut. It was much worse than a punch or kick to the gut. If It hurt me that bad, I couldn't imagine how other people had dealt with it. Just those three little words had made me feel like I would never amount to anything, and that I wasn't worth anyone's time. My counselor had basically said that I was nothing. And that there was no reason to set my sights on going to college. I didn't know if what he said would come true. But despite what he had said I had other plans and they had nothing to do with what he had suggested.

When it was time for graduation we wore our caps and gowns proudly as we walked across the stage. We shook hands with the principal, putting the tassel from one side to the other as we received our diplomas. The entire faculty was there. As I stood waiting for my turn to walk across the stage I looked over to where the teachers stood and found my counselor. The more students that crossed the stage, the angrier the look that he wore became. As soon as I received my diploma and had placed my tassel on the other side I looked in his direction pointed my diploma at him and gave the biggest smile that I could, just for him. Noone even paid any attention. Everyone's eyes were on their own friends and relatives who were also walking across the stage. But he saw me and he saw what I did. He saw that I had graduated to prove him wrong. I knew that he had seen me pointing my diploma towards him because after I did it I saw him leave the auditorium, slamming the doors behind him as he left.

He didn't break me I had won! I didn't have poor self-esteem; I had anything but that. That was for the weak! It was too bad that he didn't know me very well. That night after everything was over and I lay in bed holding my graduation cap I thought to myself, I still have more diplomas to earn, and more colleges to go to earn them!

The next evening I saw one of Tommy's gang members, Cisco. I asked him if he was in the building. Cisco said, "Naw he at Renee graduation want me to tell him somum?

"Yes, just tell him that I asked about him."

"Yeah okay."

So Tommy was still with Renee. Could it be that Mr. I don't love no woman have forgotten what he had told me? It had been over a year since he had started seeing Renee. Since he had been gone I never saw Deidra outside. She didn't even hang out near the benches or at the back of the breezeway. I guess she was biding her time and waiting patiently for him to come back to her. He had not tried to get in contact with me to meet with him to read for almost four months. I wondered if he had ever told Renee that there had been a time when he couldn't read well. Na, Tommy had too much pride for that; He would never let her know that. I hoped that was the case but I doubted it. He had just been having so much fun with Renee that he had let the time slip by. They say, Time flies when you're having fun. The last time that I had seen Tommy he was having the time of his life!

Chapter Sixty-Two: The Fight of My Life

Summertime! Freedom! I had graduated and I didn't have to go back. I didn't have to listen to pieces of Black history; I could go to the Library on my own and read about what the Black teachers in my school couldn't talk about and what the white teachers didn't want us to learn about. The one sad thing was that Brenda and her family had gone away for the weekend. Before she left she said, "I'll be back before you know it!" So there I was counting the days while playing softball with the other girls who came down from their floors and played when there was nothing else to do.

I had started dating one of Jean's brothers but never felt the way that I had about Mark. I also spent time hanging out with her sister Diane, who wasn't in the gang and had told me long ago when I first met her that she didn't want to have anything to do with them. She had gone to school. She had graduated and walked across the stage of my graduation class. As I was walking half way over to her building, I heard someone call me. I looked across the street and there were Bay-Bay and her girls. They stopped walking and she motioned for me to come across the street. After getting over to the other side to see what they wanted looking at them I could see the tiredness from taking care of their babies and what the constant drinking was doing to their faces. Bay-Bay spoke first, "Hey girl, where you been, we ain't seen you since the git together. Where's yo friend? why ain't she with you?"

"She's gone for the weekend. What's up? I was just on my way to your house Jean to see if your sister was at home." Everyone started looking at Jean because she hadn't told them that I came over to her house every now and then to shoot the breeze with her sister. Jean looked at them while hunching her shoulders to look as if she didn't know. Sweet looked like she wanted to eat Jean up on the spot.

Sweet told Jean, "We'll discuss this later." Jean turned her head as if she didn't want the others to know that I was associating with anyone in her house.

Carolyn spoke, "Oh we didn't tell you, we got a part-time girlfriend named Kathy here, she's visiting her cousin Patricia that lives on the Jean's floor." Kathy said "Hey! You the one they call Yella Girl?

"Yeah, but I don't like being called that, I'd rather be called by my name." Bay-Bay nudged Kathy who glanced back at her then quickly back at me.

"Okay, cool I don't want to start no problems on the first day that I'm here."

I gave her a sarcastic look, "What you want to wait till you've been here awhile?"

All of Bay-Bay's girls started laughing. Everyone was laughing except Kathy. I had a feeling that they had already told her about me and in knowing that she didn't like me from the moment that she laid eyes on me. I started thinking, there's gonna be more to this than I thought. When she spoke I was looking at her. She had her hair pulled up tight with an afro puff attached to it at the top. One of her front teeth was missing which gave her a real bad looking mouth. She wore her short sleeved blouse with the buttons opened where you could see a part of her breast. Her blouse had pockets and I could see her pack of Kools sticking half way out. She also had on a pair of short, very tight cutoff jeans. She wore slouch socks and gym shoes called "Keds" which were worn by just about everyone, both boys and girls. She looked like a gang-banger and before I could ask she immediately told me that she was from the Westside. People from the Westside were said to be tougher than people who lived on the Southside. But that was a point that was always debatable depending on where you lived.

Bay-Bay said, "We going up to the drug store to git some smokes and maybe some beer. Wanna hang out?"

"Naw, I'm good."

"Okay we'll smell you later." They started to walk across the gravel in the direction of the drug store. As I watched them walk away, a thought came to my mind. *Here's your next fight.* I shrugged it off and went back to sitting on a bench to think instead of now going to visit. I didn't even know her but just the way that she had looked at me and the feeling in the pit of my stomach told me that I was going to get to know her very well and; very soon.

I got bored and went upstairs to get cleaned up for dinner. Later I watched a little television, took a bath and called it a night. It was late. Everyone in my house was asleep but I couldn't all I found myself doing was tossing and turning so I got out of bed and lay on the couch by the window. The light from the

television usually made it easier for me to go to
sleep. Just as I had dozed off there came a tapping at
my window. It didn't startle me because I had gotten
used to Tommy sending for me that way. I stepped into
my house shoes and followed his gang member. Crap! I
thought this was over since he was with Renee. When we
got to the sixteenth floor I knocked on the laundry
room door, he kept saying, "Hurry up! Hurry up an come
in!" Once I came inside he kept telling me to hurry
up and sit down was flashing a huge grin. He said "com
ere I got some-um to sho yu." I walked over and from
the back of his pocket he pulled out his own library
card. I looked at him and told him that I was proud of
him. Then I looked at the name on it and it wasn't
his. "Who does this belong to?"

"Don't worry bout that, I plan to git something
in a week and I- ma git you really surprised. My boy
gone give you a note when I'm ready. I just want to
let yu know what yu gonna see an he-a." He was
grinning like a schoolboy. His gang member walked me
back to my house. I didn't care how good he had gotten
I still hated him for the things that he had done.

Brenda and her family came back a day earlier. I
had seen them get onto the elevator so I ran up the
stairs to meet her. I made it up there just as the
elevator opened. As soon as Brenda's mother saw me she
said, "Brenda can't come out for a few days okay hon?"
I looked at her then at Brenda She spoke silently as
she stood behind her mother as she put her pinkie and
thumb, next to her ear to let me know me know that
she would call me later. I half smiled, nodded and
walked up the stairs to my house. Later that night
when she called me I asked her what had happened. She
laughed and told me that she and one of her uppity
cousins had gotten into an argument, which turned into
a fight and the fight had almost turned into a family
square off. Then she asked me what I had been up to. I
told her about seeing Bay-Bay and her new recruit.
What the new girl looked like and what she said to me.
"Sounds like they trying to give you a heads up on
your next opponent. We'll keep an eye out. Call me and
let me know when you get off of lockdown."

"Will do." We both laughed as we hung up the
phones. Brenda was still on punishment so I had
started to visit Jean's brother. We had been dating
and become an item. I stayed at their house for a
while then I went back to my building. Although I knew

274

more people now than I did before. Even though my building was facing theirs for some reason I just didn't feel comfortable when I was over there. A couple of days later I was going to walk to the drug store to get myself a pack of cigarettes because Brenda was still on lock down. Half way across the school yard going in the same direction that I was were Bay-Bay and her girls again they were on their way to the same store that I was. I was going for cigarettes; they said that they were going for alcohol and cigarettes.

It was the usual light weight talk as we walked the two blocks from State Street to Michigan Avenue. Once we got there I bought my pack of Kools, they bought Kools and a half pint of White Port. Kathy told them it was her treat and paid for their purchase. I thought to myself, no wonder they were so tight with her. And I didn't know that Jean had introduced Kathy to Carlos until later.

I listened from a short distance as she repeatedly mentioned to them how she was such a great fighter in her gang. And she constantly bragged about her affiliation. She impressed them all by using profanity that I don't think that any of us had heard used before. On this particular day she had just worn her Ked sneakers without any socks to show her tattoo, a cross that she had on her ankle. Bay-Bay had one but hers was not as large as Kathy's. They all fussed over her hair, her clothes and the way she cursed. I wasn't impressed and said very little. I thought that she had a foul mouth and couldn't think of any situation where I would want to use the type of language that she did. I wasn't an angel, far from it, but I didn't feel the need to do and say what she did to make friends or to impress anyone. Then again maybe she wasn't trying to impress them. Maybe for her it was who she was and how she really talked. Bay-Bay and her girls just thought that she was the shit.

Kathy paid for their purchase it was when she reached for the bag that I noticed the initials C.W on the topside of her hand. Bay-Bay and her girls had the type of tattoo with their ex-boyfriends initials like she had on their wrists. The ones on their wrist weren't real like the one that Kathy wore on her ankle. The way that Bay-Bay and her girls made their tattoos were by taking the eraser from a pencil and continuously going over on their skin for the initials they were trying to make, and after doing this over and over it would rub the skin away. After a scab had formed they would pick it off and the initials were there. It gave the look the look that it was homemade, one could tell that it hadn't been done by a professional person.. Jean's sister had told me that Kathy's last name was Lloyd. Without thinking I asked her who the initials that she was wearing belonged to. I don't know why I asked her, I guess I was just curious. Since she was from the Westside, since I didn't know anyone from there I didn't think that it would matter. She laughed and put her wrist close to my face.

"It's Jean's brother." Then she pointed to Jean and started laughing. Jean's eyes grew large as she looked at me. "I ain't in it, I own know nothing bout it!"

"You're lying again Jean and you know it. Why didn't you tell her?"

Kathy said, "Tell me what?"

"That I was going out with C.W!

Kathy interrupted as I spoke, "You mean, **was** goin outwit- em, **was** means past tense!" I lunged past Bay-Bay and grabbed her blouse. Her buttons popped off and scattered on the floor. The gang separated us to keep us from fighting. Some of them walked in front with her, the others stayed behind, walking beside me. That's the way we walked all the way back to the building. No one smoked; no one said a word.

I was going to tell him that he had been busted. As I got into the playground Kathy caught a glimpse of her male cousin. She turned around and immediately started to dared me to come closer, then started threatening me and then telling me all of the things that they had done together. I put my middle finger up and said what it meant out loud. Then I told her, "I don't need this shit! You can have him! I'm outta here!" and turned around and started walking back to my building. That's when I heard Carolyn say, "Don't hit her Kat just let her walk away." By the time I heard Carolyn say it; I was already feeling the punch from Kathy directly into the middle of my back. It was so hard that it pushed me forward, but not hard enough to make me fall. Now it was on. Back again into the old mode, the one that Tommy had taught me except now I didn't have the time to drop my hands down and take the deep breath to ready myself as I had been able to

276

so many times before. She kept motioning me to come to the playground and It I had to get her there then that's exactly what I was going to do.

I could see people running from everywhere towards what had become a large circle. "Damn it! Does this ever stop? Here I go again and I know that Bay-Bay had set it up." Now we were in the middle of the playground, it had started to look like an arena. I took my stance, closed my hands slowly and made both into fists. I had one up to guard my face but then noticed that Kathy had also done the same, stance and all. This was going to be ugly. The crowd got so large that it started moving us toward the chain link fence. I threw the first punch it met its target but she came up much faster than I thought. When she came up she was smiling. It seemed to be something that she was used to and had been wanting ever since she had met me. Bay-Bay and her girls had blended themselves into the back of the crowd leaving Jean in the front to fend for herself.

I didn't see Jean but one of the girls from my building knew her she was holding her by the arms. I didn't even know who she was but I was grateful for it.

We had been moved by the crowd to the other side of the playground; to the side where we usually played softball. I saw Kathy as she made the fist and threw the punch toward my face. I pulled back my hand to make a fist but as I pulled my hand back before making the fist and then my fingernail got caught in the cross wire at the top of the fence. I pulled so hard to return the punch that my finger got caught in the cross wires it ripped off my whole fingernail from my finger. I glanced back quickly at the fence and saw my fingernail hanging from the top of it but there was nothing that I could do. I didn't feel any pain but moved my body and was able to push the crowd back just enough for me to be able to hit her in the jaw. Her head went to the left and I followed through by bringing up my right fist, another hit to her face and a hit to the stomach. She went down on both knees but got up on her feet slower; I kicked her in the mouth and saw that she was wearing a set of false teeth from the bottom of her mouth and sent them flying out of her mouth on the ground! The crowd screamed in laughter pointing and teasing her.

Tommy had taught me how to stay out of arms

reach and then to move in and jab. I did it and as she lost her balance and fell down. She leaned on one knee to get up but when she did, I saw her pull something from her waistband in the back of her jeans. Before I could move back the crowd pushed her towards me and I couldn't dodge her or step back. I only saw a glimpse of it as she swung her arm towards me. It happened so fast and quick that it only felt like a paper cut. It started to sting and I saw the blood on my shirt and continued to flow. I saw what she had used. We called them "razor backs" but men who went to the barbershop called them "straight razors." The cut from the razor side starting behind my ear and angled itself a couple inches from my jaw bone. The adrenalin burst from seeing so much blood all over me made me forget about what Tommy had taught me. Now all I could think of was getting this over with.

If what I saw worked for Shannon, when she had fought Tommy then I knew it could work for me. I had seen up close and had seen every move that she made when she hit him. I moved in and used it. Right punch, left punch then another right to set her up and the fourth punch to take her out. It worked perfectly. It always did. The fight was over and I was totally spent. Kathy was stretched out on the ground. Out cold.

Chapter -Sixty-Three: The Set Up

Out of nowhere came the sound of breaking glass. Bottles were being thrown from the porches from different floors of her building that Jean lived in and I was trapped in the middle of the circle! Kathy's cousin and some other boys had come to help carry her away from the playground. There were so many people that I couldn't see above them. I kept looking for Brenda couldn't see her face in the crowd, not that she would have been able to get to me anyway, and the crowd was so tight. As the bottles and whatever that could break kept being thrown down, people started running away. I bottle was thrown and broke right next to me. I looked up, instead I saw a large chain being swung in the air like those were on TV when they lassoed the horses. The chain was coming directly toward my face and just as it was about to hit me, a large dark skinned, muscular arm reached up and the chain wrapped itself around it. I tried to duck. The chain wrapped around the arm. It was Tommy's! The chain made a blowing, swooshing type sound as it went around his arm. Had it wrapped itself around my neck, when snatched back it would have taken my head off. Thank you Lord! I didn't even know that Tommy or his gang was there, or how long, but here he was and he had saved my skin again. Then someone screamed, "Look out! Somebody threw a bat!" I ducked and covered my head. Tommy ducked too and the bat missed us but it did hit one girl in the face and knocked her out cold. Her whole face was covered in blood. Someone ran through the crowd, picked her up and carried her out of the playground. Tommy put his fingers in his mouth and whistled. Its sound was long, loud and sharp, a sound that signaled every gang member that there was trouble. It was returned by other whistles to let him know that he had been heard and was on their way. Some of Tommy's boys were already there with him as he was watching me fight; the returning whistles let him know that his signal had been heard and that they were on their way. As I stooped down, I turned to saw boys coming out of the stairwell in Jean's building and the same was happening from mine. It all happened so fast. Once they met in the playground everyone started fighting. Tommy yelled at me, "Run girl" and before he could turn his head back he was sucker punched by a boy that was standing next to him; it didn't faze him.

I looked at him but I couldn't move. Still squatting down trying to cover my head, I looked around and tried to understand how my fight with Kathy had turned out the way that it did. I knew the first time I threw that punch at Kathy had been a stupid move. Not that I felt wrong for protecting myself, but there was no reason or to justify what was happening now. A fight had started over a stupid boy that had cheated on me, who I didn't like enough to fight over and definitely not enough for it to cause this. I heard a popping sound, a familiar sound. Someone had started shooting. Behind that came a series of sounds, POW! POW, POW, POW, POW! All in a rapid succession.

Everyone knew when those sounds started things didn't end well and started running for their lives. I wasn't trying to think about where the shots were coming from. The echoes from the shots made it sound like they were coming from everywhere and they were all coming down like rain into the playground. It had to be from Oswald's gang there was no one else. Then I knew it wasn't about me it had been a set-up to catch Tommy and his gang out in the open. The fight, my fight had given Oswald's gang the opportunity to make it happen. Tommy had come to help me. I heard a louder, closer shot; it went right over my head but the bullet went straight into Tommy's. I was standing right next to him.

I saw his eyes open wide; He looked over at me as his mouth parted slightly, he fell to the ground in what seemed to take forever to me in slow motion. As I bent down and held his head in my hands I could see the neat round hole in his forehead. Then I heard another of his boys scream out, "Oh Shit"! The knees of his pants seemed to blow apart. He fell to the ground as the blood spewed from the holes in his pants. There was the sound of another shot, he grabbed his chest and he lay on the ground. Still. One of the gang members who were closest to the entrance of the playground was trying to crawl out as a gunshot stopped him cold.

As shots from the other building continued, I saw four more of Tommy's gang fall and lay still. Two members from the other building walked right into the playground holding shot guns, walked right up to two of Tommy's gang members and shot them point blank. Every one of Tommy's gang-members who was in the playground was being hunted down and killed. Two of

Tommy's gang, Andrew and Roy, was kneeling near the
monkey bars; as soon as they pulled their guns from
the waistband of their pants they were shot. NO one
had had a chance because in the playground there was
nowhere for Tommy or his gang to hide. They were being
hunted down like ducks in a barrel. Cisco ran into the
playground shooting wildly he was shot so many times
that he seemed to dance like a puppet before falling
down. Dead. I heard T-Bone holler from the bottom of
the stairs telling Tommy that he was coming but the
people from the building held him and Emmett everyone
knew that neither of them would have a chance as soon
as they stepped into the playground. After Tommy and
the majority of his gang had been cut down by the
gunfire the shooting stopped. Their dead bodies lay in
the playground were they had been shot. With Tommy,
there were twelve in all.

Chapter Sixty-Four: Death in the Playground

I sat there holding Tommy's head in my lap; I waited for the shot that would take me with Tommy. I closed my eyes and hoped that my death would be like the rest who lay dead in the playground, quick and painless. I kept waiting; after a moment I opened my eyes but my mind was still waiting for the shot that I knew would come. As I slowly looked around at the bodies I kept thinking that they might have been the last. No goodbyes to my family, no goodbyes to my friend Brenda, No being able to apologize for the things that I had done. Through tears, I thought that I saw something. So much had happened that I didn't believe what my eyes were seeing. In my mind I remember when I had been sitting on the porch listening to the two women who had talked about The Grim Reaper. They had said that if you can see the Reaper when he comes around and he sees you, then there was no reason to run. He would find you and take you. That's what he did. They said, he only took the souls of the dead.

My eyes had been the lens; my mind became the movie projector, taking frame by frame in slow motion zooming in to show a close up of the shock, surprise, pain, disbelief and the death of those who had fallen to the ground all around me. My mind recorded the bullets finding their marks and how the bodies had reacted to the intrusion of the bullet to their body. How the accuracy of a bullet found the face of Tommy and some others. Two young girls who were trying to run out of the playground were also struck down. Every sound stopped, I heard no words, I noticed no one, and my world and my mind went blank.

I wonder if Tommy saw Death when he walked into the playground. I wonder if any of his gang did, or if they even knew who or what the faceless form wearing the black hooded robe carrying the stick that had on the end of it had a curved blade. Like a character from a horror movie that maybe he or his gangmembers had seen. Only they were looking at but not knowing who they were looking at. I knew, it had been Death and he had sat in the playground, waiting patiently until it was his time. He knew that it was all over. I watched him walk slowly to each body and gently touch it with his scythe never stopping to look at who he touched. Then he came to where I sat holding Tommy's head. As he touched his arm with the scythe; I looked up at him and he looked down at me, walking slowly past me to continue to do the job that he was there to do. Then, the sound of what seemed to be a hundred police sirens started to come closer and closer. Someone put a bandana around my neck as a second pair of hands went under my arms and lifted me up, letting Tommy's head drop from my lap to the ground. I grabbed the package of Kools out of his rolled up sleeve. I guess I needed to have something to remember him by. As I was being half dragged, half carried away from the playground I kept looking at Death as he continued to make his rounds. I didn't bother to look at who was helping me. Then I saw him stop. He turned his body in my direction. We both knew that I had seen him.

I had held Tommy in the playground, he had plenty of opportunity to touch me with his scythe but he hadn't. Now he was facing me as I was being taken away. For a second, he didn't move he just looked in my direction and I kept watching him.

I wondered if he had been disappointed in having to let me go. Then again I didn't think so. He had collected more than enough souls that day and he didn't need to chase me. He would always know where to find me. That was his job. I knew that I would see him again one day. Suddenly I heard a voice scream, "Come on we gotta get out of here and we gotta do it now! The police are getting out of their cars and coming to the playground!"

I looked up; it was Brenda and her brother who were half carrying me to the building. We got to the fourth floor, but how I don't remember. As we looked through the fence I saw that Death had left with what he came for. We could see the police checking each of the bodies before putting them into body bags and placing them into the paddy wagons. I looked at my ring finger where the nail was torn off; it was bleeding all over my clothes. Brenda's mother took the bandana off of my neck and put her hand over her mouth. She and her son helped me into their house. She told him to put me on the couch while she made a call. Brenda and her brother sat down on the couch next to me, Brenda held a cold towel against my neck. Her brother held one on my finger. The ride that Brenda's mother had called for came and we were driven to the hospital. I sat on a gurney in one the emergency rooms. While waiting for the doctor I heard other people crying and screaming in pain. The killings happened in the projects, where I and others had lived. There were those who were in worse shape than I was. That was all I needed to know.

That's when it all came flooding back, but now things that I hadn't seen were all appearing as the pieces of a much larger picture and the picture became complete when it all ended. Sitting alone on that gurney I closed my eyes and allowed my mind to slow down as I started to put everything into a frame as though they were negatives from a camera although my subjects had been in color. I remembered taking one last look at the playground. Tommy and his gang had been set up. Right down to the fight with me. Kathy had been the key in the plan. It had been her job to find someone to fight and fortunately for her with everyone knowing about the fight with Bay-Bay's girls, I was the perfect one.

That's probably why they were in such a hurry to introduce us, their way of getting their revenge. With me, it was almost like a guarantee that Tommy and his gang would come to my rescue to make sure that if it was a girl's fight it would be fair. It had worked perfectly. Once Tommy and his gang were in the playground they became sitting ducks. Oswald had known people in Patricia's and Jean's building. I know that he knew Patricia's brother because I had seen them sitting on the side of the building smoking cigarettes and talking a couple of times, when I had played softball. I had seen her brother standing behind Kathy. It was after her having seen him that she started to call me out. At the time I didn't think anything of it. Tommy had killed Oswald.

The question that kept coming to my mind was why did Oswald's gang wait so long to go after them? There would be no answer to that question because only they knew. Kathy had been a decoy and didn't know it she could have been expendable if needed. Then again, I could have been wrong. It may have not been that at all. It may have been just a coincidence in the way that the shootings happened. The shooters were never identified. It was that way in all of the projects. This was no different. As I sat in the little room, I wanted to believe that no matter how bad Tommy was he would have taken a bullet sooner or later, and it had come sooner. I will always remember the bad things that he did in the past, but this time he died doing a good thing, trying to rescue me, not dying because he was involved in a gang fight. He had played chess with The Reaper for a long time. To the Reaper it was a game, it always was for those who somehow tried to outwit him. He had waited patiently and now it was time. He came and collected everyone with Tommy, including Tommy that day. The game was over. As always the Grim Reaper had won and now it was **check mate.**

Bright's mother had said, "You can't cheat death." Tommy had, for a long time, but today his time was up. After the doctor sewed me up, giving me ten stiches he told me how lucky I had been that day. He put iodine and something else on my finger and placed it on a splint before putting a bandage on it. He didn't ask me how I got hurt or what had happened and I felt no need to tell. The Doctor assumed that Brenda's mother was mine since she had brought me in. Brenda told me afterwards that the doctor told her mother that if the slash had been two millimeters more it would have cut into the main artery and she would have been making funeral arrangements for me. After returning to Brenda's house her mother told me what the doctor had told her. Brenda was crying and hugging me. I lost count of how many times she had said to me how glad she had been that I was alright. But I wasn't alright. What she was looking at was only the shell of who I was. On the inside, I was back in the playground. In my mind the scenes continued to play like a loop, going from the beginning to the end. Then it would start all over. Brenda and her mother held me and constantly told me that what had happened was not my fault. But they had not been there; they had not seen what I had seen. And I couldn't tell them about the Grim Reaper for fear that after all that had happened I probably had in some way, was going crazy and feared that I was going to lose my mind.

Chapter Sixty-Five: The Sleep Over

Brenda's mother had called my mom and asked her if I could stay over because she was having a sleep over. My mother knew how close Brenda and I were, But she still asked to speak to me. I took the receiver and my mother reminded me of knowing how much she disliked to be asked to give permission to do anything at the last minute. She allowed me to stay because Brenda's mother had asked. She felt okay with it because she felt that it was going to be supervised. After hanging up, I breathed a sigh of relief. My mother had met Brenda's mother once and appeared to have been comfortable with her. That night, everyone sat up as I went from beginning to end of what had happened. . I lay awake all night wondering how if I had done something different what the outcome would have been. I felt the tears as they rolled down my face because I felt that I was just as guilty because Tommy had come to my rescue again and this time he had paid for an act of kindness for me with his life. Now I knew how Mark felt... I knew exactly how he felt. And I like him would have to live with this for the rest of my life. That night I cried hard into the pillow knowing that Tommy had died trying to save me. But it wasn't just Tommy it was the rest of his gang. Although they were following his lead, they all had died the same way. I had hoped that the people in the building had seen it differently. The How's of what happened but not The Why's.

Chapter Sixty- Six: Dead But Not Over

I told them what I had heard and seen while I was in the emergency room where they had not been allowed. I told of hearing how every family that lost a member to Death had been plunged into deep sadness and despair. After the doctor had finished with me I walked out of the room and heard the screams of Tommy's and Deidra's mothers. All of their family members were crying and screaming in disbelief. I saw Tommy's mother falling on the floor not wanting to believe her son was gone. Deidra stood silently by, looking but showing any emotions at all. Relatives of the other gang members had come to identify their bodies. None of the mothers whose son's had died would ever believe that their sons had killed, raped, robbed and beat others. Some of those people's only crime against the gang was having been in the wrong place at the wrong time. Even people like Deidra who had loved Tommy but had still felt the force of Tommy's wrath. To those mothers, those were their sons, their babies. What they had seen was only the good that their sons had done, helping to carry the groceries by hand and by cart up and down the stairs when the elevators didn't work. How they helped others who needed help with their groceries too. How they had protected the kids who lived in the building from people like the Wa Who Ba Man and other predators. The good that these young men had done was of little comfort to them now.

Putting the services and Funerals together and trying to help those who didn't have enough money like Candy was going to be needed. I wanted to if only for Tommy. I just didn't want to be a part of it. It hurt too much and my mind and heart could not bear another bad thing. It would be long, so very long because there were so many to prepare for, twelve in all.

I stayed with my grandmother just so I didn't have to be involved. My family told everyone that I was out of town which would be excusable by all. Everyone knew that no one had any say so when a parent told them that they were going to a relative's house for whatever the reason. I just couldn't bear to see the activity. I wanted to stand alongside of Tommy's casket and say thank you to him but I couldn't. I wouldn't be able to stand and look at him while saying goodbye.

I finally came home after all of the services and funerals were over. That night as I sat in my bed looking out of the window, I looked up at the moon. The sky was clear; I crawled of my bed and got the pack of Tommy's cigarettes that I had hidden in the back of my dresser drawer. Inside of the wrapper I found the white slip of paper that had been folded in half, it was the slip of paper that Tommy that had teased me about when we were to meet. I opened it slowly and with the moonlight it was easy to read. I could tell from the way that it was written that he had really taken his time to write it. It said, "Moby Dick." Immediately I put my head down on the window sill and started to cry. I wanted to think in my own way that GOD was trying to show me something. Maybe he led Tommy to protect me or, maybe he was there all along. Winning didn't teach me anything. You win that's it end of story but the losing part and what you took from it, that's the interesting part. That's the lesson, that's the challenge. There had been twelve bodies for the funerals. Afterwards the buildings were ghostly quiet. It was hard to believe that they were all gone. My mother called all of us together after dinner and announced that we were going to be moving out of the projects into our own home. They were very excited because we were going to be moving into our own home, away from the fear of any of us getting killed every day and all that went along with it.

The next day I went down to see Brenda. We walked over to our regular spot across the street and sat against the wall of the school. She asked, "What's wrong?"

"My family's moving."

Tears started running from her eyes. "Damn." We sat by the school not speaking, only smoking for an hour. Brenda got up and said, "I gotta go."

"Okay, I understand. Hey, if it's worth anything I'm hurting too." Brenda walked to the street, looked both ways then crossed to go home without looking back. I could see from a distance that she was wiping her eyes. I was wiping mine too. After she was out of sight I lit a cigarette, brought my knees up and crossed my arms on them. As I inhaled, I looked up at my building. In spite of all that had happened to me, this was my home. Everyone that I knew lived here. It had been really bad most of the time but there were many good times too. I didn't want to go.

I slept very little if any that night. Just when I thought it was going to be okay, I got another unexpected kick to my stomach. All night I cried. I had so much to cry for. The next day I went down to Brenda's house and we sat on her porch. She told me that at Tommy's funeral, Deidra had been hysterical. She had always told everyone including me some time ago that she couldn't get pregnant. But after having missed one period too many, she had gone to the Doctor and had found out that she was four months pregnant. Deidra had been so excited that she had raced home to tell Tommy hoping that this would make him leave Renee. She thought after telling Tommy about the pregnancy they would be a family and she would surely win him back. She hadn't heard about the fight or deaths of Tommy and his gang. She had been at the Doctor's office all day. Brenda told me that at the funeral she had held her stomach because even though she had known about Renee and although Tommy was gone but she had something that Renee didn't have, a part of Tommy.

Later, after all of the funerals were over, it was whispered that there were a lot of parents who felt that Tommy and his gang got what they had deserved. I did know some of the bad things that he had done, probably more than I should have. But what I did know was that he had saved my ass more times than I could count. Tommy and his gang died that day for me, or maybe it was for other reasons that none of us will ever know. He treated me with kindness and even gave me respect. And sometimes he treated me like I was a piece of shit. He did a lot of things for me that I have never figured out why. It was a relationship for convenience, he needed me and I certainly needed him. Almost like a little sister, I think that the way he did show kindness even a bad way was because it was the only reason that he knew how. The one thing that I do know is Tommy and his gang, like members of other gangs that die' did so because they took their mortality and the thought of being invincible for granted. For the things that he did it was a surprise to me that he had lived as long as he had. Tommy had been illiterate when I met him, but he had had great survival instincts and had even showed a desire to improve himself, for that reason I did know why because I had been a part of that project. Tommy

had been cunning, fearless and up until he lost the
only member that he thought of as a brother, had only
taken calculated risk for his gang members. After
losing K.C he became careless, reckless and cruel. His
anger had been seething and eventually erupted. He
felt vindicated when he killed Oswald. It was his
personal revenge. The Grim Reaper had been watching
his every move and when the time was right it came for
him as I sat in the playground he let me see and watch
him collect all the souls of those that he had watched
and waited for so long which now belonged to him.

Chapter Sixty-Seven: Memories

My family moved after that. I had on occasion returned to see those that I had left behind. But as I walked into the building it didn't feel right, I felt like a stranger, an outsider, even scared. So I never came back until I heard about them tearing down of the buildings. Now I was watching them as they were tearing down mine. There was one last thing that I had to do before I could pack away all of the memories that I had locked away for so many years away. Standing there looking across the street at the last few floors that the wrecking balls were knocking down, and the trucks as they hauled the rubbish away I started to make my very last walk, using my eyes and mind to take me back into what was, and what and where it used to be.

Behind the building where the parking lot used to be, was now an empty space. I envisioned the strip mall which was also gone. With the help of my memory I could see where the grocery store called, "Nationals" had stood. Next to it had been the small darkly lit lounge that never had a sign over it, a laundry-mat, and a small carry out liquor store, a small fast food place and at the end, a clinic that was attached to a Walgreens drug store.

The hot dog stand that was dedicated to Muhammed Ali was gone. I didn't know when it was taken away. Through all of the emptiness I could see the whole area as though it were still there the way it was when I had lived there. At the corner was fifty-First Street was the last remaining building.

As I looked west the infamous police station that sat directly in front of the viaduct on Wentworth Avenue was still there. I think it will always be there. I crossed the street staying on the east side. At the corner is a currency exchange; the only place that was still there. I continued to walk along places that were once store fronts or small houses. These were gone and the rest of that block it was all empty space. I stopped at the place that used to be a large grocery store called, "Red Rooster." With all of the empty space that it sat on it was hard for me to remember that it had been so large. I stopped at that point and turned to go back in the other direction because The Red Rooster was usually as far as I would go as a kid. I didn't know anyone south of the store and I never felt comfortable near the white buildings.

At the corner going north was The John G Farren Elementary School it was still there. A short distance was where the graveled area started. It covered the whole area from where the DuSable U.G.C. sat all of the way to the DuSable High School it too is was still there. I remember having liked DuSable Upper Grade Center which was still there. I learned so much because it was where my Biology classes took field trips, and yes, it too was there. To get from The DuSable Upper Grade Center to the DuSable High School there was enough gravel to cover a half of a football field. Walking along the school's walls, I touched one of the bricks and paused to think about the four years that I had spent there. Even with the good and the bad, DuSable had been the place that had inspired my thirst for more knowledge. It had been the place that I remember vividly watching the R.O T.C as they went through their maneuvers, the basketball team, and the softball team.

As I looked at what was left of my home, I could also see the places where all of the other buildings used stood. I shivered as I looked at the playground and remembered holding Tommy's head in my lap. Instantly, the tears welled up in my eyes and I had to continue walking. Standing there any longer would have brought back too much. I had to quickly shake away that memory and move on. Once I got to the end of the school, I stopped at the corner and looked down towards the next block. I could see nothing but a block of empty lots. Just space with lots of nothingness. It was up to my memory again to sort out the vast emptiness ahead of me.

Right at the corner as I crossed the street was a small take out hamburger stand. It was called Hot Potato. There were no seats inside. You went in, placed your order, paid for it and left. The menu showed hamburgers, hotdogs and polishes. The French Fries were drenched in ketchup. They also sold different brands of canned pop. The food was good and what made it even better was that it was cheap. Another thing was, it was directly across the street from the high school. It was open early in the day and would close late at night. In all of the years that I went to school not once did I ever hear of it having been robbed? Behind it was a short makeshift walkway that had a bin for the garbage. A short walk away was two buildings. One had an apartment on top with a liquor store on the first floor. The next building, which sat beside it, was a ragged two flat. The stairs were made of wood and lots of them had rotted out and were missing.

At the house that had the liquor store, you would always see the wino's carrying their purchase in a brown paper bag. They would take the top part of the bag and wrap it around the neck of the bottle and then pushing it quickly into the back of the waist band of their pants pockets or in a pocket that was inside of their ragged coats. They would usually buy and drink the cheapest wine that they could afford. Depending on who you asked, it was called, "wino's wine, Bums wine or Street wine." The wines were the drinks of the day, Wild Irish Rose, White Port, and Gordon's Gin. The bums would take the White Port and add Kool-Aid and it was called, "A Brick." Last but not least was Thunder-Bird. It was strange how details like that came to mind. For them, drinking was their way to escape from the sad realities of life. When the street lights came on men would start to congregate around the light post and greet each other. One would greet one of his drinking buddies by holding up his bag like it was a trophy. It would be funny to watch them greet each other but they didn't care. Each would give the other a high five then do a low five. The one with the bottle would say,

"What's the word?"
"Thunderbird"
"What's the price?"
"Forty twice."
"How's it sold?"
"Good and cold."
"Can I git it?"
"Not less u wit it."

As each bum took a long swallow (swig) they would make a face like they had sucked on lemons shaking their heads as each would say, "Damn that's good!" They would lean on each other and laugh until you would see them wiping a tear from their eyes. They slowly walked behind the Hot Potato's building laughing and joking with each other to where they had put old cardboard boxes and mop buckets they had

found. They sat there and had some sort of privacy.
They could pass their bottle back and forth and talk
about how things used to be. They didn't realize that
when they got drunk they would talk so loud that
everyone knew who was back there. But they didn't
bother anyone and no one really cared. As the time
passed you would see others gradually go behind the
building and then all you could hear was laughing and
cursing. To them it was all in fun, probably the only
pleasure that they had in their miserable lives. As it
started to get dark, they would come out and stand
near the light pole on the corner and try to sing and
harmonize to the do-whop songs that were popular in
what they referred to as, back in the day. It would be
hilarious to watch them snap their fingers while
making dance moves which made them look like they were
taking two steps to the right trying to push an
invisible wall, then repeat it going to the left. One
bum would take the lead to try to sing Jackie Wilson's
song, "Lonely Teardrops", or "Save the Last Dance for
Me." by 'The Drifters.' Because not one of them could
hold a note, I smiled as I could see them. The ghostly
figures were still smiling and singing. I felt the
sadness from what used to be, coming back as I watched
them, and then slowly fade away.

Moving further down, there used to be two
dilapidated two story houses. In the first house on
the first floor was where the candy store was. It was
so small that having twenty of us inside at one time
would have you sweating and gasping for air after
pushing your way out. In order to get any candy before
the owner sold out for the day, as soon as the bell
rang signaling the end of the school day, you had to
run as fast as possible to try to outrun the other
kids in order be able to get in line first. If you
didn't, you would end up getting caught up in the
crowd hopping up and down waving your hands and
screaming for the owner to see you. That store sold
penny candy that most of it really did cost just a
penny. The old man in the store sold Nutchews, Mary
Janes, Sugar Babies' Suckers, Bubs Daddy Bubble Gum
that was sold in the form of a rope. There was candy
called, Now and laters, Good and Plenty's, coconut
long johns. The list of your favorite candy went on
and on. I remember some girls would put their money
together and buy a pickle. They were so large that
they looked abnormal, but once the old man stuck that

peppermint stick down in the middle, abnormal or not, you would find yourself wiping the dribble from your mouth as you waited for your turn to get a bite. One of the big favorites was what we called a nickel bag of potato chips. He would put the chips in a brown paper bag and he would drench them with ketchup, hot sauce, or both. Nothing in the world was better than that. There was no place to equal that store anymore. There are still a lot of the different types of candy that we had then that are still around but they don't taste the same it seems that the candy companies are not putting in the same ingredients and that same candy has almost tripled in price.

Still walking, I looked at the large lot that was where the A&P grocery store sat. The parents of everyone that I knew of in the red buildings, shopped there. I never refer to the white buildings because since I only knew a few, people who lived in them so I couldn't say if they did shop there or not. The A&P was known for giving you a book and an S&H green stamp when you spent a certain amount of money on groceries. With each purchase you could either save that book or wait until you had enough filled books. To trade them for free items. Toasters, coffee makers, glass sets, irons. The list went on and on. They even had luggage. Sometimes when two or more mothers would shop one would say, "Yeah, like after we get this luggage we'd have someplace to go with it!" Both women and anyone else who had been within hearing distance would join in laughing along about the joke.

As my walk continued, I looked further back in the next vacant lot. Near the back of it was where the Burger King used to be. It was said to be the home of the Whopper. When the hamburgers first came out the commercial used to say, "It takes two hands to handle a Whopper," and it really did. They were gigantic after all of the fillings were added. Two people could eat off of one burger and walk out full as a little tick.

Closer to the front of the street there had been two more houses. One house had a resale shop on the first floor. We called it the hand me down store, but it wasn't for us to decide if your mother took you there to buy clothes because she couldn't afford any new ones then that's where you would go. When your mother was finished, you would go out with your head down, praying that none of your friends would see that

your mother had shopped there. If by any chance you
had been seen, you would never hear the end of it.

Two more places to remember that weren't there
either the funeral home. This never held any good
memories for anyone; it only held tears and sorrow for
all who went there. Those who went to see the dead and
those who were already dead who lay in their caskets
on view. Every memory that I had, I intentionally
blocked out; there was no need to stop.

The funeral home sat next to an alley. The last
business on that street was a Clark gas station.
Everyone went to it. People from the red buildings as
well as those from the white. It was the closest one
for either ones to use. I looked across the street as
I turned to make my way back, it was still there! The
Fir men's house. It was still there! I could feel big
smile come across my face.

Flooded with the memories of the safe haven it
had been in summer day camp. It meant going swimming,
visits to the museum, to places where we had picnics.
We even went to Lincoln Park Zoo. Those happy memories
were welcome. I was young, no gangs, no worries, no
nothing. Just waiting for the next day to come to see
what they had planned for us that day. Sometimes we
didn't go anywhere at all. We stayed there and the
people who worked there let us watch movies, play
Ping-Pong and provided lots of other activities. It
was okay to go there and have something to do rather
than be somewhere else with nothing at all to do.

As I continued on my walk back, I received
another surprise. Beethoven Elementary school, my
school was still there! Lunchroom cookies, Sloppy Joes
with mashed potatoes, cold weather, hot weather kids
playing in the playground! I could remember it all; I
could almost see it all. But then as I looked at where
the grass ended and the asphalt should have begun,
there was nothing. Nothing and more nothing, Just
patches of sparse grass and dirt. If you looked you
can see all of the way across the field from State
Street over to Federal Street. It was all gone, from
Forty-Seventh Street all the way to Fifty First Street
with the exception of what was left of my building,
where the back hoe continued with its work filling the
trucks which hauled out the bricks. There was one last
white building waiting to come down. I considered mine
already gone. It had come down to just a matter of
days.

Chapter Sixty-Eight: It's Over

Now while standing in front of the school, I had let my memories succeed in taking me to the places that I had vowed never to go to again. I ended up feeling glad to have done so. Those memories took me to places that I didn't remember and had made me remember things that I thought that I had forgotten. Now having been an adult for more years than I would care to tell, I know why this happened. When years before people only knew bits and pieces of what's and the whys of the projects. At that time only the important people who sat behind closed doors made the decisions and knew the how and whys. At that time they had no one to answer to but themselves. The one true thing was that those decisions at the top had nothing to do with us, the people who lived in The Robert Taylor Homes. The people who made the decisions made it into what it became.

They were the influential people who ran the city and they succeeded in turning their backs on the people of the projects. In return, we the people in the projects turned our backs on them. As I turned to walk back to my car I took one last glance at what had been, at what used to be at what would never be seen again. I realized there were tears in my eyes. They were there without my having noticed. I guess they came from the memories. In my mind as a child and even later as an adult it never dawned on me that the projects would ever change.

Realistically my tears had been of joy for the others who had lived there for so long and hopefully had found a new and better place to live. All along I had been walking and reminiscing about the past. It was nostalgia. Something that you would hear older people talk about, the good old days. I had lived there and had experienced a little of both. As I made my way to my car I smiled, because in my heart I would always remember The Robert Taylor Homes as they had been. The good part was that it will always be the place that gave me my beginning, my beliefs and self-esteem. It was also where I watched it being torn down to die.

Chapter Sixty-Nine:
Who Was Robert Taylor?

Robert Taylor was the first African American whose work had been publically acknowledged in the United States. He designed most of the buildings that were housed on the campus of the Tuskegee Institute and served as second in command to another famous African American, Booker T. Washington was the founder of, and president of the Tuskegee Institute. Taylor was awarded an honorary doctorate by Lincoln University in Pennsylvania. He served on the Mississippi Valley Flood Relief Commission (appointed by President Herbert Hoover) and was chairman of the Tuskegee chapter of the American Red Cross. Dr. Robert R. Taylor, an honored and highly regarded member of the colored race. After his death, both the white and Negro citizens lose one whose place will hardly be filled.

Dr. Taylor was a man of fine character, strict integrity, progressive, of quiet mien, and one who held a fine sense of civic obligation and responsibility. It was a privilege for the leaders of the white race to confer with Dr. Taylor on frequent occasions relative to questions and problems affecting community racial relations. He was always sane and sensible in his viewpoint and ever actuated by a spirit always to cement friendly and cordial relations between the races.

Robert Robinson Taylor probably would have opposed the project named in his honor.

Robert Taylor's Resignation

In 1942 he, Robert Taylor, along with the other members of the Board, sat and listened to the architects who expressed great concern about having to construct buildings 16 stories high and the risk in using steel and concrete construction citing how unsafe it would have been and building to build that high and how it would put thousands of the tenants lives at risk.

Engineers involved in the job, as well as the fire department, all agreed. Upon reflection the other members of the board agreed with Dr. Taylor when he presented the idea to have the buildings only four stories high and spread out in other communities where the lower income tenants could interact with other blue collar working communities.

There was one member who was absent a lot due to political obligations: The Late Great Richard J. Daley. When he found out what the members of the board had decided, without notifying him, he became so incensed at the very idea that he immediately vetoed it. He grew up and was raised in Bridgeport and as mayor, it had been said that he did not want to be disgraced with the idea of even having an African American population being able to work and definitely not allowed to be housed in his area. This was considered a nearby resource Rich Area.

Mayor Daley's blatant discrimination was not what Dr. Taylor expected to hear. It was said that mayor Daley would overlook the decision to integrate the housing decision if Dr. Robert Taylor would inform him of the members on the board who had agreed with the decision. Instead he refused and on that day resigned. In the 1950's the majority of the white ethnic gangs had faded away, their members finding jobs through patronage in the Democratic machine, often as police. His position was becoming stronger. After Dr. Taylor's seat was vacated until a predecessor could be appointed Mayor Daley proceeded to prevent the possibility by continuing with the original plan to ensure that the integration of blacks and whites would never happen..

He immediately commissioned and found two architects, Shaw, Metz, and Associates and contractor Gust K. Newberg who had just finished building The

McCormick Place to build a bridge or what was later
considered by the African American community a barrier
over what is known today as The Dan Ryan Expressway.
Comiskey Park was more accessible this way but it is
not known if this was part of the reason for the
bridge. Afterwards he had a meeting with the board to
made it known that he did not want the African
American population going over the bridge. This same
crew would construct The Robert Taylor Homes.

The Robert Taylor Homes Construction

After Robert Taylor's resignation, the CHA went full force in getting the buildings in place. The construction of the development was started in 1960. It was considered the biggest construction year in CHA history, with a total of 8,000 units along with other projects. The Robert Taylor Homes projects originally contained 4,415 units figure was reduced to 4,312 units through the conversion of some apartments to school and nonresidential use. The site, which covered ninety-five acres, was only a quarter of a mile wide, but was two miles long. It ran from Stat Street west to the Rock island Railroad tracts, which in turn was adjacent to the Dan Ryan Expressway and from Pershing Road south to 54th Street. It was a straight line geographical extension of Stateway Gardens.

The housing was contained in twenty-eight identical U-shaped groups of three. They were completely undistinguished, with red or yellow brick veneers, central elevator shafts, and fenced galleries. Because of the magnitude of the project it was built in 4 stages. The First covered the area from 47th to 51st street. It included eight apartment buildings, a management, maintenance building, a community center that was leased to the Chicago Park District and thing plant for the entire project. The Second stage covered the area from 43rd to 47th street, The Third and last stage was from 51st to 54th street.

It was documented that The Chicago Housing Authority, under the direction of Richard J. Daley Sr. had 2,000 construction workers pouring concrete frames at the weekly rate of 16 floors, and laying one- half million bricks per week. The land cost was 7.3 million. Taylor Homes was completed in November 1962, eleven months ahead of schedule. It originally had 800 residential units and small business and a number of junk yards. Its size was broken by 2 small shopping centers. One of the centers was at 51st street, the other at Pershing Road. The total development for this monstrosity was 75 million or after being broken down, in the annual cost section was 16,988 dollars per unit. At the time of its demise it contained close to 27,000 people, 20,000 said to be children and babies. There were roughly 5.8 people per unit.

The Chicago Housing Authority's Justification

The Chicago Housing Authority's justification for high rise public housing was a myth. In an open letter, the Authority's board chairman "wrote that virtually all new construction in the city was high rise. Families who either must or wanted to live in any urban area would have to learn to live with the high rise buildings for all large centers of population needed to accommodating an ever increasing number of people within a prescribed land area." It was said that that statement demonstrated an almost complete ignorance of the conditions in Chicago.

The CHA's statement to better support the high rise was to placate those who knew better. There was no money being made from the residents having a lot of residents in one place satisfied members of the board, That the Blacks could be contained in the units, thus keeping segregation alive, satisfying Mayor Daley and with that, it would never offer any hope or any incentive for anyone to get out.

When the board decided to go ahead with the plan to continue with making the projects higher than was originally suggested The Planning Committee of Chicago chapter of the American Institute of Architects had pointed out the numerous faults and structural problems that could have been eliminated had already fallen on death ears. The wheels had already been put in motion.

The Chicago Authority's Mission Statement

To minimize Racism

Provide jobs and job training for all who wished to work.

To provide upscale jobs and also doing the same for the school system.

To fund adequate social and recreational services and controlling crime.

Each annual report by the CHA, because the commitments had not been met stated that it (CHA) would continue to strive to make reasonable improvements.

The Chicago Housing Authority's Failure

After all was said and done, the one thing that was for sure was that the CHA failed. It failed to live up to its mission statement because when clear alternatives were presented to them they ignored them, resulting in a domino effect magnifying the problems that continued to grow with poverty, violence and the overcrowding. This in turn allowed gangs to expand and eventually take over.

To be clear, The Robert Taylor Homes didn't meet its fate because of any inherent flaw in its design as thought by the engineers who had opposed it. In 1980 the CHA's engineers later said that the housing development would have lasted. "As long as the Empire State Building, if it was maintained properly.

Even when I lived there, talk of the Robert Taylor Homes had gone on for so long that the people who lived there had started to make jokes about it. It was all talk. Little did anyone know that plans to demolish the projects had been in the works for years.

The CHA explained to the US congress when they were required to show whether it would be fiscally prudent to rehabilitate or destroy the structures that the CHA had let the 2 buildings deteriorate and with the remaining budget there would be no way that they would be able to rehabilitate them.

They told Congress but they didn't tell the tenants of the Robert Taylor Homes of their decision to demolish in February 2002. The families that were still living in the Robert Taylor Homes were given a 180-day notice of eviction. In 6 months the buildings, my former home, the homes of enemies, friends, and communities that had been homes for generations to families were to be demolished. In the end it was called, "The Dislocation of The Robert Taylor Homes. On March 8, 2007 the last remaining building was demolished. How sad it seemed that the honorable name of a widely recognized African American man, an Architect, would forever be synonymous with what was perceived as the largest public housing deviation from the national culture and not as an example of it. The buildings were later referred to as, "The Projects."

In October 2010, The Chicago Housing Authority, along with a development team comprised of related Midwest, Heartland Housing and several other associates stated that they would in the future build as envisioned a redeveloped site for a modern urban community. This would offer housing that would be affordable to families across a broad income spectrum. Along with schools, parks, community space and accessible retail businesses all of this would be within close proximity.

Wasn't that the original Mission statement when the CHA opened in 1962?

Epilog

In chapter sixty, after accepting the invitation to the girl gangs get together, my friend Brenda asked me why I had accepted, knowing that I was being set up. I told her that I had to play the hand that I had been dealt. I knew how to play poker, and to make my point clear that I wasn't going to run from them any more I chose to take that chance, to play my hand. Not knowing whether I was holding a winning hand or a losing hand and the way that things had been happening to me my hand could have been no better than a crap shoot. I walked inside of that apartment.

Not with luck, but with protection and something that all of the riches in the world could not have helped at the time. But I walked in and came out with what GOD had given me all along; Courage and protection, how awesome is he? The very beginnings I have had some type of dialog with GOD. I asked him many questions but never understood how to wait to hear his word. I was angry because I felt that he didn't hear me, but how could he not? You see what I have learned in the thirty-plus years and still counting. Is that on the night, that I felt that I had a losing hand it didn't matter, The hand that we're dealt in life is a matter of faith because in the end, It is GOD who holds all of the chips. I smile sometime when I think of all of the fights that I was involved in, to protect my family and to protect myself. I did my best, GOD did the rest. Need I say more? They say that GOD takes care of fools and babies;

I was definitely a lot of the first probably a little bit of the second. Thirty plus years and counting it is still slowly coming together. One Sunday while flipping the channels on the television, I happened to catch a sermon. Ordinarily I don't watch them, but it was what this pastor said that left me in awe. He said, "If your dream is not hard then you're not struggling hard enough." He was so right. My dream after graduating high school was to help others who were too sick to care for or help themselves. It became more than a dream; it became a passion to strive to accomplish. It was to become a Nurse. My mantra was to Believe Big-Pray Bold! My life has been a time of testing but I have to remember to trust GOD's timing. To be thankful always-Believe that GOD loves you and hears you. Be grateful for what you have today and for how far that he has already brought you. And think about what you've been through!

You may not be where you are, but it doesn't mean that you haven't made it! And if you didn't make it how much prouder could you be if your children have picked up where you left off? In life we will meet all types of people, those who may try to do you physical or mental harm, those who are toxic. Some will tell you pretty lies but is that what you really want or need to hear? There may have been closed to you for years. There is going to come a time when those doors will open for you, don't be surprised! Realize what you've gone through! YOU DESERVE IT! Start Soon!

To My Readers

For those of you that have read this book to my path and the journey from my memories from the beginning to the end is but one small chapter of many in my life, And I thank you. I do have one request. Below I have listed a small selection of songs that were the best in what we used to call "back in the day." Read the names, smile, nod your head, and tap your feet, maybe you will find the name of one or more of the songs that you liked. Let it into your memory, take that walk and see what you remember when that song came out.

Who you were dating, whose quarter parties you attended what you were doing in school. If you lived in The Robert Taylor and you attended DASABLE UGC AND HIGH School, what you can say is "It may not have been that good but, as you sing one of these songs you'll think to yourself, it certainly wasn't all that bad. And *no matter how far I go* in life, I'll always remember where I came from to get there.

"I'll Always Remember, The Robert Taylor Homes." It is history now. Of mine and of everyone that lived there. It will always be remembered by those of us who lived there, it will never be forgotten.

The Oldies

Let's Stay Together---Al Green

Let's Get It On---Marvin Gaye

Me and Mrs. Jones--Billy Paul

Low Rider---War

ABC---Jackson Five

Hot Pants---James Brown

Ball of Confusion---The Temptations

Fire---Ohio Players

Keep on Truckin---Eddie Kendricks

Some Day We'll be Together---Diana Ross and Supremes

Ain't No Sunshine---Bill Withers

Oh Girl---Chi-Lites

Benny and the Jets---Elton John

Disco Inferno---The Tramps

Just my Imagination---Temptations

Respect---Aretha Franklin

Backstabbers- The O'Jays

Thank you for letting me be myself Again---Sly and the Family Stone

Freddie's Dead---Curtis Mayfield

The Worm--- The Ohio Player

Super fly---Curtis Mayfield

Shining Star---Earth, Wind and Fire

Mr. Big Stuff---Jean Knight

My Girl---The Temptations

Tracks of my Tears---Smokey Robinson and the Miracles

It's Your Thing---Isley Brothers

One Nation under a Groove---Parliament Funkadelics

Jungle Boogie---Kool and the Gang

Uptight Everything's Alright--- Stevie Wonder

I'll Take You There---The Staple Singers

Love Train---The O'Jays

Lean on Me---Bill Withers

Duke of Earl---Gene Chandler

Poppa's Got a Brand New Bag---James Brown

Shining Star---Earth, Wind and Fire

Mr. Big Stuff---Jean Knight

My Girl---The Temptations

Tracks of my Tears---Smokey Robinson and the Miracles

Love on a Two Way Street-The Moments

Betcha by Golly Wow-The Stylistics

Books about the Robert Taylor Homes
And The Chicago Housing Authority

Morton Newman-wrote the seven part series on the Robert Taylor Homes where he quoted persons who wanted to remain anonymous in the Chicago Daily News.

D. Bradford Hunt wrote "Blueprint for Disaster; The Unraveling of Public Housing." Mr. Hunt is Associate dean and professor of social science at The Roosevelt University in Chicago

Robert Weaver wrote "The Negro Ghetto-1948"

Sudhir A. Venkatesh wrote; The American Project (ISBN 0674008308) A professor of Sociology of Columbia. His book was the winner of the 2000 Association of the Publishers Inc. Award.

Alex Kotlowitz; There are no Children Here

The Internet under Robert Taylor Homes

Made in the USA
Monee, IL
19 July 2024

62119639R00173